BIBLICA ET ORIENTALIA

(SACRA SCRIPTURA ANTIQUITATIBUS ORIENTALIBUS ILLUSTRATA)

46

Para John ... ...

biblica et orientalia – 46

MARTIN ALONSO CORRAL

EZEKIEL'S ORACLES AGAINST TYRE

Historical Reality and Motivations

EDITRICE PONTIFICIO ISTITUTO BIBLICO – ROMA 2002

ISBN 88-7653-349-4

© E.P.I.B. – Roma – 2002

Iura editionis et versionis reservantur

EDITRICE PONTIFICIO ISTITUTO BIBLICO

Piazza della Pilotta, 35 - 00187 Roma, Italia

"It is sometimes not so much the sources themselves as the ability

of the historians to ask questions that is threatened by exhaustion"

(P. Briant, *Rois, tributs et paysans*)

Acknowledgements

The present monograph was submitted originally as a doctoral dissertation to the Skirball Department of Hebrew and Judaic Studies at New York University in May 2000. It is published here in revised and updated form.

It is a pleasure to acknowledge those persons and institutions that have offered their support during the completion of this project. Baruch Levine, who served as my dissertation adviser, provided new ideas, insights into the text, and was a decisive influence at crucial stages of research and writing. His patience, positive attitude, and, most of all, his love of learning have been a source of inspiration for me during these years as a Ph.D. student and will continue to be so in the years to come. Daniel Fleming helped me ground my study of Akkadian. I am very thankful for his criticism of earlier drafts. His comments were always insightful and to the point. Günter Kopcke provided the historian's perspective needed in a project of this nature. His notes on Phoenician art were most useful at the early stages of my project. Larry Schiffman helped me at different stages in my progress as a Ph.D. student. I am deeply indebted to these four scholars. Where the study that follows is found wanting, the responsibility is mine alone.

My gratitude goes also to Larry Stager whose advice and orientation were decisive in deciding the direction of my work. S. Ribichini was very helpful in suggesting a number of articles on Tyre published in the *Rivista di studi fenici* and specially in securing the latest issue that contained an article relevant to my study. J. D. Muhly helped me understand the importance of lead isotope analysis applied to provenance studies and Seymour Gitin shared with me the results of the lead isotope analysis done on a number of silver pieces from silver caches found at Ekron. My gratitude should include the University of South Africa at Pretoria and the University of Tübingen in Germany. Both of them reproduced for me unpublished dissertations not readily available. I also want to thank Fr. Agustinus Gianto, S.J., editor of *Biblica et orientalia*, for his kindness in including my work in the series and for his useful comments and suggestions.

ACKNOWLEDGMENTS

The Spanish Foundation "La Caixa" and NYU through the Skirball Department of Hebrew and Judaic Studies provided support in the form of doctoral fellowships. I am very grateful for the assistance of these two institutions.

I wish to express my gratitude to my dear friend Henry Resnick for his support during these years as a Ph.D. student. Henry kindly read several chapters of my dissertation offering insightful comments.

I would also like to express thanks to members of my immediate family for their support and encouragement. To my mother I offer thanks for the countless hours of conversation, dedication, and unfailing encouragement of any and all of my academic pursuits. Completing this dissertation would have not been possible without her constant love, dedication, attention, and care. This study is dedicated to her as a token of filial devotion.

Martin Corral
New York
March, 2002

Contents

Abbreviations

ABD	D. N. Freedman, ed. *The Anchor Bible Dictionary*
Ag. Ap.	Josephus, *Against Apion*
ANET	J. P. Pritchard, ed. *Ancient Near Eastern Texts*, 3rd ed.
Ant.	Josephus, *The Antiquities of the Jews*
ARAB	D. B. Luckenbill, *Ancient Records of Assyria and Babylonia*
BA	*Biblical Archaeologist*
BAR	*Biblical Archaeology Review*
BDB	F. Brown, S. R. Driver, and C. A. Briggs, *Hebrew and English Lexicon of the Old Testament*
BHS	*Biblia Hebraica Stuttgartensia*
CAD	*Chicago Assyrian Dictionary*
CAH	*The Cambridge Ancient History*
CIS	*Corpus inscriptionum semiticarum*
CPP	V. Krings, ed. *La civilisation phénicienne et punique: manuel de recherche*
DCPP	E. Lipiński, ed. *Dictionnaire de la civilisation phénicienne et punique*
GKC	*Gesenius' Hebrew Grammar*, ed. E. Kautsch, trans. A. E. Cowley
HALOT	L. Koehler and W. Baumgartner, *The Hebrew and Aramaic Lexicon of the Old Testament*
IEJ	*Israel Exploration Journal*
JCS	*Journal of Cuneiform Studies*
JNES	*Journal of Near Eastern Studies*
KAI	H. Donner and W. Röllig, eds. *Kanaanäische und aramäische Inschriften*
KTU	D. Dietrich, O. Loretz, and J. Sanmartín, eds. *Die Keilalphabetischen Texte aus Ugarit*
RSF	*Rivista di studi fenici*
TA	*Tel Aviv*
TLOT	E. Jenni and C. Westermann, eds. *Theological Lexicon of the Old Testament.*

ZA   *Zeitschrift für die alttestamentliche Wissenschaft*

ZÄS   *Zeitschrift für ägyptische Sprache und Atertumskunde*

1
Introduction

One of the most impassioned, mysterious, and singular prophets of ancient Israel, Ezekiel, lived through the greatest crisis of ancient Israel's history: the destruction of Jerusalem and her Temple, the loss of national independence, the end of the Davidic monarchy, and the Exile (2 Kgs. 25; Jer. 39-41, 52; Lam. 1-5; 2 Chr. 36). An Israelite leader in the Exile, he was frequently misunderstood and unfairly treated. He stood for righteousness and justice and promised a better future to Judah after a time of exile and national crisis. He favored total submission to the Neo-Babylonian empire realizing very early that Egypt could not, and would not help the weakened, diminished, and endangered Judean kingdom. He was unpopular. Many considered his message treasonous to his people and nation.

And, in a period of "bipolar politics," as Jeremiah before him, Ezekiel had an accurate picture of the historical circumstances and precarious balance of power between Babylonia and Egypt, the two "superpowers" of his time. He realized that the battle of Carchemish (605 BCE) had marked a turning point in this balance of power. Total submission to the rising Neo-Babylonian empire was Judah's only choice. Relying on Egypt for support would unleash a process that would mean Judah's utter destruction and the end of her national existence.

The book of Ezekiel has three major sections. Each of them reflects different aspects of Ezekiel's ministry: the first one in chapters 1-24 contains prophecies of judgement against Israel that help Israel understand why YHWH let Jerusalem be destroyed. The second section in chapters 26-32 includes the oracles against foreign nations. They affirm the values presented in the rest of the book showing the fate of other nations to be "just as much divinely ordained as the fate of Israel."[1] They "serve as a prelude to the establishment of a new kingdom of Israel by announcing punishment of all who oppress God's people."[2] The third

---

[1] Renz, *Rhetorical Function*, 1999, 101.
[2] Boadt, "Ezekiel," *ABD*, 2.711.

section in chapters 33-48 proclaims Israel's future salvation and focuses on the new order YHWH will establish for Israel.

Seven are the nations condemned in the second section of the book: Ammon (Ez. 25:1-7), Moab (Ez. 25:8-11), Edom (Ez. 25:12-14),[3] Philistia (Ez. 25:15-17), Tyre (Ez. 26:1-28:19), Sidon (Ez. 28:20-23), and Egypt (Ez. 29-32). The oracles against foreign nations in Ezekiel and in Isaiah, Zephaniah, and Jeremiah are "apparently considered transitional." They link "words of woe with proclamations of good news."[4] The nations Ezekiel condemned represented Israel's enemies. The oracles portray them as the objects of YHWH's judgment. Thus a divine judgment on them also served as a message of hope.[5] The oracles against Tyre and Egypt are by far the longest. Both Egypt and Tyre stood in Nebuchadnezzar's path. They constituted the main obstacles to Nebuchadnezzar's complete domination of the area. At the same time, they were the two major regional powers. Egypt's power was both political and military. Tyre's was economic and, to a certain extent, political as well. Ezekiel considered Egypt an unreliable political ally (Ez. 29:6). The country played a persistent role in instigating Judean uprisings, only to fail to support the Judeans adequately for a successful outcome. Tyre, the second major regional power, represented an amazing history of economic and political success. She had built an impressive trading network, monopolized trade, collaborated with the major empires of the period, and managed to maintain her political independence at the same time.

As part of the oracles against foreign nations, Ezekiel 26:1-28:19 presents a series of oracles against the city of Tyre. Chapter 26 depicts Nebuchadnezzar's siege and destruction of Tyre and its consequences. Chapter 27 is a lamentation (קינה) over Tyre in which the city is depicted as a mighty ship. Verses 12-25a present an impressive picture of Tyre's commercial empire mentioning trading partners and

---

[3] The prophecies in Ezekiel 35-36 include a second oracle against Edom and a prophecy of restoration of the land of Israel.

[4] Block, *Ezekiel 25-48*, 1998, 3.

[5] Some scholars have related the oracles against foreign nations to the "execration texts" in Egypt suggesting that the ritual cursing or prophetic threatening of enemies may have had a definite place in the cult (see Bentzen, "Ritual Background," *Oudtestamentische Studiën* 8 [1950]: 85-99).

commodities traded. Chapter 28 has two oracles: one against the haughty prince of Tyre (1-10) and another against the king of Tyre (11-19). Both of them contain mythological themes.

Both textual sources and the archaeological record show that Judah's neighbors were taking advantage of her situation in the period immediately before and after the destruction of Jerusalem.[6] Among the seven nations Ezekiel mentions in his oracles against foreign nations Tyre is the only exception: Tyre and Judah shared no common boundaries, they never had territorial disputes, and maintained good relations during most of their history. Tyre did not participate in or instigate Jerusalem's destruction, she was not an unreliable ally, and no obvious reason for rivalry, resentment, or anger is discernible in the Tyrian oracles. For these motives it is surprising to see Tyre in a list that includes Judah's worst enemies (Ammon, Edom, Moab, and the Philistine cities). What is more important, Ezekiel devotes three chapters

---

[6] The clearest evidence of hostile acts against Judah comes from Edom. Arad ostracon # 24, line 20 mentions an Edomite advance in the Easter Negev c. 598 BCE. The Bible blames Edom for having annexed Judean land (Ez. 35:10) and for being guilty of violence (Ez. 25:12; 35:5; Joel 4:19). The Edomites may have even assisted the Babylonians in the sack of Jerusalem (Obad. 11, 13, 14; Ps. 137:7; Lam. 4:21-22). The nature of Ammon's and Moab's acts against Judah is less clear. 2 Kgs. 24:2 indicates that, after Jehoiakim's rebellion against Nebuchadnezzar, Nebuchadnezzar retaliated by sending Babylonian units together with bands of Arameans (or Edomites according to an emendation), Ammonites, and Moabites against Judah (c. 598 BCE). No extrabiblical source mentions such an attack. In any event, all Transjordanian states (Edom included) seem to have enjoyed a relative prosperity in the period around the destruction of Jerusalem and to have been spared from destruction. According to Ez. 25:3, 6, Ammon rejoiced at the destruction of the Temple, the desolation of the land of Israel, and the exile of the Judeans. For its part, Moab showed a disdainful attitude toward Judah (Ez. 25:8). Jer. 49:1 condemns Ammon for having seized one-time Israelite territory. The Philistines were also Judah's traditional enemies. Similarities of vocabulary link the oracle against Philistia in Ezekiel 25:15 to the Edomite oracles in 25:12 and 35:5 in which acts of vengeance against Judah were condemned. For its part, Egypt is accused of being an unreliable political ally (Ez. 29:6). Egypt constantly instigated Judean uprisings, only to fail to support the Judeans adequately for a successful outcome in their revolt. Tyre is an exceptional case among the foreign nations condemned in these oracles. No obvious reason for rivalry, resentment, or anger is discernible in the Tyrian oracles. Sidon's condemnation can be related to Tyre's. These two Phoenician cities are regularly paired in the oracles against foreign nations, as, e.g., Jer. 27:3 and Joel 4:4 (see below, under 2.9).

(26-28) to condemning Tyre while Ammon, Moab, Edom, and Philistia, Judah's worst enemies, get just one chapter (25) combined. Only the oracles against Egypt in chapters 29-32 are longer than the Tyrian oracles. But in Egypt's case, the accusation of political unreliability is clearly stated in the prophecy itself.

Tyre's unique situation among the seven nations condemned in Ezekiel demands a detailed reconstruction and analysis of her actions in relation to Judah during the end of the 7th century and the beginning of the 6th century. The inescapable conclusion is that Tyre was somehow harming Judah.[7] At this point a number of questions need to be raised and answered. These questions include: What was Tyre doing to Judah? In what way(s) was Tyre harming her? What were the reasons for Tyre's condemnation? What core of historical events does the prophet refer to and what set of historical circumstances does the prophecy echo? What is the historical reality of the prophecy? Why did Ezekiel consider Tyre a threat? In what way was Tyre a threat to Judah? Finally, why would Tyre want to harm Judah?

The motives for Tyre's condemnation offered in the numerous studies of the book often are just a repetition of those stated in the oracles themselves. Some of them are Tyre's desire to profit from the destruction of Jerusalem, Tyrian greed, the haughtiness and self-deification of Tyre's ruler, religious and theological reasons. Too often the oracles have been interpreted without taking into account their historical background. The following pages will discuss the causes proposed in such studies.

One of the most often repeated explanations for the Tyrian oracles by both commentaries on Ezekiel and historical surveys is that Tyre saw the destruction of Jerusalem as an opportunity to expand her commercial activities. The supporters of this theory suggest that Tyre sought to benefit from Jerusalem's fall by controlling trade coming to and through Jerusalem (Ez. 26:2).[8] Jerusalem, they say, could serve Tyre

---

[7] To my knowledge, no scholar has so far alluded to the possibility that Tyre was somehow directly harming Judah.

[8] Katzenstein, *History*, 1997, 322; Zimmerli, *Ezekiel 2*, 1983, 40; Greenberg, *Ezekiel 21-37*, 1997, 530, 540; Block, *Ezekiel 25-48*, 1998, 32, 36. The textual support for this explanation is Ez. 26:2. The present discussion will offer a new interpretation of this

as an important trade center on the route from Phoenicia to the Red Sea and the southern Arabian Peninsula.[9] No historical or archaeological evidence is presented in support of these allegations and it is difficult to imagine how Tyre could possibly benefit economically from Jerusalem's fall. Tyre was a major trading empire and Jerusalem only the capital of a backward, tiny state with no major trade routes traversing it. The actual archaeological evidence coming from Judah contradicts this interpretation as well. Nebuchadnezzar's campaign of 587/6 BCE represented a major destruction of the area.[10] If there were trade, it would have left traces in the archaeological record. The positive side of this suggestion is that it takes into account economic considerations, which I consider very important, but it contradicts both the historical events and the archaeological record. It can thus be easily dismissed.

Tyre's greed, a motive ultimately connected to the city's desire to benefit from Jerusalem's fall and to moral considerations, is often presented as a reason for her condemnation.[11] The criticism of the previous suggested motivation applies to the one of "greed" as well.

Arguments of a moral nature have often been proposed as well. The two oracles in chapter 28 present a haughty ruler/king of Tyre. This fact has led scholars to suggest that his arrogance, pride, and haughtiness[12] were the reasons for the oracles. To this, it must be said that arrogance, pride, and haughtiness are commonplaces in the oracles against foreign nations.[13] They constitute literary devices, stereotypes,

---

crucial text that is in line with the historical and archaeological data at our disposal (see below, under section 4.1.a).

[9] Block, *Ezekiel 25-48*, 1998, 32 (see also Greenberg, *Ezekiel 21-37*, 1997, 530).

[10] Mazar (*Archaeology*, 1990, 458-460) and Stern ("Israel," *BA* 38 [1975]: 26-55; *Archaeology*, 2001, 323-25) present the archaeological evidence for this period. Most of the Judean cities and fortresses excavated in the Shephelah, the Negev, and the Judean Desert were destroyed. Jerusalem, Ein Gedi, Arad, Kadesh Barnea, Ashkelon, Ekron, Timna, and Tell Sera' are among the cities destroyed in the early 6th century.

[11] Katzenstein, *History*, 1997, 322 comments that Tyre's "arrogance and greed demanded an imperative punishment." Similarly Zimmerli (*Ezekiel 2*, 1983, 40) states that "Tyre [...] remained commercially calculating. [...] Those who were calculating in Tyre thought that they could calculate their future and their life."

[12] Zimmerli, *Ezekiel 2*, 1983, 80, 95; Block, *Ezekiel 25-48*, 1998, 86-87.

[13] The same motives are used against Moab (Jer. 48:29); Ammon and Moab (Zeph. 2:10); Assyria (Zech. 10:11); the Chaldeans (Isa. 13:19); Egypt (Ez. 30:6, 18; 32:12); and Philistia (Zech. 9:6). Insolence, arrogance, self-exaltation, superiority, are regular

and cliches. From a historical point of view, these alleged causes are difficult to substantiate. Furthermore, no evidence is presented in support of such motivations.

Related to the previous set of alleged causes is the *hubris* motive according to which the Tyrian king's self-deification is the ultimate reason for the oracles. It is indeed very likely that the Tyrian kings were considered incarnations of Melkart, the city god.[14] But in the oracle against Egypt, Pharaoh is also portrayed as saying "The Nile is mine, I made it" (Ez. 29:3, 9),[15] and yet we know that the true reason for Egypt's condemnation was not Pharaoh's self-deification but Egypt's unreliability as a political ally.[16] If Tyrian religion had a primary role in the oracles against Tyre, one would expect constant references to Tyrian religious practices.[17] One finds an extended, colorful, impressive

---

terms, literary devices used to portray those enemies of Israel considered superior politically or economically. There was a certain literary convention on how to depict the enemies of Israel and the above terms were regularly used in the prophecies against these states.

[14] See Ribichini, "Melqart," in *DDDB*, eds. Van der Toorn et al., 1999, 1056-58. Greenberg (*Ezekiel 21-37*, 1997, 577), points out that certain classical sources report that the Phoenician royal family claimed descent from the gods adding that "Israel's prophets ascribed self-deification to pagan kings as an expression of their supreme arrogance and self-reliance." In line with this declaration, Block (*Ezekiel 25-48*, 1998, 88) states that "human hubris must be answered by divine judgment."

[15] The Egyptians worshiped the inundation of the Nile and its personification *Hapy*. The river was often called "father of gods." Pharaoh, the son of the sun-god Ra, was thought to be the incarnation of the falcon-headed god Horus the successor of Osiris. His image was often placed in temples among those of other gods (see Miosi, "Re," *ABD*, 5.624-25; Te Velde, "Nile," in *DDDB*, eds. Van der Toorn et al., 1999, 626). The perception of the king's divinity among the Egyptians was of a rather limited sort; he was seen chiefly as an intermediary between the gods and humanity (see eds. O'Connor and Silverman, *Egyptian Kingship* [1995]).

[16] Ez. 29:6 states the real motive for Egypt's condemnation by saying that "Egypt had been a staff of reed to the house of Israel," i.e. an unreliable ally. A similar description applied to Egypt appears in 2 Kgs. 18:21 as part of Sennacherib's mockery of Hezekiah's equally vain reliance on Egypt. The text reads as follows: "You are relying on that broken staff of reed, on Egypt, wich will pierce the hand of anyone leaning on it: so is Pharaoh, king of Egypt, to all that rely on him." See chapter 2 for a detailed discussion of Egypto-Judean relations during the period leading to the destruction of Jerusalem in 586 BCE.

[17] Notice for example the total absence of allusions to Tyrian idolatry, to sacrifices of infants, or to any other Tyrian religious practices (Block, *Ezekiel 25-48*, 1998, 32).

description of Tyre's economic activities and trade instead. This, in fact, shows that economic and, to a lesser degree, political reasons, not religious motivations, were the underlying factors for the oracles. Religious and moral factors were only of secondary importance in the prophecies. They were just one element in a much larger picture of Tyrian oppression (cf. section 3.14).

Finally, on theological grounds, it has been advanced that Nebuchadnezzar was YHWH's agent of judgement upon Judah and that attempts by any nation to oppose Babylonian domination in the Levant were perceived as "defiance against the irrevocable divine decree."[18] The Tyrian oracles may also be conceived as an answer to Nebuchadnezzar's failure to destroy Tyre when all other nations mentioned in Ezekiel's oracles were destroyed or defeated.[19] Did this mean that Melkart, Tyre's city god, was superior to YHWH, the god of Judah? Or had YHWH failed Judah? Arguments based on theological grounds, even though valid, are by their very nature subjective and speculative. Even if we accord validity to them, they do not preclude the existence of other underlying factors for the oracles. Theological causes on the one hand, and economic, political, and historical factors on the other, do not exclude each other, on the contrary, they supplement each other.

When it comes to evaluating the actual historical events the prophet refers to and the prophecy echoes, authors are deliberately vague. None other than W. Zimmerli considers Tyre's deeds in the late 7th century and early 6th century as beyond historical corroboration.[20]

---

[18] Block, *Ezekiel 25-48*, 1998, 32. After the destruction of Jerusalem in 586 BCE, only Egypt and Tyre were still resisting the Babylonians.

[19] After the battle of Carchemish (605 BCE), Nebuchadnezzar neither destroyed nor defeated Egypt. In his attempt to invade Egypt in 601, he suffered heavy losses and was finally repelled by the Egyptian army. Jeremiah (Jer. 43:8-13) and Ezekiel (Ez. 29:17) predicted a Babylonian occupation of Egypt (c. 570) but no reference to such occupation exists in Babylonian, Egyptian, or Greek histories. In other words, Tyre and Egypt were in the same category of undefeated states (on this matter, see discussion in Wiseman, *Nebuchadrezzar*, 1985, 39-41). During this period Egypt was a major naval power and probably supported Tyre by sea.

[20] Zimmerli, *Ezekiel 2*, 1983, 24. Zimmerli's words are: "To what extent also particular relationships between Jerusalem and Tyre (from as early as the time of Solomon?) have to be taken into consideration remains completely obscure."

Among the studies of the so-called prose section in Ez. 27:12-25a, where a list of trading partners and commodities traded appears,[21] the situation is not much better. These studies have focussed on a number of issues such as (1) the dating and authorship of the section and its relation to the poetry section which precedes and follows it; (2) the identification of trading partners and products; and (3) the explanation of Phoenician technical terms. These studies never take economic and political factors in the period immediately before and after the destruction of Jerusalem as the determining reasons for Tyre's condemnation. They do not seem to realize that the emphasis on Tyre's economic power indicates that economic reasons were part of the motivations for the oracles, in fact, they were one of the major causes for them.

It is the purpose of the present discussion to deal with the aforementioned unanswered questions. The study will determine the ultimate causes of Tyre's condemnation, the historical events the prophet refers to, and the historical reality of the prophecy.[22] Answers to these questions are complex. They have several faces involving political, economic, and social factors. In the end, Judah's restraint of trade and economic stagnation were the direct result of Tyre's economic policies and trade practices.

A discussion of different works on Ezekiel and Phoenician history is necessary at this point. It will proceed from general studies to specific works beginning with commentaries on the entire book followed by studies on Ezekiel 26:1-28:19 and discussions of Ezekiel 27. An assessment of historical works, necessary to reconstruct the historical events to which the oracles refer, comes next. It includes Phoenician and Tyrian history, archaeological findings, recent studies, and a history of the relations between Phoenicia and Judah.

---

[21] Most authors consider this trade list a prose section. Following Greenberg, I see Ez. 27:12-25a as a poetic adaptation of a commercial inventory (see Greenberg, *Ezekiel 21-37*, 1997, 566).

[22] It is important to notice at this point that we need to read between the lines in biblical interpretation. Very seldom the oracles against foreign nations give the explicit motives for the condemnation of these nations. As commented earlier, certain rhetorical conventions such as moral motives are part of the genre. When we go beyond these moral terms, we always find that the nations condemned either were hostile to Judah or threaten her in some way.

a) Works on Ezekiel

1) General commentaries on Ezekiel

Ezekiel 26-28 as well as the rest of Ezekiel's oracles and, indeed most aspects of his career and ministry, have been the object of extensive study, scrutiny and criticism. W. Zimmerli[23] wrote the most comprehensive and monumental commentary on the book. He explores the book's textual transmission, readings, variants, and versions, tries to reconstruct the basic form of the prophecy, and traces its subsequent elaboration. On form-critical and traditio-historical grounds, he proposes numerous emendations and alternative readings to the text.[24] Two important, recent, and more conservative studies of the book are Greenberg's [25] (1983, 1997) and Block's[26] (1997, 1998).

---

[23] Zimmerli, *Ezekiel 1* (1979); idem, *Ezekiel 2* (1983). Cooke's commentary (*Ezekiel* [1936]) is still a useful tool in the study of these oracles though somewhat outdated.

[24] On the assumption that the prophet was a poet, Zimmerii assigns a core of oracular poetic fragments and especially the lamentation (קינה) sections to Ezekiel himself. The existing text, nevertheless, incorporates many later accretions by Ezekiel's "schools" (see Zimmerli, *Ezekiel 1*, 1979, 68-74).

[25] Greenberg, *Ezekiel 1-20*, (1983); idem, *Ezekiel 21-37* (1997). Greenberg's approach differs radically from Zimmerli's. He views the text synchronically, describes his method as "holistic," and seeks to reconstruct the perception of the text by an ideal reader living at a time when it reached its present form (Greenberg, "Holistic Interpretation," in *The Divine Helmsman*, eds. Crenshaw and Sandmel, 1980, 148). Greenberg recognizes Ezekiel's hand in virtually the entire book and maintains that the chronology of the oracles and the historical circumstances they reflect show the oracles were written in a single life span. In his opinion, the oracles present a coherent world-view contemporary with Ezekiel and consequently must have been directly shaped by him if not his very words (Greenberg, *Ezekiel 1-20*, 1983, 26-27).

[26] Block, *Ezekiel 1-24* (1997); idem, *Ezekiel 25-48* (1998). Block adopts a position closer to Greenberg's. In his opinion, indications of the prophet's own hand in the book's composition are as follows: 1) the prophecies are written in the first person. 2) Ezekiel is commanded to record information he receives from YHWH on several occasions. 3) The prophet's emotional response has left its mark on the confused and erratic shape of some texts. 4) The practice of transcribing oracles immediately after they have been received from a deity, with the prophet's name attached to them, is attested in extrabiblical sources. Recorded oracles provided a test of the truth or falsehood of Ezekiel's claims (Block, *Ezekiel 1-24*, 1997, 20-21). Block admits the difficulty of proving further involvement of Ezekiel in the book. While defending the overall integrity of the text as it has been transmitted, Block recognizes the prophet may

2) Studies on Ezekiel 26:1-28:19

A more specific work dealing with Ezekiel chapters 26-28 is H. J. Van Dijk's[27] *Ezekiel's Prophecy on Tyre* (1968). The book is a philological and linguistic study of Ezekiel 26-28. Following M. Dahood, Van Dijk constantly uses Northwest Semitic parallels.[28]

3) Studies on Ezekiel 27

Chapter 27, with its many *hapax legomena* and Phoenician technical terms, has attracted the attention of scholars. The largest concentration of these terms appears in verses 12-25a where a list of trading partners and commodities traded is presented. Some of the most important studies on this chapter are as follows:

H. P. Rüger's dissertation,[29] *Das Tyrusorakel Ezek 27* (1961), is one of them. In his study, Rüger dates the lamentation in 27:3b-11 to Ezekiel's time,[30] discusses the technical terminology and the countries mentioned in verses 12-24, correlates products and suppliers with an established system of trade routes,[31] and dates verses 12-24 to the Persian period (5th century).[32]

---

have inserted glosses in earlier oracles in the light of later prophecies or events. Later editors may have contributed other editorial comments as well (Block, *Ezekiel 1-24*, 1997, 22-23). My own position on the formation of Ezekiel 26-28, the subject of the present study, is closer to Greenberg's and Block's than to Zimmerli's.

[27] Van Dijk, *Prophecy* (1968).

[28] In the preface to his book (p. VIII), Van Dijk states that his purpose is to establish the "soundness" of the Massoretic text and prove the need for having recourse to other Northwest Semitic dialects. Van Dijk admits the self-imposed limits of his study by saying that he prefers not to deal with questions going beyond the philological and syntactical problems.

[29] Rüger, *Tyrusorakel* (1961).

[30] Between 586/85 and 574/73 BCE (Rüger, *Tyrusorakel*, 1961, 48, 50).

[31] Rüger finds behind the list in verses 12-24 a system of four trade routes: 1) 27:12-15 is the Persian royal route depicted by Herodotus (*The Histories*, 5.52-53). 2) 27:16-18 describe the great road along the main watershed of the west-Jordan mountains in its two branches: a) one on the western side of the Jordan and b) another on the "King's Highway" east of the river. 3) 27:19-22 is the incense route from South-Arabia. 4) 27:23 is the ḫarrān šarri, "road of kings" from Assur to Carchemish (pp. 116-17). His reconstruction is unconvincing on several grounds. First, his division of the chapter into

E. Lipiński's article,[33] "Products and Brokers of Tyre according to Ezekiel 27" (1985), concentrates on several Phoenician technical terms. Lipiński aims at examining the intermediary role of the nations as presented in Ezekiel 27 and establishing "the meaning of the terms ʿizĕbōnīm and maʿărāb, which designate the wares put on sale by Tyre or exchanged for foreign goods."[34]

Liverani's study,[35] "The Trade Network of Tyre according to Ezek. 27" (1991), discusses the resources in materials and men for the functioning of trade as presented in verses 1-11 and arranges them in three concentric belts.[36] Then he deals with the geographical picture of Tyre's external trade partners, distinguishing four different belts.[37]

---

two sections, one in poetry (27:3-11) and a second one in prose (12-25a) is artificial and arbitrary. Even if such a division is accepted, it does not follow that the two parts come from different periods or settings. Rüger also overlooks the fact that the road system used by the Persians existed long before the rise of Persia and that the Persian empire never extended as far as Tarshish. Furthermore, as Zimmerli has pointed out, if the author of the list had trade routes in mind, "one would have expected a much more concise mention of specific places" and "a properly ordered sequence of places" (Zimmerli, *Ezekiel 2*, 1983, 71).

[32] Rüger dates the list in verses 12-24 to the time after the Egyptian and Babylonian revolts against Xerxes in 484 and 482 BCE. At that time, Rüger continues, the economy of the two countries was so weakened that the absence of both Egypt and Babylon from among Tyre's trade partners would not be surprising (see Rüger, *Tyrusorakel*, 1961, 122-23). The mention of Egypt in 27:7 demonstrates that Ez. 27:3-11 and Ez. 27:12-24 are two parts of one and the same composition, a diptych. The presence of Cyprus in 27:6 reinforces the same conclusion. Babylon was absent for obvious reasons: Nebuchadnezzar was besieging the city of Tyre.

[33] Lipiński, "Products," in *Phoenicia and its Neighbors*, eds. Gubel and Lipiński, 1985, 213-20.

[34] Lipiński, "Products," 1985, 213.

[35] Liverani, "Trade Network," in *Ah Assyria*, eds. Cogan and Eph'al, 1991, 65-80.

[36] Liverani, "Trade Network," 1991, 67.

[37] 1) The inner belt (Judah, Israel, Damascus) supplies agricultural products. 2) A second belt (Beth-Togarma, Arab, Qedar) provides animals and animal products. 3) A third belt (Yawan, Tubal and Meshek, Dedan II, Edom, Eden-Harran-Assur) supplies manufactured products. 4) The outer belt (Tarshish, Sheba and Raʿma, Dedan I, again Edom) provides metals and luxury goods (p. 73).

Finally he dedicates a section to trade terminology and products traded and dates the oracle to the period c. 610-590 BCE.[38]

I. M. Diakonoff's article,[39] "The Naval Power and Trade of Tyre" (1992), is a most important study. Diakonoff isolates technical terms and translates them. He identifies the nations and countries the text mentions, and determines the historical setting of the data in question. His article, full of insights and appealing suggestions, is an invaluable tool in searching for historical reality in the Tyrian oracles. In it, he shows an immense erudition, identifies every single commodity mentioned in the text, defends the overall integrity of the Massoretic text, and, at the same time, is persuasive in the few emendations he proposes. Diakonoff's overall reasoning and command of the facts are more solid, his proposals more persuasive, and his determination of the historical data in question more accurate than any other article written on chapter 27. Unlike most authors, he recognizes the importance of Tyre's military power as depicted in Ezekiel 27 and finds elements of realism that illustrate Tyre's political stature as a regional power in it. Marveled at Ezekiel's exceptional knowledge of Tyre's naval and land forces and trading activities, Diakonoff suggests that the prophet lived in Tyre for a long time gathering information about it. In his opinion, this took place in the period before the siege of the city in 585 BCE, the *terminus ante quem* for acquiring such information.[40]

Diakonoff's method and suggestions have served as a blueprint in the quest for historical reality in the Tyrian oracles this discussion has set up to establish.

General studies on the Phoenicians are also relevant to the discussion on Ezekiel 27. G. Bunnens' work,[41] *L'expansion phénicienne en Méditerranée. Essai d'interprétation fondé sur une analyse des*

---

[38] Liverani, "Trade Network," 1991, 71. Liverani states that the list in Ezekiel 27 was composed c. 610-590 BCE and inserted in the book soon afterwards. In his opinion, the document refers to Tyre's trading activities during the same period.

[39] Diakonoff, "Naval Power," *IEJ* 42 (1992): 168-93.

[40] The suggestion appears in the final section called GENERAL REMARKS, SOURCES OF INFORMATION AND SUMMARY (Diakonoff, "Naval Power," 1992, 191-92). Diakonoff's article has been the guide for the present work in its quest for historical reality in the Tyrian oracles. However, not all his conclusions have been accepted in the present study.

[41] Bunnens, *L'expansion* (1979).

traditions littéraires (1979), is the most comprehensive study of the textual traditions on the Phoenician colonization. It includes a section on Ezekiel 27 in which different conjectures and theories on the oracle are examined and the chapter's overall reliability evaluated.

The most important treatment of the establishment and development of the Tyrian settlements in the Iberian Peninsula is Maria Eugenia Aubet's *The Phoenicians and the West: Politics, Colonies, and Trade* (1993).[42] In reconstructing the Phoenician presence in the Iberian Peninsula, Aubet made use of both archaeological data and documentary sources. Her study confirms the Phoenician abandonment of the Peninsula at the beginning of the 6th century BCE.

b) Historical Studies

The study of the Tyrian oracles is incomplete without a look at the history of the city and, in fact, of the whole area. Determining the setting of the oracles and the historical situation and circumstances they refer to makes necessary a good command of the events that took place in the period immediately before and after the destruction of Jerusalem and the siege of Tyre. This knowledge is the prerequisite for dating the oracles since they are perfectly datable to Ezekiel's time from a historical and literary point of view.

The main problem in reconstructing the history of Tyre, or Phoenicia in general, is the absence of annals or records. To trace the history of Tyre or Phoenicia, we rely on the Bible, the Neo-Assyrian and Neo-Babylonian Chronicles, the testimony of classical historians, Josephus, and an analysis of the archaeological record.

1) General histories of the Phoenicians

In 1962, D. Harden wrote *The Phoenicians*.[43] The book is still the most comprehensive history on the Phoenicians. The study is organized

---

[42] Aubet, *West* (1993). A collection of useful essays on the Phoenician colonization of the Iberian Peninsula by different scholars is presented in ed. Bierling, *Phoenicians in Spain* (2002).
[43] Harden, *The Phoenicians* (1962). Markoe has published recently a general history of the Phoenicians (*Phoenicians* [2000]).

thematically rather than chronologically. It is an important source for most aspects of the Phoenician colonization and culture. Many new studies have appeared since 1962. J. C. L. Gibson published in 1982 a selection of Phoenician inscriptions.[44] S. Moscati edited the important catalogue of the exhibit *The Phoenicians*.[45] The catalogue covers all major aspects of Phoenician history and culture, religious beliefs, main colonies, architecture, arts and crafts, city planning, army, etc. The series of seminars called *Studia Phoenicia* (1983-2000) are a major source of information on all aspects and periods of the Phoenician and Punic Civilizations.[46] The first dictionary on the Phoenician Civilization was released in 1992,[47] and the first research manual in 1995.[48] The first journal dedicated to the study of the Phoenician World, *Rivista di studi fenici*, appeared in 1973 and has been published on a regular basis ever since. In addition to all this publication activity, several congresses on Phoenician studies have taken place since 1979.[49]

2) General histories of Tyre, archaeological findings related to the city's history, and recent studies

H. J. Katzenstein's *The History of Tyre*[50] is the standard history of the Phoenician city. The book covers Tyre's history from the earliest times to 539 B.C.E. Katzenstein's massive work was first published in 1973 and, due to the absence of archaeological data at the time, relied

---

[44] Gibson, *Textbook*, vol. 3 (1982).

[45] Ed. Moscati, *The Phoenicians* (1988).

[46] *SP*, vols. 1-15 (1983-2000).

[47] *DCPP*, ed. Lipiński (1992).

[48] *CPP*, ed. Krings (1995).

[49] *Atti del I Congresso internazionale di studi fenici e punici. Roma, 5-10 novembre 1979*, 3 vols. (1983); *Atti del II Congresso internazionale di studi fenici e punici, Roma 5-10 novembre 1987* (1991); *Atti del III Congresso internazionale di studi fenici e punici, Tunisi, 11-16 novembre 1991*, 2 vols. (1995). Two more congresses on Phoenician studies have taken place: the *IV Congresso internazionale di studi fenici e punici* (1996) and the *V Congresso internazionale di studi fenici e punici* (2000). They have not yet been published.

[50] Katzenstein, *History* (1997). A previous history of Tyre by Fleming (*History of Tyre* [1915]) is totally outdated.

heavily on written sources.[51] He gathered together all textual and archaeological references to Tyre available at the time, interpreted them, and arranged them in chronological order. The last chapter of the book is dedicated to Tyre in the Neo-Babylonian period and traces the interactions of Babylon and Egypt, the two major powers of this period, in relation to each other and to the other satellite states (Judah, the Philistine cities, Moab, Edom, and the Phoenician cities).

Important new studies have appeared since 1973. Archaeological excavations and discoveries[52] have taken place in Tyre,[53] Ashkelon,[54]

---

[51] The second edition of the book (1997) is just a reprint of the first edition with bibliographical addenda.

[52] For general surveys, see the pertinent entries in ed. Stern, *New Encyclopedia* (1993); Meyers, *Oxford Encyclopedia* (1997); Stern, *Archaeology* (2001).

[53] Since the publication of Katzenstein's history, important archaeological discoveries have taken place. The typology of Tyrian pottery was established in 1978 when Bikai published *The Pottery of Tyre*. The texts on Ṣurru, a city of Tyrian exiles, were released in 1982-1987 (see Joannès, "Localization," *Semitica* 32 [1982]: 35-42; idem, "Trois textes," *Revue d'assyriologie et d'archéologie orientale* 81 [1987]: 147-58). A *tophet*, the first one discovered in Phoenicia, with two hundred funerary stelae, many of them inscribed, was found in Tyre in 1991. The discovery generated a strong controversy (see Moscati's article "Tofet," *RSF* 21 [1993]: 147-51).

[54] Lawrence Stager has been directing the land excavation at Ashkelon since 1985. Phoenician Red-Slipped Ware, "Samaria ware," and Red and Cream-Polished Phoenician ware have been found in large quantities in Ashkelon (604 BCE destruction debris) and Ashdod (c. 600 BCE destruction debris). These findings demonstrate important trade connections between Phoenician and Philistine cities in the 7th century. A Phoenician inscription written in the late 7th century script was found in Ashkelon as well as a Phoenician (?) royal dedicatory inscription in Philistine script in Ekron (7th century) (see Stager, "Fury of Babylon," *BAR* 22 [1996]: 59-69, 76-77 and "Archaeology of Destruction," *Eretz-Israel* 25 [1996]: 61-74). An exciting discovery was announced at a press conference in Tel Aviv on June 23rd 1999. At the end of a three-week underwater search, Lawrence Stager and *Titanic* discoverer, Robert Ballard, announced they had located two of the oldest deep-sea shipwrecks ever found. The larger is about 58 feet long and the smaller 48 feet long. Each of them carried a crew of six or more and at least ten tons of wine in several hundred amphoras in perfect state of conservation. Using *Jason*, a deep-sea diving robotic craft equipped with multiple cameras, they were able to photograph and videotape the ancient shipwrecks and to raise a number of artifacts from the two wrecks: twelve amphoras, three cooking pots, a mortarium, and an incense altar. The two ships set sail from Phoenicia (Tyre?) sometime between 750-700 BCE bound for Egypt or Carthage (see *Semitic Museum News, Harvard University*, vol. 3, # 1 and 2, December, 1999, 3-5). Lawrence Stager and Robert Ballard intend to continue their underwater excavations in the Black Sea.

Ekron,[55] Carthage,[56] Cyprus,[57] and elsewhere.[58] New inscriptions have also been found.[59] These finds, ongoing projects, and discoveries give us a more accurate picture of Tyre's role in the end of the 7th century and beginning of the 6th century. They confirm, among other things, the massive destruction the Neo-Babylonian take-over of the region represented and its effects in the Philistine and Phoenician coast as well as in Judah and the Transjordanian states. They call for a new fresh look at the oracles against Tyre and for a reevaluation of Tyrian history at the same time.

In spite of all these discoveries, our knowledge of Tyre's history is still in its infancy. Two formidable obstacles make difficult any progress in our knowledge of Tyre's history: the impossibility of excavating Tyre due to the fact that the modern city is built on top of the old one and the permanent instability of the area.[60] In the absence of Tyrian annals, some of the kings for the 7th-6th centuries are but a name in a list. Nothing else is known about them. Not even their names are known for some years.[61] In any case, to the extent that it is possible, it is

---

Due to the absence of oxygen in the waters of this sea, they expect to find ships and their entire crews intact.

[55] See Gitin, "Ekron of the Philistines," *BAR* 16 (1990): 33-42, 59; eds. Heltzer and Eitam, *Olive Oil in Antiquity* (1987).

[56] Joseph Greene and Lawrence Stager are now preparing the final report on their excavations in the Carthage Tophet (1976-1979). Current excavations are underway at the site by G. Mosca as well.

[57] See for example, Karageorghis, *Phoenician Discoveries in Cyprus* (1976).

[58] Similar finds have taken place in Dor, Sarepta, Sidon, and other places. For a description of the findings, see *CPP*, 1995, 564-69.

[59] Notice for example the discovery in 1980 of the Phoenician inscription from Cebel Ires Dağy. The inscription is dated on paleographical grounds c. 625-600 BCE and demonstrates the extent of Phoenician cultural influence in Cilicia (see Mosca and Russell, "Phoenician Inscription," *Epigraphica Anatolica* 9 [1987]: 1-28). One of the most important inscriptions ever discovered in Anatolia is the Incirli (Zincirli) Stele dated to the second half of the 8th century and written in Phoenician, Luwian, and Greek. Stephen Kaufman and Bruce Zuckerman are working on the translation of this boundary stele. Both of these two inscriptions illustrate Phoenician penetration in Cilicia.

[60] To these two factors, one should add the prevalence of illegal, unsupervised excavations. Thousands of new objects appear every year in the black market.

[61] The main sources for the Tyrian kings are the Phoenician inscriptions, the Neo-Assyrian and Neo-Babylonian Chronicles, the Bible, and Josephus. Josephus is the

necessary to correlate the events referred to in the Tyrian oracles with historical facts.

3) Studies on the history of Judah and her relations with the Phoenicians

The best study of the relations between the Phoenician cities and Israel and Judah is F. Briquel-Chatonnet's *Les relations entre les cités de la côte Phénicienne et les royaumes d'Israël et Juda* (1992).[62] Briquel-Chatonnet's study covers political, diplomatic, and commercial relations, together with religious, technical, and artistic influences. Her excellent study, however, is more relevant for the relations between the Phoenician cities and the Northern Kingdom of Israel than for those between the Phoenician cities and Judah.

Supplementing Katzenstein's and Briquel-Chatonnet's studies, A. H. E. Asher's unpublished dissertation,[63] *Judah and her Neighbours in The Seventh Century BCE* (1996), evaluates a century of Judean history and international politics. Asher's study covers the period between the death of Hezekiah in 687 BCE and the final fall of Jerusalem in 587 BCE. Asher draws largely on A. Malamat's articles on the history of this crucial period.[64] Even though her work does not pay much attention to the Phoenician cities, it is very useful for reconstructing the events that led to the destruction of Jerusalem and her Temple.

The aforementioned works on Ezekiel and historical studies have dealt with a variety of issues and questions ranging from philology to history. No commentary on Ezekiel, history of Tyre or specific study (biblical or Phoenician) has provided a satisfactory answer to the actual or ultimate cause or causes for Tyre's condemnation. Furthermore, no

---

single most important source for the first half of the 6th century BCE. To illustrate our absolute lack of information for some periods, the names of the Tyrian rulers for the years 660-591 BCE are unknown to us.

[62] Briquel-Chatonnet, *Relations* (1992).

[63] Asher, *Neighbours* (1996).

[64] Some of Malamat's articles are as follows: "Last Wars," *JNES* 9 (1950): 218-27; "New Record," *IEJ* 6 (1956): 246-55; "Last Kings," *IEJ* 18 (1968): 137-56; "Josiah's Bid," *JANES* 5 (1973): 267-79; "Last Years," in *World History of the Jewish People*, ed. Malamat, 1979, 4.1.205-21; "Small State," in *Text and Context*, ed. Classen, 1988, 117-29; "Between Egypt and Babylon," *Studia theologica* 44 (1990): 65-77; "Caught," *BAR* 25 (1999): 34-41, 64.

study has taken into account economic and political considerations and
applied them fully as the underlying reasons for these oracles. No work
has correlated known historical and archaeological data with Tyre's
commercial and trading policies in an attempt to explain the ultimate
reason(s) for Tyre's condemnation. It is the goal of the present
discussion to accomplish such a task.

After a historical survey of the main events between 626 and 573
BCE,[65] the study examines the reasons for Tyre's condemnation
analyzing all the underlying factors, the historical reality motivating the
oracles and showing that economic and political factors are the main
causes for the Tyrian oracles. Social and religious factors are also present
but of secondary importance.

Judah's economic stagnation was the direct result of Tyre's
economic policies and trade practices. Metals and horses were the
commodities Judah needed most and Tyre had a practical monopoly over
their trade and distribution. Tyre's trading policies enabled her to partake
in the Assyrian oppression, to establish alliances with Egypt and
Babylon, to enter into trade partnerships with the Philistines, to entertain
economic relations with Edom, to have a share in the lucrative Arabian
trade, and to extend her commercial influence into Judah itself. Tyre
participated in the slave trade and may have even sold Judean slaves in
the wake of Jerusalem's destruction in 586 BCE.

Social factors are present as well. Tyrian products (ivory, purple,
cedar, fine oils, perfumes...) were viewed as status symbols. They
represented the oppression of a dishonest Tyrian merchant elite that sold
itself to the highest bidder. A clear link between Tyre's religion and her
economic activities is also observable. Tyrian colonizing activities were
a continuation of her Canaanite religion under the patronage of Melkart,
the city god.

A new interpretation of Ezekiel 26:2, the clue for understanding
the oracles, confirms its economic nature and demonstrates that the
expression דלתות העמים means "peoples' ports" and that ירושלם
stands for the entire territory of Judah. The text thus describes the

---

[65] The year 626 BCE marks the beginning of the rapid decline of the Assyrian empire
with the death of the Assyrian king Assurbanipal. 573 BCE is generally accepted as the
date for the end of Nebuchadnezzar's siege of Tyre. At that time all the Levant was
under Neo-Babylonian control.

situation of desolation and ruin that resulted from Nebuchadnezzar's destruction of the Philistine ports at the end of the 7th century. Throughout most of her history, Israel lacked an exit to the sea. The Philistine cities were the natural outlet for import and export of products and commodities. Tyre anticipated a major trade shift to the North, to her own ports. This trade shift would mean Judah's economic ruin.

The study concludes with a discussion of the economic focus and political status of Tyre as reflected in Ezekiel 26:1-28:19 and a new interpretation and dating of the Tyrian oracles on historical and literary grounds.

2

Historical Setting of Ezekiel 26:1-28:19

1. The End of the Assyrian Empire (626-610 BCE)

Ezekiel's oracles against Tyre describe Nebuchadnezzar's siege of Tyre that took place in the early part of the 6th century BCE. Beginning in 604 BCE, the Levant came under Neo-Babylonian control. The history of this period can be reconstructed by using Neo-Babylonian sources, the Bible, classical sources –especially Herodotus' information on the Egyptian Saïte Dynasty-[1] and a small number of inscriptions. Archaeological remains can supplement the information provided by the written sources.

The Neo-Babylonian Chronicle is our main source of information. It covers the years 626-594 BCE. The entries for the years 622-617 BCE are missing and the Chronicle breaks off after 594.[2]

The weakening of Assyrian control in the Levant after Assurbanipal's death (627) opened up the way for the intensification of the Egyptian presence in the area. At the same time, all the petty states of the region tried to share in the spoils of the languishing Assyrian empire. As a result, Tyre was able to regain its former possessions on the mainland and became the leading city on the Phoenician coast. Carthage in turn became the naval and military protector of Tyre's colonial empire in the West.[3]

When the Chronicle starts in 626, we find the Assyrian King Sin-šar(ra)-iškun seeking to subdue the Babylonians who were striving to regain their independence. On the twelfth of the month of Tisri (August, 626 BCE) an Assyrian army advanced on Babylon and was decisively beaten in what was the last Assyrian attempt to gain control of Babylon.

---

[1] Contemporary documentation of the Saïte dynasty is very scarce (see Redford, *Egypt*, 1992, 431).

[2] Wiseman published it in 1956 (*Chronicles* [1974]). Grayson made a revision in 1975 (*Chronicles* [1975]).

[3] See Katzenstein, "Tyre," *ABD*, 6.690.

Six weeks later, Nabopolassar (626-605 BCE) "sat upon the throne in Babylon."[4] An alliance with the Median King Cyaxares (c. 625-) was instrumental in the Assyrian defeat. From then on the Assyrians were only fighting in defense of their own homeland. Nabopolassar gained control of Nippur (622) and of the districts of Suḫu and Ḫindanu (616) and defeated the Assyrians in Qablinu (616).

The same year the Egyptian Pharaoh Psammetichus I (664-610 BCE) appears on the Euphrates as an ally of the Assyrians. The reasons for this Assyro-Egyptian alliance are obscure. Psammetichus may have wanted to reestablish the balance of power in Mesopotamia threatened by the Medo-Babylonian alliance and the subsequent Babylonian advance. Fear of a Babylonian domination over Assyria's former colonies, among which was Syria, now in Egypt's control, is a likely explanation for this Egyptian intervention.[5]

The Medes began the siege of Assur in 615. They conquered and looted it in 614 BCE. Subsequently, Nabopolassar and Cyaxares concluded a peace treaty there. The fall of Nineveh, the Assyrian capital, to Nabopolassar, Cyaxares, and their allies, the Umanmanda,[6] came next in 612 BCE. After a siege of three months, the city was destroyed and her temples looted. Cyaxares retreated to his homeland. Sin-šar(ra)-iškun died during the same year[7] and Aššur-uballiṭ II, the last king of Assyria, fled to Harran where he established an Assyrian government in exile. Nahum 2-3 contains a superb description of Nineveh's assault, panic, humiliation, and downfall.

In 610 the Babylonians and Medians marched to the Upper Euphrates unopposed and took Harran. Aššur-uballiṭ[8] abandoned the city and retreated to Syria.

---

[4] Wiseman, *Chronicles,* 1974, 51

[5] Asher, *Neighbours,* 1996, 31. When Assyria retreated from *ebir nāri* (beyond the river), according to Asher, she turned these territories over to Egypt. Allegedly the Egyptian takeover took place after the Babylonian revolt of 626 and the outbreak of civil war in Assyria in 623 (Asher, *Neighbours,* 1996, 36).

[6] Umanmanda is an Akkadian general term meaning "tribal hordes" applied to various enemies including the Cimmerians and Scythians.

[7] It is not clear whether he died during the siege or was able to escape it. He was never heard of again (see Oates, "Fall," in *CAH*, eds. Boardman et al., 1991, 3.2.180).

[8] No Egyptian forces are mentioned in the Babylonian Chronicles from 615 to 610 BCE.

A text of Herodotus (2.112)[9] apparently referring to Psammetichus I has been used to suggest the existence of an Egypto-Tyrian alliance (c. 630-610 BCE).[10] The text in question reads as follows:

> To this day there is in Memphis, south of the temple of Hephaestus, a particularly fine and well-appointed precinct which was his. The houses around this precinct are inhabited by Phoenicians from Tyre, and the whole district is called the Tyrian Camp.

In relation to this precinct, Tyre is credited with the manufacturing of silver bowls of Egyptian style from the later 7th century found at Praeneste among other places.[11] Tyre gave pharaoh "a (royal) domain of cedar" in Lebanon or a small district in the forest of Lebanon in return.[12]

2. Egyptian Control of the Levant and the Scythian Presence

Sometime in the second half of the 7th century the Scythians, sometimes identified with "the enemy from the North" of Jeremiah and Zephaniah's prophecies,[13] reached "Syrian Palestine."[14] The eradication of the Scythian presence in the Levant came at the end of Psammetichus I's reign.[15] The chronology of this presence is based on spotty

---

[9] I use R. Waterfield's translation of Herodotus, *The Histories* (1998).

[10] Katzenstein, *History*, 1997, 298-300.

[11] See Katzenstein, "Tyre," 1992, 690; Harden, *The Phoenicians*, 1962, 189.

[12] According to a fragmentary inscription on a statue of Hor, an army commander at Heracleopolis (see ed. Breasted, *Ancient Records*, 1962, 4 # 967 [p. 494, note g] and 970).

[13] Yamauchi, *Foes*, 1982, 87-97.

[14] Herodotus (1.104-05) states that, after defeating the Medes, the Median empire crumbled and "from there they marched on Egypt. When they reached Syrian Palestine, the Egyptian king Psammetichus came to meet them." See Malamat, "Historical Setting," *IEJ* 1 (1950/51): 155.

[15] No archaeological evidence for the Scythian presence in the Levant has been found. The term "Scythians" is used to describe a specific tribe which inhabited the area North and East of the Black Sea. The Scythians first appear in written history in Esarhaddon's annals (681-668 BCE) and seem to be centered at that time in what is today Northwest Iran. The finding of a number of arrowheads of a type called "Scythian" in Jerusalem in

documentary evidence, primarily Herodotus. In *The Histories* 1.104-06 he wrote:

> The Medes and the Scythians clashed; the Medes lost the battle, their empire crumbled and the Scythians occupied the whole of Asia.
> From there they marched on Egypt. When they reached Syrian Palestine, the Egyptian king Psammetichus came to meet them. With a combination of bribery and entreaty he persuaded them not to go any further and they turned back. On their way back they came to the town of Ascalon in Syria. Most of the Scythians bypassed the town without doing it any harm, but a few of them, who had fallen behind the main body, plundered the sanctuary of Heavenly Aphrodite. [...]
> The Scythian domination of Asia lasted twenty-eight years.

The correlation of Herodotus' testimony with other evidence indicates that a longer period was required for these events. The Scythians were an Asiatic nation of horse-rearing seminomads residing in the steppes of southern Russia. They displaced the Cimmerians, another nomadic people that lived in the steppes of Russia, southward (c. 750). The first Scythian inroad in Assyrian territory took place in 676 BCE when Esarhaddon beat them. Subsequently the Scythians invaded Urartu (674) and subjugated it. Then Mannaea and Media came under Scythian domination (c. 652). After an Assyrian-Scythian alliance and the Assyrian defeat of Media (653-652), the Scythians under king Barbatua (c. 678-c. 645 BCE), dominated Media with Assyrian permission. Later Media was liberated from Assyrian domination in 625 when Cyaxares II ascended the Median throne. The Scythians reached the summit of their power in Western Asia between 650 and 645. It is at this time that the twenty-eight year period Herodotus referred to must have started.

---

the destruction layer (586 BCE) has prompted Yamauchi (*Foes*, 1982, 97, 99) to suggest the Scythians were mercenaries in the Chaldean army. But different peoples used this kind of arrowhead at the time. Some types of ivories have also been identified with the Scythian presence in the Levant. It is not clear whether there was a permanent Scythian presence in the area of Syria-Palestine or just sporadic raids. It is not even clear they ever reached the Levantine coast.

Barbatua's son, Madyes, defeated the Cimmerians sometime after 650. Under his reign the Scythians reached the Egyptian border (Herodotus, 1.105). The Scythian change of sides documented in Babylonian records from 615 BCE onwards, was a decisive element in the disintegration of Assyria. At that time the Scythians appear as allies of the Medes. Their domination of Asia came to an end with the Median annexation of Mannaea and Urartu (609-585).[16]

Herodotus' account on the Scythian domination of the Levant is not universally accepted. Many scholars have a skeptical attitude towards it. Some see it as patterned on the Cimmerians' depredations in Asia Minor and dismissed it as fictional. Others consider it a distortion of a historical assignment of Scythian mercenary troops in Assyrian service to posts in Palestine and their subsequent clash with Egypt. Some contemporary Bible commentators doubt the historicity of the Scythian invasions as well rejecting previous interpretations of Jeremiah's earliest oracles according to which the oracles were prompted by the Scythian incursions.[17]

Psammetichus I died at the end of 610 BCE after a long reign of fifty-four years. According to Herodotus (2.157), "For twenty-nine of these years [...] [Psammetichus] maintained a siege of the great Syrian city of Azotus [Ashdod], until the city fell."[18] The final destruction of a gate (area M, stratum VII) can be related to this siege or to a subsequent one by Nebuchadnezzar around 600 BCE.[19]

Some scholars have supposed an extension of the Egyptian Saïte empire into Phoenicia by the end of Psammetichus I's reign. Redford, for example, states that "Psammetichos's direct control [...] extended along the coast as far as and including Phoenicia, where he boasts that his

---

[16] See Sulimirski and Taylor, "Scythians," in *CAH*, eds. Boardman et al., 1991, 3.2.564-67; Redford, *Egypt*, 1992, 438-41.

[17] See Redford, *Egypt*, 1992, 440.

[18] A number of different interpretations of the fragment have been proposed. Tadmor, for example, suggested the figure "29" to be considered as the regnal year of Psammetichus I or 635 BCE (Tadmor, "Philistia," *BA* 29 [1966]: 102; Cogan and Tadmor, *II Kings*, 1988, 300). Other scholars have connected the twenty-eight years of Scythian domination of the Levant with this datum and suggest that the siege of Ashdod happened in the years following the Scythian defeat by the Egyptians (see for example Malamat, "Last Wars," 1950, 218).

[19] Dothan, "Ashdod," *ABD*, 1.481.

officers supervised timber production and export."[20] Others reject the possibility that Egypt pursued a policy of direct annexation in the Levant.[21] The data may just show an intensification of Egyptian trade and economic relations with the Phoenician cities.

3. Necho II's and Josiah's Encounter at Meggido – Josiah's Death

Psammetichus I's son Necho II succeeded him. Necho ruled for fifteen years from 609-595/4 BCE. In early summer 609 BCE, in collaboration with Aššur-uballiṭ, Necho tried to recapture Harran and failed. Pharaoh "Necho [...] went up to fight at Carchemish on the Euphrates, and Josiah went out against him"[22] (2 Chr. 35:20). The account in 2 Kgs. 23:29 states that "in his [Josiah's] days, Pharaoh Necho, king of Egypt, went up to the king of Assyria to the river Euphrates. When King Josiah went against him, [Necho II] put him to death at Megiddo as soon as he saw him."

The historic core and interpretation of this event has long puzzled scholars and is a matter of dispute to this very day. The difficulties in interpreting the passage are related to a second question that has to do with the limits of Josiah's kingdom and whether Megiddo was under Judean control at the time.

The biblical background to this story is as follows: Josiah (640-609 BCE) was made king at the age of eight after his father's murder in 640 BCE by the "people of the land" and reigned for thirty-one years (2 Kgs. 21:24; 22:1; 2 Chr. 33:25; 34:1). The information provided in 2 Chronicles indicates that in the eighth year of his reign (c. 632), he began to seek the God of David (2 Chr. 34:3a). The twelfth year (628/7) marked the beginning of his reform. He started by purging Judah and Jerusalem of the high places (2 Chr. 34:3b). Afterwards he extended his reform to the "towns of Manasseh, Ephraim and Simeon, as far as Naphtali" (v. 6). Finally, with the discovery of the Book of the Law in

---

[20] Redford, *Egypt*, 1992, 442. Redford refers here to the statue of Hor mentioned in note 12 (Breasted, *Ancient Records*, 1962, 4 # 967 [p. 494, note g] and 970). The inscription refers to cedar from the royal domain.

[21] See for example Asher, *Neighbours*, 1996, 37.

[22] Unless stated, translations of biblical passages are my own.

the Temple in the eighteenth year, his reform program hit full swing (2 Chr. 34:8-35:19).[23] The reform in his twelfth year coincided with the beginning of a civil war in Assyria between Sin-šum-lišir and Aššur-etel-ilāni.[24] Evidently, Josiah took advantage of the weakening of the Assyrian empire to assert his independence.

To a great extent the reconstruction of the geographical extension of Josiah's kingdom depends on the texts cited in the previous paragraph. Archaeological evidence is ambiguous. As Asher pointed out, all attempts at reconstructing the borders of Josiah's kingdom beyond Judah and its vicinity are speculative. Such attempts depend upon ambiguous sources. Maximalist and minimalist interpretations of the geographical extension of Josiah's reform have been proposed.[25]

The minimalist approach would limit the extension of Josiah's kingdom to the area between the Beer-sheba Valley and Beth-el. Most of the minimalists would limit annexations in the north to the area of Mount Ephraim alone.[26] In its most extreme formulation, the maximalist approach assumes that Josiah attempted to restore the kingdom of David in all its glory.[27] Intermediate positions between these two also exist.[28]

---

[23] 2 Kings only mentions the reform in this year and includes the "cities of Samaria" i.e., the Northern Kingdom (2 Kgs. 22:3; 23:19).

[24] Cross and Freedman, "Josiah's Revolt," *JNES* 12 (1953): 56-58.

[25] For a review of the two approaches, see Asher, *Neighbours*, 1996, 111-114.

[26] For example Mazar, Malamat, and Kallai consider that the expression "from Geba to Beer-sheba" in (2 Kgs. 23:8) reflects the limits of the reform. Rose and Nelson question the extension of Josiah's reform to the former Northern kingdom. Na'aman thinks the town lists of Judah and Bejamin in the book of Joshua indicate the extension of the kingdom of Judah in Josiah's time (Na'aman, "Judah," *TA* 18 [1991]: 57). Asher follows Na'aman's minimalist assessment.

[27] On the basis of Jeremiah 49 (oracle against Ammon) and Is. 9:1-7, Ginsberg suggests that Josiah controlled not only the former territories of Judah and Israel but also the three Transjordanian states (Ginsberg, "Judah," in *Alexander Marx Jubilee Volume*, ed. Lieberman, 1950, 347-68). Katzenstein (*History*, 1997, 303-04) proposes that Necho II demanded the surrender of the former Assyrian provinces (Megiddo, Samaria). On the basis of 2 Chr. 34:6, Mitchell includes Gilead among the territories occupied by Josiah (see "Judah," in *CAH*, eds. Boardman et al., 1991, 3.2.386). The presence of Hebrew inscriptions at Meṣad Ḥashavyahu (Yabneh-Yam) has prompted some scholars to think that North Philistia was under Josiah's control (Naveh, "Hebrew Letter," *IEJ* 10 [1960]: 129-139) and to accept the possibility of a "substantial advance in the N territory" (Althann, "Josiah," *ABD*, 3.1016).

Various interpretations of the events at Megiddo have been suggested. For the most part, they assumed the historicity of the account in 2 Chr. 35:20-24 according to which there was a military clash between Egypt and Judah at Megiddo in 609 BCE. Such a military encounter, however, is not borne out in 2 Kgs. 23:29, which has led some scholars to doubt the military background of the episode.[29] Several interpretations are as follows:

1) Josiah saw Necho II's move as a threat to Judah's newfound independence and hurried to occupy Megiddo, which had been left vacant by the Assyrian departure (Asher).[30]

2) Josiah wanted to delay Necho II long enough to ensure the defeat of his archenemy, Assyria and of her king Aššur-uballiṭ II (Rowton)[31] or to prevent an Egyptian "prop up of the hated Assyrians" who were in sharp decline (Mitchell).[32]

3) Josiah was a tributary of Psammetichus I and Necho II came to Palestine to receive the oath of loyalty of the vassal kings, among them Josiah. The oath had become invalid on Psammetichus' death in 610. By killing Josiah, Necho wanted to force the Judeans to abide by his instructions (Na'aman).[33]

---

[28] In some cases it is difficult to determine whether a scholar is minimalist or maximalist. Malamat, for example, accepts that Josiah extended his dominion to the territories of the former Assyrian province of Samaria and excludes Galilee at the same time (Malamat, "Josiah's Bid," 1973, 271).

[29] The account in 2 Kings is the only contemporary evidence of this event (see Cogan and Tadmor, *II Kings*, 1988, 300-02). The account is laconic and offers no explanation for the events at Megiddo. No extra-biblical reference to the event has been found. It is generally thought that Josiah died trying to stop Necho II (see Malamat, "Josiah's Bid," 1973, 278). The capture of the Assyrian stronghold of Harran and the fact that Necho was a new, untried pharaoh may be the reasons for Josiah's attack. For a discussion of the main conjectures proposed, see Asher, *Neighbours*, 1996, 125-34.

[30] Asher, *Neighbours*, 1996, 128.

[31] Rowton, "Death," *JNES* 10 (1951): 128-130.

[32] Mitchell in "Judah," 1991, 391. To Redford the reasons behind this action of Josiah have to do with Judah's "sharing a community of interest with Babylon in international politics" for over a century. Josiah, according to him, "simply saw himself as an ally of the forces of right in the final destruction of Assyria" (Redford, *Egypt*, 1992, 448). Josiah may have expected Babylonian recognition of his hegemony over Israel (see Asher, *Neighbours*, 1996, 131).

[33] Na'aman, "Judah," 1991, 52.

4) Necho II wanted the fortress of Megiddo for himself and killed Josiah treacherously. He was unwilling to allow the existence of an ally who might change sides and block his retreat (Nelson).[34]

In the final analysis and despite all the scholarly conjecture, what happened at Megiddo remains a mystery. Any scenario proposed for the circumstances surrounding Josiah's death is based on speculation.[35]

The archaeological evidence for Josiah's annexation of Meggido is limited. It depends on the existence at the old Assyrian capital, Megiddo, level II of a newly built fortress. The correlation is made on textual, not historical or archaeological grounds.[36] The fact that the fortress was apparently built according to a "reed" commonly used in Palestine based on the cubit of 44.5 cm suggests the fortress was of Egyptian or Israelite foundation.[37] The archaeological evidence thus is indecisive: stratum II at Megiddo can be equally regarded as Israelite or Egyptian.[38] The same conclusion applies to Meṣad Ḥashavyahu, an Egyptian or Judean fortress with Greek mercenaries.[39] Finally the association with Josiah of one or the other of two minor destructions in level VI of Shechem is highly unlikely.

Textual and archaeological data suggest that Josiah's kingdom was a weak one. The destruction brought up by Sennacherib's campaign of 701 BCE remained evident until the very end of Josiah's reign when many sites destroyed in 701 BCE were still unsettled. Even though Judah enjoyed a period of peace and prosperity in the 7th century BCE under Assyrian rule that enabled her to recover gradually, restore some

---

[34] Nelson, "*Realpolitik*," in *Scripture in Context II*, eds. Hallo et al., 1983, 188.

[35] Asher, *Neighbours*, 1996, 134.

[36] Thus Amiran and Dunayevsky, Albright, Kenyon, Yadin.

[37] Malamat, "Josiah's Bid," 1973, 268ff.

[38] Malamat speculates that Assyria had transferred Megiddo to Psammetichus I to serve as a logistic base or vital way station for the Egyptian army in its Syrian campaigns (Malamat, "Josiah's Bid," 1973, 267-78). After evaluating all possibilities, Asher concludes that Megiddo became an Egyptian base at sometime between 646 and 616. For a full discussion of the evidence, see Asher, *Neighbours*, 1996, 37-41; Stern, *Archaeology*, 2001, 313-14.

[39] An alliance between Josiah and Psammetichus I would explain the mixture of Judean and Egyptian material in the fortress. Josiah may have controlled it allowing Psammetichus to use the coastal route for his military operations in the north (see Cazelles, "Vie," in *Le Livre de Jérémie*, ed. Bogaert, 1981, 31; Nelson, "*Realpolitik*," 1983, 183-89).

settlements, and rebuilt her economy, the same is true of Judah's eastern and western neighbors. The expansion of these neighbors was to exert a considerable impact on Judah's fate at the end of her existence.[40]

After Josiah's death, his body was taken to Jerusalem for burial and "the people of the land" made his youngest son, Jehoahaz, king (2 Kgs. 23:29-30).[41] He was twenty-three and reigned for three months (June-August 609) (2 Kgs. 23:31). Meanwhile Necho II established his headquarters at Carchemish to protect his interests in Syria and support the Assyrians. The Euphrates became the border between Egypt and Babylonia for the next few years. Necho took up residence in the province of Hamath in Riblah. Then "Pharaoh Necho imprisoned him [Jehoahaz] at Riblah in the land of Hamath, so that he might not reign in Jerusalem, and imposed a tribute on the land of one hundred talents of silver and a talent of gold" (2 Kgs. 23:33). Necho made his elder half-brother Eliakim king with the name of Jehoiakim (609-597 BCE). Jehoiakim taxed the people of the land in order to raise this tribute (verse 35). Jehoahaz, for his part, was sent to Egypt where he died (2 Kgs. 23:34; 2 Chr. 36:4). It is not clear whether Necho's actions were motivated by an anti-Egyptian policy on Jehoahaz' part. Jer. 22:10-12 alludes to his exile in a dirge. Jeremiah announced that Jehoahaz would die in exile. Jehoahaz's exile meant the end of twenty years of Judean independence.

An episode that took place in Jehoiakim's first year (609) illustrates the attitude toward the prophets of YHWH at the closing years of the monarchy. After proclaiming the destruction of Jerusalem and the Temple if people failed to obey God's law in a temple sermon, Jeremiah narrowly escaped death (Jer. 26:1-24). Another prophet, Uriah, fled to Egypt and was extradited and executed for delivering a similar message (Jer. 26:20-23). The intervention of Ahikam ben Shaphan spared Jeremiah's life.

---

[40] Asher, *Neighbours*, 1996, 32.
[41] He is called Shallum in Jer. 22:11.

4. The Last Years of the Egyptian Dominion of the Levant and the Battle of Carchemish in 605 BCE

The Babylonian advance continued in 607. In that year Nabopolassar captured Kimuḫu on the west bank of the Euphrates river. Kimuḫu was a strategic site commanding a river crossing which guarded against any Egyptian attack down the river and represented a threat to the Egyptian communication line from Hamath to Carchemish. The Egyptians recaptured Kimuḫu and defeated the Babylonians in Quramati in 606.

The following year, Nabopolassar stayed in Babylonia, and Nebuchadnezzar (605-562 BCE), the crown prince, replaced him as commander in chief. In a decisive battle, the Babylonian army faced the Egyptians at Carchemish[42] (June-July 605 BCE).[43] According to the Babylonian Chronicle,[44]

> The crown-prince, mustered (the Babylonian army) and took command of his troops; he marched to Carchemish which is on the bank of the Euphrates, and crossed the river (to go) against the Egyptian army which lay in Carchemish, ... fought with each other and the Egyptian army withdrew before him. He accomplished their defeat and to non-existence [beat?] them.

Egypt stood alone, for nothing is heard again about an Assyrian army. The Egyptian defeat at Carchemish was decisive; the Egyptian troops were annihilated. Nebuchadnezzar pursued them to Hamath, defeated them there, and conquered the entire region of Hamath. It is likely that this area "extended as far as Qadesh on the R. Orontes and included

---

[42] Carchemish, a trade center on the west bank of the Euphrates river at one of the main fords of that river, was important both commercially and militarily. A principal trade route ran from Nineveh up to Harran then crossed the Euphrates at Carchemish, and continued on to the Orontes River Valley in Lebanon. From there other routes led to the Mediterranean, Palestine, and Egypt.

[43] For a discussion of the precise date of the battle of Carchemish, see Wiseman, *Nebuchadnezzar*, 1985, 16.

[44] Wiseman, *Chronicles*, 1974, 67. Josephus also mentions the battle in his *Ant.*, 10.6.1 (84).

Riblah, the town taken by the Egyptians with Carchemish, in 609 BCE."[45] Riblah became the Babylonian base of operations in southern Syria. From there Nebuchadnezzar directed the collection of tribute and the dispensation of justice (see Jer. 52:10-11).[46] No Egyptian historical record of the battle has been found. No siege of Tyre or Jerusalem, a preliminary step to any large-scale assault against Egypt, took place at this time. With Assyria destroyed and Egypt without any credibility in Syria-Palestine, Carchemish sealed Babylonia's ultimate victory.

The Babylonians would eventually take all of Syria-Palestine, but there was a brief delay. Nabopolassar died soon after the battle of Carchemish and Nebuchadnezzar had to return to Babylon, where he was crowned king.

Nebuchadnezzar took captives after the battle of Carchemish. Berossus states that, after receiving news about his father's death, Nebuchadnezzar,[47]

> Set the affairs of Egypt and the other countries in order, and committed the captives he had taken from the Jews, and Phoenicians, and Syrians, and of the nations belonging to Egypt, to some of his friends, that they might conduct that part of the forces that had on heavy armor, with the rest of his baggage, to Babylonia; while he went in haste, having but a few with him, over the desert to Babylon.

The book of Daniel (Dan. 1:1-4) mentions a siege of Jerusalem in the third year of King Jehoiakim of Judah (605). After the siege, Daniel states, Nebuchadnezzar took some of the vessels of the temple and deported, among others, Daniel and his friends. There is no reference in the Babylonian Chronicle to any siege of Jerusalem in this year but only

---

[45] Wiseman, *Chronicles*, 1974, 17.

[46] This may indicate that the Egyptian dominion in the Levant was more nominal than real. Evidence of Egyptian domination of Phoenicia is meager. A fragmentary basalt stele from Sidon kept at the British Museum (# 25094) with a text of Necho II is often presented as a proof of such domination (Mitchell, "Judah," 1991, 391). The inscription is rather a proof of the good relations existing between Egypt and the Phoenician cities at this time.

[47] As quoted by Josephus in *Ag. Ap.*, 1.19 (137). Josephus' quotes are from W. Whiston's translation, *Works of Josephus* (1995).

of operations against Ashkelon whose city was captured in Kislev (November/December 604 BCE). In Judah a fast was called the same month showing the concern felt there (Jer. 36:9). Jehoiakim's violent reaction to Jeremiah's warnings about the imminent destruction of Judah by the king of Babylon (Jer. 36:29) suggests that Jerusalem had not yet given in to the Babylonians.[48] Since no other record of a siege of Jerusalem at this time has been found, it has been suggested that Dan. 1:1-4 refers to the year 604.[49] Dan. 1:1 does not say that the city was captured or that Jehoiakim was taken prisoner. Josephus' reference to Jewish prisoners after the battle of Carchemish and his exclusion of Judah from the territories Nebuchadnezzar conquered after the battle seem to support this suggestion.[50] The vessels of the Temple could be part of the tribute referred to in the Babylonian Chronicle.

The importance of the battle of Carchemish as a turning point in the Egypto-Babylonian struggle for control of the Levant did not go unnoticed by the Israelite Prophets. Jeremiah realized Babylonia would take control of the whole Levant (25:1-14; 46:1-12) and advocated submission to Nebuchadnezzar (36:29). Echoing these momentous events at Carchemish, Jer. 46:1-12 betrays the Judeans' initial joyful reaction to the liberation from Egyptian domination. The judgment on Egypt starts as follows: "Concerning Egypt, about the army of Pharaoh Necho II, king of Egypt, which was by the river Euphrates at Carchemish and which King Nebuchadrezzar of Babylon defeated in the fourth year of King Jehoiakim son of Josiah of Judah" (Jer. 46:2). Jeremiah goes on picturing Egypt as having lost its power and rejoicing at its powerless situation (Jer. 46:11-12).

The battle of Carchemish meant the end of the Egyptian domination of the Levant. 2 Kgs. 24:7 summarizes well the outcome of the battle: "Never again did the king of Egypt leave his country, for the

---

[48] Wiseman, *Nebuchadnezzar*, 1985, 23.

[49] Dan. 1:1 says: "In the third year of the reign of Jehoiakim king of Judah, Nebuchadnezzar king of Babylon came to Jerusalem and besieged it." See Wiseman, *Nebuchadnezzar*, 1985, 23; Mitchell, "Judah," 1991, 394-95. The book of Daniel is taken to follow the Judean (autumn-autumn) calendar (Mitchell, "Judah," 1991, 394).

[50] The text reads "So the king of Babylon [...] took all Syria, as far as Pelusium, excepting Judea" (*Ant.*, 10.6.1 [86]).

king of Babylon had taken all that belonged to the king of Egypt, from the Wadi of Egypt to the River Euphrates."[51]

Carchemish happened in the aftermath of the disintegration of the Assyrian empire. The reasons for its sudden instability are complex and much debated.[52] Assurbanipal (668-627 BCE) controlled the greatest empire ever, yet within twenty years Assyria had ceased to exist. The main reasons are as follows:

1) The very small size of metropolitan Assyria determined that the prosperity of the country could only be supported by the tribute of territories far beyond the natural borders of Assyria whose resources were exhausted.
2) Huge military expenditures resulting from the extension of the Assyrian empire well beyond its borders and the ensuing considerable strain on the economy.
3) A brutal imperial policy consisting of the exaction of huge amounts of tribute and manpower and the practice of mass deportation.

5. The Babylonian Domination of the Levant (605-597 BCE)

In his accession year (605), after the battle of Carchemish, Nebuchadnezzar "marched unopposed" through the "Hatti-land"[53] and took the heavy tribute of the Hatti-land to Babylon. In the following year (604) Nebuchadnezzar returned to the Hatti-land. He claims that "all the

---

[51] Wiseman (*Nebuchadnezzar*, 1985, 24) gathered external evidence for the Egyptian retreat. The evidence comes from Arad. According to him, the fortress, destroyed by the Egyptians in 609 BCE (Stratum VII), was rebuilt c. 604 BCE (Stratum VI). A letter from one Eliashib, a Judean official, shows the interruption of supplies to the "Kittim" or Kittiyim (*lktym*). This is a term originally designating the inhabitants of Citium in Cyprus; it "came to refer to the Greeks that settled there in large numbers and by extension to Greeks and Graecicized peoples throughout the Mediterranean" (Mitchell, "Judah," 1991, 399). Three seals belonging to "Eliashib son of Oshiahu" have also been found at one of the South rooms of the site together with ostraca listing commodities in Egyptian hieratic symbols. For a different view according to which the site was under Judean control, see Manor and Herion, "Arad," *ABD*, 1.331-36. They notice Israelite scribes had "adopted hieratic symbols for numbers, measures and commodities" (334).
[52] I follow Oates, "Fall," 1991, 180, 183.
[53] Wiseman, *Chronicles*, 1974, 69. The term Hatti-land in Neo-Babylonian inscriptions is an imprecise term designating the whole area of Syria and Palestine.

kings of Ḫatti land came before him and he received their heavy tribute."[54] Jehoiakim of Judah (609/8-598/7 BCE) was among the kings that paid tribute to Nebuchadnezzar and remained his vassal for three years (2 Kgs. 24:1). Subsequently, according to the Neo-Babylonian Chronicle, Nebuchadnezzar,[55]

> Marched to the city of Ashkelon and captured it in the month of Kislev [November/December 604]. He captured his king and plundered it and carried off [spoil from it...] He turned the city into a mound and heaps of ruins and then in the month of Sebat he marched back to Babylon.

The city of Ashkelon was utterly destroyed[56] and the population and Aga, their king, were deported to Babylonia where a community calling itself "Ashkelon" existed in the 6th century.[57] In the wake of Nebuchadnezzar's attack against Ashkelon, Jehoiakim proclaimed a fast in Judah (Jer. 36:9).[58] Chapter 36 of Jeremiah tells how the prophet had his secretary Baruch read a scroll of utterances in public, in the Jerusalem Temple. The book was confiscated, read to the king, and destroyed. Jehoiakim ordered the arrest of Jeremiah and Baruch, who went into hiding.

In the next three years (603-601) Nebuchadnezzar marched every year to the Ḫatti-land. These annual expeditions seem to have aimed at maintaining political pressure and Babylonian prestige on the kingdoms

---

[54] Wiseman, *Chronicles*, 1974, 69.

[55] Wiseman, *Chronicles*, 1974, 69.

[56] Nebuchadnezzar's strategy consisted in opening up the road to Egypt. In order to do this, he needed to neutralize and reduce the Philistine plain and the coastal highway to Egypt. For the destruction of Ashkelon, see Stager, "Fury of Babylon," 1996, 59-69, 76-77; idem, "Archaeology of Destruction," 1996, 61-74.

[57] Tadmor, "Philistia," 1966, 102, note 62; Zadok, "Phoenicians," *BASOR* 230 (1978): 61; Oded, *Mass Deportations*, 1979, 25, note 34.

[58] Some scholars date this fast to Jehoiakim's eighth year (601) when a decisive battle between Babylon and Egypt took place at the Egyptian border. The basis for this dating is an emmendation of the Massoretic text from the "fifth" to the "eighth" year following the Greek text (see Holladay, *Jeremiah II*, 1989, 255-57).

of Syria and Palestine and helping in the collection and dispatching of the annual tribute to Babylon.[59]

The entry for the year 603/2 describes the siege of an unknown city (there is a lacuna in the text). The Chronicle mentions siege towers and a powerful army. It is generally assumed that Nebuchadnezzar was once again in the west. The city in question has often been identified with a Philistine or a Phoenician city. A letter from a local ruler named Adon to his overlord in Egypt, found at Saqqara may refer to the same event. The letter reads in part as follows:[60]

> That [I have written the Lord of Kings is to inform him that the forces] of the King of Babylon have come (and) reach[ed] Aphek...[...] they have seized ... for Lord of Kings Pharaoh knows that [your] servant [...] to send a force to rescue [me]. Do not abandon [me, for your servant did not violate the treaty of the Lord of Kings] and your servant preserved his good relations. And as for the commander [...] a governor in the land. And as for the letter of Sindur ...[...]

On paleographical grounds, the letter is dated to the end of the 7th century. The identification of the city in question is much in dispute. Philistine cities such as Gaza, Lachish, Ashdod, and Ekron and even Phoenician cities such as Byblos, Sidon, and Tyre have been proposed.[61] The identification depends on the location of the Aphek mentioned in the letter. Porten's reexamination of the letter established the existence of a line in Demotic at the reverse of the letter containing the name Ekron.[62]

---

[59] Wiseman interprets these annual marches as "implying the regular enforcement of law and order in the dominions he had inherited from his father rather than specific military mopping-up operations" (Wiseman, "Babylonia," in *CAH*, eds. Boardman et al., 1991, 3.2.231).

[60] Porten, "King Adon," *BA* 44 (1981): 36.

[61] For a survey, see Porten, "King Adon," 1981, 36-52; Wiseman, *Nebuchadnezzar*, 1985, 25-26. The letter shows traces of Phoenician syncretism such as the mention of Baal-Shamen, a Phoenician deity who was one of the guarantors of the treaty between Baal of Tyre and Esarhaddon. Adon is a Semitic name. The letter illustrates also the relation of these petty border states with Egypt and their information-system (see Katzenstein, *History*, 1997, 309).

[62] See Porten, "King Adon," 1981, 43ff.

The letter reflects the existence of a formal treaty relationship between Adon and Egypt. There is no evidence of an Egyptian [Necho II's] response to Adon's plea. The fate of Adon is unknown. It is not unlikely that other cities entered the same kind of treaty relationship.[63]

In 601 Nebuchadnezzar attacked Egypt. Necho II (610-595 BCE) mustered his army and both met in open battle. Both sides suffered heavy losses. The Chronicle states that "the king of Egypt heard (it) and mustered his army. In open battle they smote the breast (of) each other and inflicted great havoc on each other."[64] The Babylonian army experienced such heavy losses that in the following year Nebuchadnezzar was not able to campaign in the Ḫatti-land. He stayed in Babylon where he "gathered together his chariots and horses in great numbers."[65]

The Neo-Babylonian Chronicle does not give the location of the battle and there are no Egyptian references to this clash. A passage in *The Histories* of Herodotus[66] is sometimes considered to refer to the same battle. Herodotus says that "Necho [...] engaged the Syrians on land, won a battle at Magdolus, and then took the important Syrian city of Cadytis." It is generally admitted that Cadytis is Gaza although Kadesh has also been proposed.[67] The identification of Magdolus is more complicated. Some relate it to Meggido, others to Migdol in the Nile Delta. Those that prefer the former possibility connect Herodotus' story with the death of King Josiah of Judah in 609 BCE at Necho II's hands.[68]

---

[63] Redford, *Egypt*, 1992, 442ff. Redford presents testimonies hinting at an "incipient infrastructure of 'provincial' officials assigned to the new dependencies in the Levant" as early as 613 BCE (Redford, *Egypt*, 1992, 442). According to him, "Other local heads of state such as Aga of Ashkelon and Jehoiakim himself hastened to dispatch similar letters, beseeching assistance; but Necho was unable to comply." In support of his contention, Redford (*Egypt*, 1992, 455) refers to an ostracon from Arad mentioning the king of Egypt that may date from this period (see Yadin, "Historical Significance," *IEJ* 26 [1976]: 9ff. and note 51 above).

[64] Wiseman, *Chronicles*, 1974, 71.

[65] Wiseman, *Chronicles*, 1974, 71.

[66] 2.159.

[67] The latter proposal is very unlikely.

[68] See Lipiński, "War," *Annali dell'Istituto Orientale di Napoli* 32 (1972): 235, note 3 for a review of the supporters of this position. So does Katzenstein, "Before Pharaoh," *Vetus Testamentum* 33 (1983): 249-251.

A growing number of scholars nevertheless believe that Magdolus is in fact Migdol.[69]

A third text that may be connected to the two under discussion is the date formula in Jer. 47:1.[70] The text is an oracle against the Philistines "before Pharaoh attacked and captured Gaza."[71] Jeremiah refers to a specific historical setting whose determination is severely hindered by the absence of the name of the pharaoh in question. The setting of the prophecy is disputed. Possible scenarios are as follows: 1) Jer. 47:1 refers to a campaign by Psammetichus I before 610 and after his conquest of Ashdod. 2) Jer. 47:1 alludes to an attack against Gaza by Necho II just before the battle of Meggido in 609 or sometime thereafter. 3) Jer. 47:1 depicts Necho II's siege of Gaza in 601 as an aftermath to the battle with the Babylonians.[72]

The fact that Herodotus speaks of a battle between the Egyptians and the Syrians, not the Babylonians,[73] and the difficulty in determining the exact historical setting of both Herodotus' and Jeremiah's references undermines any attempt to correlate these three accounts and makes any argument based on such correlation speculative.

6. The Capture of Jerusalem in 597 and its Consequences

King Jehoiakim of Judah (609/8-598/7 BCE) refused to pay tribute to the Babylonians (c. 600). The account in 2 Kgs. 24:1 states that "in his days [Jehoiakim's], Nebuchadnezzar, king of Babylon, came up; and Jehoiakim became his vassal for three years. Then he turned and rebelled against him." It is probable that Jehoiakim paid tribute to Nebuchadnezzar in the years 603, 602 and 601 and that he withheld tribute in the year 600. He saw the Babylonian setback of 601 BCE as an opportunity to break free from Babylonian vassalage. He may have

---

[69] See Wiseman, *Nebuchadnezzar*, 1985, 29; Lipiński, "War," 1972, 236; Mitchell, "Judah," 1991, 397-98.

[70] Lipiński has insisted on correlating the three accounts (see Lipiński, "War," 1972, 240).

[71] Holladay, *Jeremiah II*, 1989, 334, renders יכה as "struck."

[72] Holladay, *Jeremiah II*, 1989, 336-37.

[73] This is a fact even if the presence of auxiliary troops from Syria in the Babylonian army is admitted (see Lipiński, "War," 1972, 240-41).

considered the Egyptians the stronger party in the Southern Levant. Egypt may have also encouraged and supported his rebellion.[74]

During the following year (599/598), Nebuchadnezzar returned to the Ḥatti-land but he took no direct action against Judah. Raiding parties were sent to take spoil from the Arab tribes.[75] Jeremiah 49:28-33 contains an oracle against Kedar and Hazor, which may be related to this campaign.[76] However, 2 Kgs. 24:2 informs us that Nebuchadnezzar retaliated by sending Babylonian units together with bands of Arameans,[77] Ammonites and Moabites against Judah. Aramean involvement, if it took place, is a result of closeness of the operation to their traditional lands. The outcome of this attack on Judah is unknown.

Tyre did not join the revolt. The reasons for this position are unclear. Tyre may have realized that Egypt was not yet ready to take positive action in Syria. Egypt had a passive attitude and did not even move its troops into southern Palestine. Instead Nebuchadnezzar showed up in the Levant once again. Tyre may have profited from the Neo-Babylonian rebuilding endeavor after the battle of Carchemish and benefited from the destruction of the Philistine cities and the subsequent shift of the southern trade that took place.[78] It is unclear whether, as Katzenstein states, Tyre maintained a position of neutrality while being closer to Egypt and paying tribute to Babylon and supplying her with cedar wood.

The entry in the Babylonian Chronicle for Nebuchadnezzar's seventh year (598/7) shows that Nebuchadnezzar decided to crush Jehoiakim's rebellion in that year. In the month of Kislev (December) he marched against Jerusalem, the Judean capital. The Babylonian Chronicle provides a terse account of the operations. It states that, after

---

[74] See Berridge ("Jehoiakim," 1992, 3.664); Cogan and Tadmor (*II Kings*, 1988, 308).

[75] Wiseman interprets this as "a holding operation until due punishment could be meted out, and it depended for its efficacy on the response to the recently invoked loyalty oaths imposed on these tribes" (Wiseman, "Babylonia," 1991, 232).

[76] Holladay, *Jeremiah II*, 1989, 384.

[77] An emmendation from "Arameans" (ארם) to "Edomites" (אדם) has often been suggested (Stade, Klostermann, Benzinger, Burney, Katzenstein [*History*, 1997, 310, note 84]). Arad ostracon # 24, line 20 may reflect an Edomite advance in the Eastern Negev. Wiseman (*Nebuchadnezzar*, 1985, 31) and Cogan and Tadmor (*II Kings*, 1988, 306) reject such emmendation on textual and historical grounds.

[78] Katzenstein, *History*, 1997, 310-11.

marching to the Ḥatti-land, Nebuchadnezzar, "encamped against the city of Judah and on the second day of the month of Adar [March 15-16, 597 BCE] he seized the city and captured the king. He appointed a new king of his own choice, received its heavy tribute and sent (them) to Babylon."[79]

The Bible account in 2 Kgs. 24:10-17 supplements the data provided by the Babylonian Chronicle. It shows that Jehoiachin (December 598-March 597), not Jehoiakim, was the king of Judah that surrendered to Nebuchadnezzar on 16 March 597 (2 Adar) and was taken prisoner to Babylon (vs. 10-11). Nebuchadnezzar, the account continues, took the treasures of the Temple and Palace and exiled the elite.[80] He appointed Mattaniah, Jehoiachin's uncle, as king and changed his name to Zedekiah (597-586 BCE) who was the last king of Judah. To guarantee Zedekiah's loyalty in the future, Nebuchadnezzar imposed his vassal covenant on Zedekiah as well (2 Chr. 36:13; Ez. 17:11-21). 2 Kgs. 24:14-17 reads as follows:

> He carried away all Jerusalem, all the officials, all the warriors, ten thousand captives, all the artisans and the smiths; no one remained, except the poorest people of the land. He carried away Jehoiachin to Babylon; the king's mother, the king's wives, his officials, and the elite of the land, he took into captivity from Jerusalem to Babylon. The king of Babylon brought captive to Babylon all the men of valor, seven thousand, the artisans and the smiths, one thousand, all of them strong and fit for war.

The siege must have been relatively short and this accords with the relatively mild treatment Jehoiachin and his court received. Apparently Jerusalem did not suffer great damage. In connection with it, Jeremiah announced Jehoiachin's inexorable punishment, exile, and death in Babylon (Jer. 22:24-30).

Josephus' account coincides with the Babylonian Chronicle and the Bible in that there was no sign of Egyptian help. His story reads as

---

[79] Wiseman, *Chronicles*, 1974, 73.
[80] The various statistics for the number of exiles contradict each other. 2 Kgs. 24:14 gives a total of 10,000; the number in the duplicate account in verses 15-16 is 8,000; another account in Jer. 52:28 lists a total of 3,023 deportees.

follows:[81] "But on the third year, upon hearing that the king of the Babylonians made an expedition against the Egyptians, he did not pay his tribute; yet was he disappointed of his hope, for the Egyptians durst not fight at this time." This passive attitude is surprising in view of the fact that, according to Herodotus (2.158), Necho II built a canal from the Nile to the Red Sea.[82] The canal had an unmistakable mercantile purpose and may have functioned as a strategic barrier sheltering Egypt against invasions from Asia.[83]

Cuneiform documents shed some light on Jehoiachin's fate in exile. The tablets, dated from the tenth and the thirty-fifth year of Nebuchadnezzar (595/4-570/69 BCE) list the rations distributed to different deportees. They mention oil rations for Jehoiachin (*Ya'u-kīnu* or *Yakū-kinu*) "king of the land of *Yahudu* (= Judah; alternately *Yaudu*, *Yakudu*) his five sons and other Judeans such as Ur(i)milki, Gadi-ilu, Qanayama, Shalamyama and Samakuyama.[84] One of the documents is dated to Nebuchadnezzar's thirteenth year (592/1). The texts indicate that Jehoiachin was treated very favorably. The fact that Jehoiachin is referred to as "king of Judah" in the texts has induced some scholars to believe the Babylonians still considered Jehoiachin the legitimate king of Judah.[85] They may have been held as royal hostages to be "displayed on state occasions but to be trained for eventual return to their land as loyal supporters of the Babylonian regime."[86] In support of this suggestion, Wiseman comments that, Zerubbabel, the leader of the Judean exiles

---

[81] *Ant.*, 10.6.2 (88)

[82] Herodotus' information on the completion of the canal is as follows: "It was Necho who made the original attempt to dig a canal through to the Red Sea; Darius of Persia, in a second attempt, completed it." The evidence from Tell el-Maskhuta contradicts Herodotus' account and confirms the existence of the canal in this period. It seems unlikely that there would have been that much Phoenician activity around Tell el-Maskhuta had there not been a means of reaching the Red Sea at this time. It is an open question whether the canal was open for long or whether it was properly maintained.

[83] Katzenstein, *History*, 1997, 312. Necho also built a fleet of triremes on the Mediterranean and the Red Sea (Herodotus, 2.159) which may have counted on Phoenician expertise and lumber from Lebanon and Cyprus. Phoenician sailors participated in the circumnavigation of Africa (Herodotus, 4.42).

[84] Weidner, "Jojachin," in *Mélanges Syriens*, 1939, 2.925-26.

[85] Thus Wiseman, *Nebuchadnezzar*, 1985, 82. Avigad has questioned Jehoiachin's royal status (see reference in Wiseman, *Nebuchadnezzar*, 1985, 82).

[86] Wiseman's suggestion in Wiseman, *Nebuchadnezzar*, 1985, 81.

returning to Jerusalem from Babylon c. 538/7 was a grandson of Jehoiachin and had a Babylonian name (Ezra 2:2; 3:2). Jehoiachin may have been held as a political hostage in case of a change of loyalties in Judah.

In any event, Jehoiachin maintained an assistant in Judah named Eliakim. A number of storage jars bearing the stamp of "Eliakim, steward of Yaukin" (לאליקם נער יוכן) have been found in Tell Beit Mirsim, Beth-Shemesh and Ramat Raḥel. Most scholars accept the identification of the Yaukin of this seal with Jehoiachin although the evidence may come from an earlier period.[87] It is possible that these royal estates were deliberately left to supply wine to the Babylonian occupation forces.[88]

In 594/3 the prophet Hannaniah prophesied that Jehoiachin would return to Judah within two years (Jer. 28:2-4). Jeremiah nevertheless strongly opposed such a view and announced that Jehoiachin would never return to Judah (Jer. 22:27). In fact, it was not until 561/0 that, according to 2 Kings, Evil-Merodach liberated Jehoiachin in the thirty-seventh year of his captivity at the age of fifty-five. Jehoiachin was given a higher status than other kings (2 Kgs. 25:27-30; Jer. 52:31-34).[89] He dined regularly at the royal table and received an allowance for the rest of his life (Jer. 52:34).

In addition to royal hostages, certain skilled foreign craftsmen were fed in this way too. Babylonian ration texts for the year 592 mention the two sons of Aga, king of Ashkelon, three mariners, eight officials and an unspecified number of musicians from the same city. Rations were issued to Egyptian officials as well. One text (A)[90] mentions 126 men from Tyre. In another (B) at least 190 mariners from Tyre are mentioned.[91] It is not clear whether these mariners belonged to a shipbuilding class as it has been suggested.[92] The number of mariners from other Phoenician cities is much smaller (eight from Byblos and

---

[87] Berridge, "Jehoiachin," *ABD*, 3.662.

[88] Wiseman, *Nebuchadnezzar*, 1985, 82.

[89] See commentary in Cogan and Tadmor, *II Kings*, 1988, 328-30.

[90] E. Weidner published a total of 4 texts (A-D).

[91] The text is partly obliterated and the number preceding 100 can not be determined.

[92] Katzenstein, *History*, 1997, 322.

three from Arwad) Artisans from Tyre, Elam, Egypt, Persia and Lydia were also the recipients of such food rations.[93]

Many authors consider the fall of Jerusalem in 597 the decisive event in the progressive disintegration of the land of Judah.[94] As a result of the king's surrender, the city itself was spared wrack and ruin. The siege, nevertheless, took a heavy toll on the city and the country. The looting of royal and temple treasuries decimated the economic resources of the tiny state and the deportation to Babylon of the Judean elite destroyed the social fabric of the Judean community.

Even though the physical destruction of Judah took place in 586 BCE, the community as such was destroyed ten years earlier with the deportation of masses of its population. The ruling classes of the state were exiled: the royal family, the wealthy, the priests and prophets, the military, craftsmen and artisans. Ezekiel was among the Judean deportees taken to Babylon at this time. Ezekiel's call came while he was "among the exiles, by the river Chebar." It took place "in the fourth [month], on the fifth day of the month [...] [in] the fifth year of King Jehoiachin's exile" (July 31, 593 BCE) (Ez. 1:1-3).

The internal situation of Judah after 597 can be summarized as follows: 1) Judah lost her political defense and was exposed to political adventurers and demagogues. 2) The exile of the property owners created economic and social confusion in Judah. 3) The exile of the fighting class prevented Judah from ensuring internal and external security.

7. The Final Years of the Kingdom of Judah (597-586 BCE)

All in all, 597 started a period of unprecedented political instability in Judah. Mattaniah - Zedekiah (597-586 BCE), the last Judean king, lacked experienced advisers. They had been deported to Babylon. He "merely continued in the heterodox policies of his nephew (2 Kgs. 24:18-20; Jer. 52:1-3), which were, in the international

---

[93] Weidner, "Jojachin," 1939, 2.925ff.; *ANET* 308; Zadok, "Phoenicians," 1978, 57-65.
[94] Asher, *Neighbours*, 1996, 189-90. During the campaign of 597, Nebuchadnezzar may have annexed Benjamin to the province of Samaria and this circumstance saved the area from the destruction that took place a decade later.

circumstances, foolish and even hazardous."[95] The presence of his nephew Jehoiachin may have compromised his position from the beginning, although in exile, Jehoiachin, was held in esteem by his fellow captives. Some circles in Judah may have considered him the legitimate king. He might have continued to hold crown property. The dates in the book of Ezekiel are based on Jehoiachin's exile. The prophet Jeremiah compared those who remained in Judah to rotten figs, unfit for eating, and saw the future as lying with the exiles (Jer. 24). He portrays Zedekiah as a weak ruler, who "oscillated between continued subservience to Babylon and open revolt"[96] (see Jer. 25-26). A wavering king, he sought Jeremiah's advice but was too weak to do what he knew was right. Under mounting pressure and wrong advise from charlatans and extremists that had replaced the old Judean nobility, he finally revolted against Babylon.[97]

Nebuchadnezzar conceivably fought the Elamites in 596/5. The Babylonian Chronicle, very fragmentary at this point, contains the name Elam. Jer. 49:34-39 presents an oracle against "Elam, in the beginning of the reign of Zedekiah" (596). It is an open question whether Nebuchadnezzar attacked Elam or vice versa.[98]

Jer. 27:3 mentions a meeting of envoys from Edom, Moab, Ammon, Tyre, and Sidon at Jerusalem. The conference, according to the Massoretic text of Jer. 27:1, took place "at the beginning of the reign of King Zedekiah" i.e., his ascension year (c. 597). On the basis of Jer. 28:1, which mentions the fourth year of Zedekiah, it is generally thought

---

[95] Mitchell, "Judah," 1991, 401.

[96] See commentary in Cogan and Tadmor, II Kings, 1988, 322.

[97] Zedekiah inquired from Jeremiah about the outcome of the siege of Jerusalem on a number of occasions. In Jer. 21:1-7 and 34:1-7 Jeremiah prophesied the famine in Jerusalem and the city's eventual destruction by Nebuchadnezzar (early part of 587). According to Jeremiah 37-38, on three different occasions Zedekiah asked Jeremiah about the outcome of the siege of Jerusalem in 587. On the first occasion, Jeremiah consistently warned him that the Egyptian army was going to return to Egypt (37:7). Afterwards, Jeremiah was accused of defecting to the Babylonians and put in prison (37:11-16). From then on, Zedekiah sought Jeremiah's opinion secretly. The second time Jeremiah told Zedekiah that he was going to be given into the hand of the king of Babylon (37:17), and the third and last time Jeremiah advised him to surrender to the Babylonians (38:14-22) to spare his life and Jerusalem and the Temple. Zedekiah was afraid of his officials and did not dare to follow Jeremiah's advice.

[98] Holladay, Jeremiah II, 1989, 388; Asher, Neighbours, 1996, 194.

that the expression "at the beginning of the reign of King Zedekiah" should be understood as the fourth year of Zedekiah (594).[99] The meeting is traditionally interpreted as a conspiracy against the king of Babylon. Under whose initiative the conference was summoned is not clear.[100] Whether the conference was intended to convince Zedekiah to join the revolt, is an open question as well. There is no evidence showing that the visit of the foreign delegates led to any rebellion in the Levant.

Jeremiah realized that any rebellion against Babylon would end up with the annihilation of Judah. He pleaded before Zedekiah not to rebel against Babylon. The prophet knew that YHWH had given "all these lands into the hand of Nebuchadnezzar the king of Babylon, my servant; and even the wild animals of the field to serve him" (Jer. 27:6). Any nation that would "not put its neck under the yoke of the king of Babylon" would perish (v. 8), he continued. As a result, Zedekiah should not listen to the prophets and diviners who were inciting him to rebel against Nebuchadnezzar (vv. 9, 12-22). It is not known whether Jeremiah was successful or not in dissuading Zedekiah at this point.

After the siege of Jerusalem in 597 BCE, Jeremiah also sent a letter to "the remaining elders among the exiles, and the priests, and the prophets, and all the people, whom Nebuchadnezzar had exiled from Jerusalem to Babylon" (Jer. 29:1). The message of the letter is similar to Jeremiah's message to Zedekiah at the international conference of 594 BCE. It was meant to counter the assurances of a speedy return of the exiles. Jeremiah estimated that the exile would last seventy years (Jer. 29:10) and advised them to "build houses and dwell in them; plant gardens and eat their fruit. [...] And seek the welfare of the city where I have exiled you, and pray to YHWH for it, for in its welfare you will find your welfare" (Jer. 29:5,7).

---

[99] Holladay, *Jeremiah II*, 1989, 112; Katzenstein, *History*, 1997, 315. Jer. 28:1 says: "It turned out in that year at the beginning of the reign of Zedekiah, the king of Judah, in the fourth year that...."

[100] Many scholars suggest the meeting was summoned by Zedekiah (see for example Wiseman, "Babylonia," 1991, 233-34). For Wiseman, the Edomite conquest of Ramat-Negeb and Arad took place at this time and was encouraged by Nebuchadnezzar in retaliation. For other authors (see for example Mitchell, "Judah," 1991, 401-02), the delegates wanted to enlist Zedekiah's participation in the rebellion against Nebuchadnezzar. In my opinion the account in Jeremiah does not support the first interpretation.

Jer. 51:59 indicates that Jeremiah sent word to the exiled community a second time. The text reads as follows: "The word which the prophet Jeremiah commanded Seraiah son of Neriah son of Mahseiah, when he went with Zedekiah, the king of Judah, to Babylon in the fourth year of his reign." The reference seems to indicate that Jeremiah was successful in his plea with Zedekiah.[101] The purpose of this visit was to renew Judah's loyalty to Nebuchadnezzar once the plot became known to him. Most scholars uphold the historicity of the account. The finding of a bulla with the name "[belonging] to Seraiah [son of] Neriah" (לשריהו נריהו) on it reinforces the overall historical reliability of the story.[102]

A number of possible reasons for the rebellion have been suggested. They come down to two: 1) *signs of weakness in Babylon*. The entry for the year 594 BCE in the Babylonian Chronicle presents a disturbing picture of Babylon. A rebellion broke out in Babylon in the tenth year of Nebuchadnezzar between December of 595 and January of 594. Nebuchadnezzar, according to the Chronicle, "slew many of his own army. His own hand captured the enemy."[103] 2) *Egyptian intrigue*. Pharaoh Psammetichus II's (595-589 BCE) ascent to power may have stirred up new hopes for Egyptian support. His successful campaign in Nubia a year later (593) certainly reinforced such expectations.

After suppressing the revolt in Babylon, Nebuchadnezzar marched to the Ḥatti-land once again later that same year (594) and collected heavy tribute. In the last year for which we have an entry (594/3), Nebuchadnezzar called out his army in the month of Kislev (c. December 594) for a further expedition to the Ḥatti-land. In Katzenstein's opinion, the recurrence in the Chronicle of the expression

---

[101] Asher, together with many other scholars, offers an alternative interpretation according to which the conference took place under Zedekiah's initiative. When Nebuchadnezzar heard of the deliberations with the surrounding states, he summoned Zedekiah and some of his ministers for a "dressing down" (see Asher, *Neighbours*, 1996, 193ff.).

[102] See Avigad, "חותמו של שריהו בן נריהו," *Eretz-Israel* 14 (1978): 86-87. A number of other bullae from persons mentioned in Jeremiah such as Baruch (32:11), Gemariah son of Shaphan (36:9-11) and Jerahmeel the king's son (36:26) have been found (see Avigad and Sass, *Corpus*, 1997, 163 [# 390], 191 [# 469], and elsewhere).

[103] Wiseman, *Chronicles*, 1974, 73. Mitchell ("Judah," 1991, 402) and others suggest a connection between the rebellion in Babylon and the conspiracy in Jerusalem.

that Nebuchadnezzar "called out his army" signals a major call-up to demonstrate force against the Egyptian plans for further opposition in the Levant following Psammetichus II's elevation to the throne.[104] After 596, the Egyptians seem to have concentrated on consolidating their position in the Levant and in continuing their alliances with the Phoenicians.

The information supplied by the tablet of the Babylonian Chronicle covering the years 605-595 concludes here. The following tablet has not been recovered and no annals have been preserved for the remaining thirty-three years of Nebuchadnezzar's reign. The long gap in the Babylonian Chronicle between the Nebuchadnezzar's eleventh year and Nabonidus' record is filled for the year 557/6 only by a tablet kept at the British Museum.[105] For events in Judah, historical reconstruction depends entirely upon the biblical data supplemented here and there by indirect references in Egyptian sources, Herodotus, Josephus, and the archaeological record.

Egyptian activity in the Levant continued in later years. In 593 Psammetichus II engaged in a successful campaign in Nubia. Graffiti at Abu-Simbel show Phoenicians among the foreign mercenaries that participated in this campaign.[106] Judean participation is also documented.[107] Two years later, according to a Demotic papyrus from the ninth year of Darius I (512 BCE), Psammetichus set out for Palestine and the Phoenician coast (Kharu in the Egyptian terminology).[108] The expedition was essentially a pilgrimage to the holy sites of the area. Jerusalem may have been one of them.[109] Psammetichus' ulterior motives are the object of different interpretations such as follows: 1) Psammetichus aimed at impressing the small powers in the area and to "lift the spirits of the anti-Babylonian resistance and to cement

---

[104] Katzenstein, *History*, 1997, 314.

[105] Nabonidus ruled from 556 to 539 BCE.

[106] *CIS* I.111-12.

[107] In a letter to Philocrates (c. 170 BCE), Aristeas mentions that the Jews had assisted the Egyptians in their wars with the Ethiopians (*Letter of Aristeas*, 13). See ed. Charlesworth, *Old Testament Pseudepigrapha*, 1983-85, 2.9.

[108] Griffith, *Demotic Papyri*, 1909, 3.92.95.

[109] Asher, *Neighbours*, 1996, 194. Katzenstein considers that "the whole affair was a peaceful voyage, apparently made by ship" and suggests that Byblos was the goal of the voyage (*History*, 1997, 317).

alliances."[110] 2) He intended to arouse Zedekiah's open rebellion against Babylonia.[111] The Judean leadership may have seen the Babylonian presence in the Levant, which after all was a new factor, as a passing phenomenon.[112]

Zedekiah did eventually rebel against Nebuchadnezzar. It has been conjectured that Psammetichus II's triumph in Nubia (593) may have stirred the hopes of the powerful pro-Egyptian party in Judea. His "Palestinian pilgrimage" may have fed the revolt movement. Psammetichus, it has been suggested, may have visited Jerusalem, conferred with Zedekiah, and entered into a treaty with him.[113] As a result of these alleged negotiations, Zedekiah may have broken his treaty with Babylon (Ez. 17:13-21). Nevertheless, no evidence has been found demonstrating the existence of such a treaty.

8. The Destruction of Jerusalem and the Temple and its Aftermath

The exact date for the outbreak of Zedekiah's rebellion is not known. In any event, sometime in the late 590s or early in the 580s, Zedekiah "rebelled against the king of Babylon" (2 Kgs. 24:20). Refusal of the annual tribute was a sign of rebellion. Ez. 17:1-10 presupposes a conspiracy between Judah and Egypt at this time. It is not clear whether an intervention of Psammetichus II (the march to Syria c. 591) took place in connection with such a conspiracy.[114] Ez. 17:11-21 shows that Nebuchadnezzar had imposed a fealty oath on him and, according to 2 Chr. 36:13, forced him to swear by his own god, that is, by YHWH.[115]

---

[110] Asher, *Neighbours*, 1996, 194-95.
[111] Greenberg, "Ezekiel 17," *Journal of Biblical Literature* 76 (1957): 304-09.
[112] Cogan and Tadmor, *II Kings*, 1988, 323.
[113] Hayes and Miller, *History*, 1986, 413.
[114] Greenberg's suggestion in "Ezekiel 17," 1957, 304-09.
[115] Invoking the vassal's gods as guarantors of the treaty oath was a common practice in Akkadian treaties (see Cogan, *Imperialism and Religion*, 1974, 46-49; Laato, *Josiah*, 1992, 159-61). On Akkadian loyalty oaths in general, in addition to Cogan (*Imperialism and Religion*, 1974, 42-49), see Parpola and Watanabe (*Neo-Assyrian Treaties*, 1988, XV-XXV); Wiseman (*Vassal-Treaties*, 1958, 1-99). For the relation of Ezekiel 17 to vassal oaths, see Tsevat, "Vassal Oaths," *Journal of Biblical Literature* 78 (1959): 199-204.

By rebelling against Nebuchadnezzar, Zedekiah had despised his oath by YHWH. As a result, YHWH would carry out a punishment suitable for the crime.[116]

YHWH's punishment in the form of Nebuchadnezzar's retaliation took place soon afterwards. The siege of Jerusalem started "in the ninth year of his [Zedekiah's] reign, in the tenth month, on the tenth day of the month," (Jan. 587 BCE) (2 Kgs. 25:1;[117] Jer. 39:1; 52:4; Ez. 24:1-2). It lasted until the 7th of Ab of Zedekiah's eleventh year (July/August 586) (2 Kgs. 25:2-3; Jer. 52:12).[118] Jerusalem withstood the Babylonians for 18 months (Jer. 39:2; 52:4-11; 2 Kgs. 25:2-3). During the siege (early part of 587) Jeremiah prophesied famine and the destruction of the city (Jer. 21:1-7; 34:1-7) and advised the people to surrender to the Babylonians (21:8-10). Under the pressure of the siege, wealthy citizens released slaves from their servitude (Deut. 15:1, 12-18) but, when the siege was temporarily lifted or relaxed, they took them as slaves once again (Jer. 34:8-22). This was the result of the intervention of an Egyptian army in Palestine. The Egyptian intervention is recorded in Jer. 37:5-11 and has no extra-biblical corroboration. During the

---

[116] As Zimmerli has pointed out, Ezekiel was aware that God's covenant had brought Israel into a sacred obligation that included avoiding any misuse of God's name (Ex. 20:7) and breaking oaths sworn by it (Lev. 19:12). Consequently, an oath taken by God's name had to be kept under any circumstances. It seems that, against Ezekiel's opinion, some among those in exile, expecting an imminent end to their deportation, saw in Zedekiah's treason an attempt at regaining their lost freedom and increasing God's honor on earth. Zimmerli's analysis of the situation is correct and to the point (see Zimmerli, *Ezekiel 2*, 1983, 366).

[117] 2 Kings 25 concentrates on the final phase of the siege and is our main source of information. The prophecies in Jeremiah 52 and Ezekiel 17 provide useful information on a number of additional circumstances surrounding the siege.

[118] It is not clear whether the account uses the Babylonian calendar starting in the spring (Nissan) or the fall (Tisri) calendar. It is also unclear which reckoning system is used: 1) The Babylonian accession year system in which the dates of the kings started to count from the first full year following the accession year. 2) The non-accession system. For this reason some scholars date the destruction to 587 and others to 586 BCE. Wiseman, for example (*Nebuchadnezzar*, 1985, 36-37; "Babylonia," 1991, 234), dates the fall to the 5th (1985) or the 25th (1991) of August of 587 BCE. Holladay also prefers 587 (*Jeremiah I*, 1986, 570; *Jeremiah II*, 1989, 34, 234). Most scholars favor the year 586 though. See for example Parker and Dubberstein (*Babylonian Chronology*, 1956, 28); Thiele (*Mysterious Numbers*, 1965, 164, 169); Finegan (*Handbook*, 1998, 259); Malamat ("Last Kings," 1968, 150-55); Cogan and Tadmor (*II Kings*, 1988, 323).

relaxation of the siege Jeremiah was able to leave the city to go to his home in Anathoth. Subsequently he was arrested, beaten, and imprisoned on the charge of defecting to the Babylonians (Jer. 37:12-16).

Egyptian involvement in the revolt is certain. After rebelling against Babylon, Zedekiah sent ambassadors "to Egypt, so that they might give him horses and a large army" (Ez. 17:15). The Lachish letters seem to confirm this involvement. Ostracon # 3 states that one Coniahu, commander of the army, had come down to go to Egypt (lines 14ff.). The Egyptian force compelled the Babylonians to relieve the siege and it enabled a few to leave the city. Jer. 37:5 informs us that "Pharaoh's army had come out of Egypt; and when the Chaldeans that were besieging Jerusalem heard news of them, they withdrew from Jerusalem." Apries (early 588-570 BCE), known also as Hophra,[119] was the pharaoh who sent the ineffective military force. He pursued a policy of active intervention in the Levant and may have convinced Zedekiah very early of his readiness to help in any uprising against the Babylonians. Ezekiel's prophecy against Egypt is dated "in the tenth year, in the tenth [month], on the twelfth day of the month" (January, 587 BCE) (Ez. 29:1). The Egyptian attack, it is generally assumed, must have taken place around this time or slightly earlier. The Egyptian intervention was rather inconsequential but may have led to a false sense of security among the Judean leadership (see Jer. 38:2, 3).[120]

In the meantime, Nebuchadnezzar worked steadily to eliminate support for Lachish especially from the southwest by which route help could be expected. Jer. 34:7 shows that Lachish (twenty-three miles southwest of Jerusalem) and Azekah (eleven miles north of Lachish) were the last fortified cities to fall in Judah. Lachish letter # 4, directed by a military outpost to the Lachish commander, reads in part: "And let (my lord) know that we are watching for the signals of Lachish, according to all the indications which my lord hath given, for we cannot

---

[119] As he is referred to in Jer. 44:30. He seems to have adopted a more aggressive foreign policy than his predecessors. See for example Kitchen, *Third Intermediate Period*, 1973, 407; Gardiner, *Egypt*, 1961, 360; Mitchell, "Judah," 1991, 403.

[120] In Redford's words the Egyptians withdrew because they "saw neither the opportunity of marching up-country to Jerusalem nor any realistic chance of overcoming the enemy in an open battle. Ignominiously the Egyptians withdrew" (Redford, *Egypt*, 1992, 466). In Ezekiel's words, God had broken Pharaoh's arms (Ez. 30:22).

see Azekah."[121] This message suggests that Lachish and Azekah were within sight or nearly so of the unnamed outpost and that Azekah had already fallen to Nebuchadnezzar. The siege was tightened by the addition of a closer siege-wall and siege towers to make a breach in the wall (2 Kgs. 25:1; Jer. 32:24; 33:4).

Herodotus states that Apries attacked Sidon and fought a sea-battle against the king of Tyre (2.161).[122] No date for this campaign is given.[123] Relying on Herodotus, Diodorus Siculus (1.68.1) supplements this information. He states that[124]

> He [Apries] made a campaign with strong land and sea forces against Cyprus and Phoenicia, took Sidon by storm, and so terrified the other cities of Phoenicia that he secured their submission; he also defeated the Phoenicians and Cyprians in a great battle, and returned to Egypt with much booty.

The nature and purpose of these operations is unclear. Were they organized to liberate Tyre and Sidon from the Babylonians? To prohibit Babylonian control of the area? To ensure an Egyptian stronghold? They have been explained in two different ways: 1) Apries was attacking the Phoenician states. 2) Apries was attacking the Babylonians.

Katzenstein is among those who think that the events in Herodotus and Diodorus refer to an Egyptian naval attack against the Phoenician cities. He connects Apries' naval campaign in Phoenicia with the Egyptian march to liberate Jerusalem, which he dates to the summer of 587 BCE. In his opinion, the purpose of this campaign was to win over the Phoenician towns to Apries' side. He suggests that Apries' intervention was prompted by "Phoenician neutrality."[125]

---

[121] *ANET* 322.

[122] Herodotus' words are as follows: "Apries [...] ruled for twenty-five years, an in the course of his reign he attacked Sidon and fought a sea-battle against the king of Tyre."

[123] Redford (*Egypt*, 1992, 465) dates it to the summer of 589 BCE. Herodotus also states that Amasis was the first person to conquer Cyprus and to make it a tributary state (2.182). No other evidence confirms this conquest (see James, "Egypt," in *CAH*, eds. Boardman et al., 1991, 3.2.725).

[124] Diodorus Siculus, *Bibliotheca Historica* (trans. C. H. Oldfather [1933-1967]).

[125] Katzenstein, *History*, 1997, 319. Katzenstein assumes that the Phoenician cities fought and suffered a defeat.

A second group of authors[126] correlate these events with two monumental undated inscriptions of Nebuchadnezzar found at Wadi Brisa near Hermel at the northern end of the Lebanon range. The two nearly identical inscriptions, "in a contemporary and an archaizing version," are partly obliterated.[127] They describe a campaign of Nebuchadnezzar to Lebanon to assure the supply of timber from the area. The inscriptions show that Nebuchadnezzar restored peace in the region and constructed a road for timber transport.[128] They mention "(this Lebanon) over which a foreign enemy was ruling and robbing (it of) its riches."[129] The foreign enemy defeated by Nebuchadnezzar is usually identified as Egypt.[130]

Jerusalem was subdued by hunger in July 586. The account in 2 Kgs. 25:3 states that "on the ninth day of the [fourth][131] month the famine became so severe in the city that there was no food for the people of the land. Then a breach was made in the city wall." The city seems to have had a fine defensive system, weak only in the north where the Babylonians may have made their breach. At that time Zedekiah escaped under the cover of the night and went out on the road of the Arabah. He was captured in the plains of Jericho and brought to Nebuchadnezzar at Riblah, his sons were slaughtered before his eyes, the Judean nobles were slaughtered as well and Zedekiah was blinded and sent off to Babylon (Jer. 39:1-7).

---

[126] Redford (*Egypt*, 1992, 465); Asher (*Neighbours*, 1996, 38-39).

[127] Mitchell, "Babylonian Exile," in *CAH*, eds. Boardman et al., 1991, 3.2.414.

[128] One of Nebuchadnezzar's inscriptions refers to the "mighty cedars of the Lebanon ...[which] with my hands I cut" (*ANET* 307). Most of the Neo-Babylonian inscriptions are building inscriptions. Many of them date to Nebuchadnezzar's time and tell us about the use of cedar wood from Lebanon in these constructions. It is unclear whether the Phoenicians felt bitter about that as Katzenstein suggests (*History*, 1997, 320).

[129] *ANET* 307. The dating of the inscription is uncertain. Other dates that have been suggested are 603 (Wiseman); 598 (Arcani); 586 (Langdon); 582 (Aharoni, Noth, Soggin); 568/7 (Mitchell). Asher dates it to 587/6 but assumes the inscriptions reflect events that took place years earlier (*Neighbours*, 1996, 38-39). For an analysis of the different dates proposed for the inscriptions, see Arcari, "Politica estera," *RSF* 17 (1990): 159-72.

[130] The "foreign enemy" may have been a Phoenician king of Tyre or Sidon instead (see for example Wiseman, *Nebuchadnezzar*, 1985, 26).

[131] According to Jer. 52:6. The Massoretic text has only לחדש "of the month."

Soon afterwards Nebuchadnezzar sent Nebuzaradan, one of his senior officers, to Jerusalem to complete the destruction of the city. On the 7th of Ab the Temple was razed and looted. Nebuzaradan then organized the removal of the cultic objects to Babylon. 2 Kgs. 25:13-17 includes a detailed list of the Temple treasures carried off to Babylon. No figure of the number of people deported is given in Kings or Jer. 39:8-10. On account of subsequent rebuilding, archaeological support for the destruction of the city is difficult to trace.[132] The palace of Ramat Raḥel fell into ruins.

Evidence of Babylonian destruction in Judea at this time is extensive. Lachish (stratum II) and Beth-Shemesh ceased to be inhabited. An ash layer at Gezer and Tell el-Hesi (stratum VII/VI) has been identified with this campaign. Most of the Judean cities and fortresses excavated in the Shephelah, the Negev and the Judean Desert were destroyed. Ein Gedi, Arad, Kadesh Barnea, Ashkelon, Ekron, Timna, Tell Sera' are some of the cities destroyed in the early 6th century.[133] Only some cities in the land of Benjamin (Tell el-Ful, Mizpah, Gibeon) escaped the Babylonian destruction. The very little Judean material that can be certainly labeled as Babylonian comes from Tell en-Naṣbeh (Mizpah). The city seems to have been spared the fate of the capital. No destruction level of the early 6th century has been uncovered.[134]

Nebuchadnezzar appointed Gedaliah over the people left in the land of Judah.[135] Gedaliah's official title, exact status, and the duration of

---

[132] Y. Shiloh found thick layers of destruction, iron and bronze arrowheads, and collapsed structures near the tower in the Jewish Quarter and on the eastern slope of the City of David (Shiloh, *Excavations* [1984]; see also Stern, *Archaeology*, 2001, 309-10).

[133] The archaeological evidence for this period is presented in Mazar, *Archaeology*, 1990, 458-60; Stern, "Israel," 1975, 26-55; idem, *Archaeology*, 2001, 323-25.

[134] Among the findings is the seal of Ja'azaniah a royal official (יאזניה עבד מלך) (see Cogan and Tadmor, *II Kings*, 1988, 326).

[135] A seal impression belonging to "Gedaliah the one who is over the house" (לגדליה אשר על הבית) was found at Lachish (c. 600 BCE). The title is generally reserved for the chief minister of the king. The Gedaliah mentioned in the seal is generally identified with the governor appointed by Nebuchadnezzar after the destruction of Jerusalem (see Gibson, *Textbook*, 1971, 1.62 [seal # 18]). It is not clear whether he acquired administrative experience under Zedekiah (Althann, "Gedaliah," *ABD*, 2.923).

his "governorship" are all unknown.[136] All evidence indicates that his was a very short interim of several months or a year at most. The capital city was established at the Benjaminite city of Mizpah (Tell-en-Naṣbeh) eight miles north of Jerusalem (2 Kgs. 25:22-26). The city had been spared from the destruction that took place during Nebuchadnezzar's campaign.

Gedaliah had some initial success in his efforts at reconstruction and encouraged the Judean troops who had escaped the Babylonians to submit to them. Among them was Ishmael son of Nethaniah and Johanan son of Kareah. The latter warned Gedaliah of a plot against him. The king of Ammon had persuaded Ishmael to assassinate Gedaliah. Gedaliah did not believe the report and failed to pay attention to the warning (Jer. 40:13-16). Ishmael son of Nethaniah assassinated Gedaliah together with all the Jews who were with him and the Babylonian soldiers stationed there (2 Kgs. 25:25; Jer. 41:1-10).[137] Gedaliah's assassination is interpreted as either a revenge against a collaborator with the Babylonian enemy (Cogan and Tadmor)[138] or as a reaction against a weak ruler (Mitchell).[139]

Two days after Gedaliah's assassination Ishmael killed seventy pilgrims on their way to Jerusalem and departed taking with him the rest of the Judeans from Mizpah. When Johanan heard about Gedaliah's assassination, he pursued Ishmael and caught up with him at Gibeon but Ishmael managed to flee to Ammon with ten men. Fearing Babylonian reprisals, Johanan decided to flee to Egypt together with his commanders and the people he had rescued from the hands of Ishmael. Near Bethlehem they asked Jeremiah what to do. Jeremiah warned them against leaving Judea for Egypt and was accused of telling a lie. They went to Egypt and finally to Tahpanhes (Tell en-Defenna/Dafna) at the eastern edge of the Nile Delta, taking Jeremiah along with them (Jer. 42:1-43:7). Babylonian reprisals took place in 582/1 when a third deportation took place. At that time Nebuzaradan, the commander of

---

[136] Cogan and Tadmor, *II Kings*, 1988, 327.
[137] Holladay assumes that Gedaliah was assassinated in September/October 587 (*Jeremiah II*, 1989, 287).
[138] Cogan and Tadmor, *II Kings*, 1988, 327
[139] Mitchell, "Babylonian Exile," 1991, 411.

Nebuchadnezzar's Imperial Guard, took 745 Judeans into exile (Jer. 52:30).

Early during his Egyptian exile while he was in Tahpanhes, Jeremiah prophesied an imminent invasion of Egypt by the Babylonians (43:8-13). Josephus mentions a successful campaign against Coele-Syria, the Ammonites and Moabites in Nebuchadnezzar's twenty-third year (582). Afterwards, Josephus continues,[140]

> When he [Nebuchadnezzar] had brought all those nations under subjection, he fell upon Egypt, in order to overthrow it; and he slew the king that then reigned, and set up another; and he took those Jews that were there captives, and led them away to Babylon.

It is not clear whether all this took place in a single year or is a general summary of Nebuchadnezzar's actions.[141] Once again, it is an open question whether Amasis' supplanting Hophra in 570 was the result of Nebuchadnezzar's campaign.[142] According to a late Arabic tradition, the invasion was the result of Nebuchadnezzar's desire to capture fugitive Jews "and to achieve his aim peacefully."[143]

A fragmentary cuneiform text (BM. 33041) dated to Nebuchadnezzar's thirty-seventh year and kept at the British Museum seems to contain a reference to a Babylonian invasion while Amasis was at war with Cyrene in 570 BCE.[144] The text, badly broken, seems to refer to an expedition whose alleged objective was "to do battle with Egypt." Whether it is so is a matter of dispute.[145] Some later traditions speak of Nebuchadnezzar as the conqueror of Libya where Cyrene was located

---

[140] Josephus, *Ant.*, 10.9.7 (182).

[141] See Wiseman, *Nebuchadnezzar*, 1985, 39.

[142] Amasis ruled from 570 to 526 BCE. Most Egyptologists and historians doubt that this invasion ever took place.

[143] Wiseman, *Nebuchadnezzar*, 1985, 39. Compare to Spalinger, "Egypt and Babylonia," *Studien zur ägyptischen Kultur* 5 (1977): 237.

[144] Cyrene was a Greek colony founded in 630 BCE on the coast of Libya. For references to Amasis' war with Cyrene, see Herodotus, 2.161-62, 181.

[145] Spalinger ("Egypt and Babylonia," 1977, 238) considers that there is no reference to a Babylonian invasion here. For Malamat ("Josiah's Bid," 1973, 278) the text is a broken list of foreign mercenary contingents in Babylonian service.

and may reflect a confusion with Cambyses' later invasion. The cuneiform text may refer to an incident following Apries failure to take Cyrene when there was civil war in Egypt.[146]

9. The Foreign Nations Mentioned in Ez. 25-32 and the Destruction of Jerusalem

As commented in chapter 1, both textual sources and the archaeological record show that Judah's neighbors were taking advantage of Judah's situation in the period immediately before and after the destruction of Jerusalem.

The four nations condemned in Ez. 25 are Ammon, Moab, Edom, and Philistia. These four nations, as Greenberg has pointed out,[147] "had at some time or other either lost territory to Israel or borne its yoke."

The clearest evidence of hostile acts against Judah comes from Edom. The Edomites seized Elat (c. 735 BCE). The city remained in their control till the end of the 6th century and gave them control of the major trade routes with the Red Sea via Gaza and Transjordan. Arad ostracon # 24, line 20 mentions an Edomite advance in the Eastern Negev c. 598 BCE. The Bible blames Edom for having annexed Judean land (Ez. 35:10) and for being guilty of violence (Ez. 25:12; 35:5; Joel 4:19). The Edomites may even have assisted the Babylonians in the sack of Jerusalem (Obad. 11, 13-14; Ps. 137:7; Lam. 4:21-22). Many articles discuss hostile Edomite actions at the fall of Jerusalem[148] and present evidence for Edom's encroachment on Judah's territory.[149]

The nature of Ammon's and Moab's acts against Judah is less clear. 2 Kgs. 24:2 indicates that, after Jehoiakim's rebellion against Nebuchadnezzar, Nebuchadnezzar retaliated by sending Babylonian units together with bands of Arameans (or Edomites according to an emendation), Ammonites, and Moabites against Judah (c. 598 BCE). No extrabiblical source mentions such an attack. In any event, all

---

[146] See Wiseman, *Nebuchadnezzar*, 1985, 39-40 for a discussion of the subject.

[147] Greenberg, *Ezekiel 21-37*, 1997, 523.

[148] See for example Myers, "Edom and Judah," in *Near Eastern Studies in Honor of W. F. Albright*, ed. Goedicke, 1971, 378-91; Lindsay, "Babylonian Kings," *PEQ* 108 (1976): 23-39; Malamat, "Last Years," 1979, 216-17.

[149] See Mazar, *Archaeology*, 1990, 444, 498-99; Dicou, *Edom*, 1994, 174ff., 182ff.

Transjordanian states (Edom included) seem to have enjoyed a relative prosperity in the period around the destruction of Jerusalem and to have been spared from the Babylonian destruction. According to Ez. 25:3, 6 Ammon rejoiced at the destruction of the Temple, the desolation of the land of Israel, and the exile of the Judeans. Moab, for its part, showed a disdainful attitude toward Judah (Ez. 25:8). No destruction layer has been found in Ammonite territory. On the contrary, Ammon experienced a period of prosperity between the end of the 7th century and the beginning of the 6th century.[150] Jer. 49:1 condemns Ammon for having seized one-time Israelite territory. In the wake of Jerusalem's destruction, Jer. 40:14 states that Baalis, king of Ammon, instigated the assassination of Gedaliah, the Judean governor appointed by Nebuchadnezzar over the people left in the land of Judah. The prosperity of Ammon and Moab was short-lived. It came to an end in 582/1 when, according to Josephus,[151] Nebuchadnezzar campaigned against Coele-Syria, Moab, and Ammon and brought them under subjection. Edom is not mentioned in this campaign.[152]

The Philistines were also Judah's traditional enemies. After Hezekiah's rebellion against Sennacherib, they had received several Judean cities in the Shephelah. This event had greatly weakened Judah economically and politically. The Philistine cities enjoyed great

---

[150] See Fisher's dissertation, *Ammon* 1996, 208-225. Recent excavations at the Ammonite capital, Rabbath-Ammon, indicate that the city experienced a period of prosperity during the 7th- 6th centuries. During this time the city was at the apex of its wealth and political power. No signs of destruction have been found c. 586 BCE but only signs of continuity. An administrative center was built c. 582 BCE at 'Umayri to organize the production of wine that was paid in tribute to Babylon. The center continued through the Babylonian and into the Persian period. Two inscriptions in Ammonite script from c. 580-560 BCE, an ostracon and a bulla mentioning the Ammonite king Baalis, were found in a pit below the foundations of the buildings of the administrative center. The presence of a number of imported Greek pottery (five to seven wares) and the finding of one bronze *thymiaterion* (lamp) of standard Phoenician type in Umm Uthainah show the relative prosperity Ammon enjoyed during this time and hint at trading contacts with Tyre (see Herr, "Ammonites and Moabites," in *Ancient Ammon*, eds. Macdonald and Younker, 1999, 228-35; Stern, *Archaeology*, 2001, 327-31, 347).

[151] *Ant.*, 10.9.7 (181).

[152] The end of the Edomite kingdom may have been the result of Nabonidus' campaigns in Transjordan and North Arabia in the year 552 BCE.

prosperity during the 7th century until Nebuchadnezzar's destruction of Ashkelon in 604 BCE and of the rest of the Philistine ports soon after.[153] Similarities of vocabulary link the oracle against Philistia in Ezekiel 25:15 to the Edomite oracles in 25:12 and 35:5 in which acts of vengeance against Israel were condemned.

For its part, Egypt is accused of being an unreliable political ally (Ez. 29:6). Egypt constantly instigated Judean uprisings, only to fail to support the Judeans adequately for a successful outcome in their revolt.

As commented in chapter 1, Tyre is an exceptional case among the foreign nations condemned in these oracles. She never had territorial disputes with Judah, apparently she had no share in Jerusalem's destruction, she was not an unreliable political ally, and no obvious reason for rivalry, resentment, or anger is discernible in the Tyrian oracles.[154]

Sidon's condemnation can be related to Tyre's. These two Phoenician cities are regularly paired in the oracles against foreign nations, as in Jer. 27:3 and Joel 4:4. In his prophecies of condemnation, Ezekiel was referring to the coast and Sidon was located on the coast. This may explain why Sidon was included in the list of condemned cities. On the other hand, the oracle against Sidon contains no specific accusation against her and could have been uttered against any of the nations addressed earlier. A quota of seven nations in the present collection may have also dictated the inclusion of Sidon in the oracles. The fact that chapters 29-32 contain seven oracles against Egypt supports this interpretation.[155]

10. The Siege of Tyre and its Consequences (c. 588/7-573 BCE)

Ezekiel 26-28 refers to a siege of Tyre in Nebuchadnezzar's time. Chapter 26:1 is dated "in the eleventh year, on the first day of the

---

[153] See for example Allen, *Contested Peripheries*, 1997, 216-77; Gitin, "Ekron of the Philistines," 1990, 33-42, 59.

[154] Only Ps. 83:3-8 documents an occasion in which Tyre is listed in a powerful group of foreign allies concerted against Israel. No extrabiblical evidence of this alliance has been found.

[155] Block's suggestion in Block, *Ezekiel 25-48*, 1998, 121-22.

month." The text does not preserve the name of the month so that the date corresponds to March-March 587-586 BCE.[156] Ez. 29:17, which is part of the oracles against Egypt, contains the latest date in the book. The oracle is dated "in the twenty-seventh year, on the first day of the month" or March-April 571[157] and is an updated version of the oracle against Tyre containing a self-correction of the prophet in 26:7-14 in which Ezekiel announced Tyre's imminent destruction at Nebuchadnezzar's hands. The oracle in 29:17 implies that the siege had already ended by then but there was no capitulation of Tyre. The destruction of Tyre did not take place after all and Egypt was going to be granted to Nebuchadnezzar instead (Ez. 29:17-19).

Josephus, quoting Menander of Ephesus,[158] provides the second historical witness of the siege. The text reads as follows:[159]

"Nabuchodonosor besieged Tyre for thirteen years in the days of Ithobal, their king; after him reigned Baal, ten years; after him were judges appointed, who judged the people; Ecnibalus, the son of Balsacus, two months; Chelbes, the son of Abdeus, ten months; Abhar, the high priest, three months; Mitgonus and Gerastratus, the sons of Abdelemus, were judges six years; after whom Balatorus reigned one year; after his death they sent and fetched Merbalus from Babylon, who reigned four years; after his death they sent for his brother Hirom, who reigned twenty years. Under his reign Cyrus became king of Persia." So that the whole interval is fifty-four years beside three months; for in the seventh

---

[156] Numerous suggestions have been proposed to account for the absence of the month but to date no solution is without problems (see Block, *Ezekiel 25-48*, 1998, 35). The dates are according to Boadt "Ezekiel," 1992, 713. For studies on the dates in Ezekiel, see Freedy and Redford, "Dates," *JAOS* 90 (1970): 462-85; Thiele, *Mysterious Numbers*, 1983, 187-91; Finegan, *Handbook*, 1998, 264-65; Greenberg, *Ezekiel 21-37*, 1997, 529.

[157] Ezekiel 29 has an oracle against the king of Egypt. Verse 1 is dated "in the tenth year, in the tenth [month], on the twelfth day of the month" (= January 587 BCE) and must be a reaction against Hophra's attack against Nebuchadnezzar in the same year.

[158] Menander of Ephesus was a Hellenistic historian who drew upon a translation of the annals of Tyre. His writings are known only from Josephus' works (see Katzenstein, *History*, 1997, 78-79).

[159] *Ag. Ap.*, 1.21 (156-59).

year of the reign of Nebuchadnezzar he began to besiege Tyre; and Cyrus the Persian took the kingdom in the fourteenth year of Hirom.

The approximate dates for the kings and judges mentioned in Josephus' quote are as follows:[160]

KINGS	Ithobal (Ethbaal III)	c. 591/90-c. 574/73	19 years
	Baal (Baal II)	c. 573/72-c. 564	10 years
JUDGES	Ecnibalus (= Yakin-baal)	c. 564/63	2 months
	Chelbes (= Caleb/Kalbay)	c. 563	10 months
	Abhar[161] (= Heber ?)	c. 563	3 months
	Mitgonus[162] (= Matan III) and		
	Gerastratus (= Ger-asthart)	c. 562-557	6 years
KINGS	Balatorus (= Baalazor III)	c. 556	1 year
	Merbalus (= Maharbaal)	c. 555-c. 552	4 years
	Hirom (Hiram III)	c. 551-532	20 years

The dating of the siege of Tyre is not fully settled. In his discussion of the unknown city Nebuchadnezzar besieged in the year

---

[160] Josephus' quote includes a fixed date and provides a synchronism. Josephus states that "Cyrus the Persian took the kingdom in the fourteenth year of Hirom." Josephus here is referring to the "kingdom of Babylon." Although the fall of Babylon took place in 539 BCE, Katzenstein understands the expression "Cyrus took the kingdom" as referring to "Cyrus' first year as king of Babylon," i.e. 538 BCE. Counting backwards, we can establish the chronology of the kings and judges mentioned in Josephus' text. I follow Katzenstein's chronology as presented in Katzenstein, *History*, 1997, 327-28. A similar chronology (off by one year) appears in Peckham, "Phoenicia," *ABD*, 5.356. The small discrepancies between the two are due to the fact that the actual total of Josephus' list is fifty-five years and three months instead of the fifty-four and three months he states in the text. Katzenstein solves this problem by adding one year to Ithobal's reign (p. 325). In any event, one has to acknowledge with Peckham that "the dates are approximate and often conjectural" (p. 355). For example, no kings of Tyre for the years 660-590 BCE are known and most of the kings in the chart are but a name in a list. Nothing else is known about them except for sporadic mentions in inscriptions. For a discussion of chronological uncertainties, see Katzenstein, *History*, 1997, 325-28.
[161] Peckham lists here 'Abiba'al (563)
[162] Or Myttyn in other versions of *Ag. Ap*.

603/2, Wiseman enumerated the arguments in favor of an early siege.[163] They are as follows: 1) in view of Nebuchadnezzar's military operations further south in the following years, it is unlikely that he would have left unchecked a powerful focus of interference of his supply lines from Riblah. 2) It is unlikely also that Nebuchadnezzar would have attempted to penetrate Egypt in 601 and 568, without neutralizing the fleets of Tyre and Sidon supporting Egypt, Babylon's main enemy. 3) The role of the Babylonians in Que (Cilicia), already in their hands in 585.

The dating of the siege rests on Josephus' text quoted earlier. Josephus, citing Menander upon whose authority he relies, says the siege took place in the days of Ithobal and lasted thirteen years starting "in the seventh year of the reign of Nebuchadnezzar." The interpretation of this text has long puzzled scholars. The precise dates for the kingdom of Ethbaal III of Tyre are taken to be 591/0-574/73 BCE.[164] The seventh year of the reign of Nebuchadnezzar was in 598/7. The Babylonian Chronicle does not mention a siege of Tyre for that year. Whether the omission is due to the fact that the Chronicle was concerned with the attack on Jerusalem is speculative.[165] Since it is estimated that the next king of Tyre, Baal II ruled from 573/2-564/3 BCE, the beginning of the siege is often dated to 588/7 and the end to 573 BCE.[166]

Babylonian texts taken to relate to the Babylonian rule by "judges" are few. One of them is a text from Nebuchadnezzar's fortieth year (565) dated at Ṣurru (Tyre). It implies the control of Tyre by Milki-

---

[163] Wiseman, *Nebuchadnezzar*, 1985, 26-28.

[164] Katzenstein, *History*, 1997, 327 and note 160 above. This identification is not entirely certain. As commented earlier, the names of the rulers of Tyre for the years 660-591 are not known. Another king with the same name could be behind Menander's tradition.

[165] Von Voigtlander (*Survey*, 1964, 134, note 23) proposed to read the seventeenth year (588/7) instead. Vogelstein spoke of a double siege, each lasting thirteen years (598-586 unsuccessful and 585-572 successful) (see reference in Katzenstein, *History*, 1997, 328, note 185). On the basis of a Latin version and assuming the existence of a haplography at a very early state in the transmission of the Hebrew text, Katzenstein interprets the seventh year as referring to Ithobaal's reign (585 BCE) not to Nebuchadnezzar's (*History*, 1997, 328). For a review of different opinions, see Eissfeldt, "Datum," *Forschungen und Fortschritte* 9 (1933): 421-22.

[166] See Wiseman, *Nebuchadnezzar*, 1985, 27; idem, Wiseman, "Babylonia," 1991, 235; Culican, "Phoenician Colonization," in *CAH*, eds. Boardman et al., 1991, 3.2.470; Eissfeldt, "Datum," 1933, 421-22.

eteri, the governor of the province of Kadesh.[167] A sale contract for the purchase of a female slave by a man from Nippur mentions a *šandabakku*-official in the following year.[168] Nebuchadnezzar himself may have been at Tyre by 564.[169]

The siege of Tyre may have been "one of containment rather than of continuous determined attack,"[170] a long blockade of the mainland opposite Tyre that required the annual replacement of the attacking troops.[171] It seems to have ended with a treaty by which the royal Tyrian house had to reside in Babylon. Together with the Tyrian king, there was a Babylonian commissioner with a seat in Ušu. The Tyrians could fetch the heir to the throne from Babylon in contrast to other royal families living in Babylon.[172]

No archaeological evidence of the siege has been discovered. But doubts about its very existence were put to rest in 1926 when a tablet containing an official receipt for provisions was published. The date of the tablet is destroyed, but its contents guarantee the dating. The text mentions provisions for "the king and the soldiers who went with him against the land of Tyre."[173]

Eleven archival economic documents from the city of Ṣurru dated between Nebuchadnezzar's thirty-first and forty-first years (573-563 BCE) give further insights into the later history of Tyre. Ṣurru seems to have been a city of Tyrian deportees situated somewhere in Central Babylon between Nippur and Uruk, near a water source.[174] With the exception of the first document dated to 573 BCE, all the texts are from

---

[167] BM 40546 dated 22 Tammuz, 40th year of Nebuchadnezzar (=July 565). See Wiseman, *Nebuchadnezzar*, 1985, 28, note 191 for full reference.

[168] Dougherty, *Archives from Erech*, 1923, 59 (# 94); Unger, "Nebukadnezzar II," *ZAW* 44 (1926): 314-17.

[169] Wiseman's suggestion (*Nebuchadnezzar*, 1985, 28).

[170] Wiseman, "Babylonia," 1991, 235.

[171] Wiseman, *Nebuchadnezzar*, 1985, 28; Markoe, *Phoenicians*, 2000, 47. This interpretation may explain why there is no mention of the siege in the Babylonian Chronicles.

[172] Josephus, *Ag. Ap.*, 1.21 (158).

[173] Unger, "Nebukadnezar II," 1926, 316; Dougherty, *Archives from Erech*, 1923, 61 (# 151).

[174] For the location see Joannès, "Localisation," 1982, 35-43. Joannès suggests the city was located by the King's Channel linking Uruk and Nippur.

after the end of the siege of Tyre. Ṣurru is not an isolated case; other places named after Phoenician and Palestinian cities conquered by Nebuchadnezzar are attested in the Neo-Babylonian and Achaemenid periods in the Nippur area. Ashkelon, Gaza, Arza, and Kadesh are among them. After Nebuchadnezzar's reign, Ṣurru disappears from economic texts to reappear in the Murashu archives as Bīt-Ṣurraya, "the city of the Tyrian domain." This village was located near Nippur.[175]

A connection between the concentration of documents in the years thirty-fourth to forty-first of Nebuchadnezzar and the fall of Tyre has been suggested[176] and it is feasible that the documents refer to a group of deportees gathered together in exile according to their city of origin.[177]

Personnel lists edited by E. Weidner show the presence of Tyrian sailors and at least 126 people from Tyre among the subordinate personnel at the palace.[178] There is nothing precluding the possibility that Nebuchadnezzar had deported part of the Tyrian population and installed it either in the palace or in the region to the south of Nippur.

The disappearance of Ṣurru from the texts in Nebuchadnezzar's forty-first year coincides with the beginning of Evil-Merodach's reign and with a change in the political system in Tyre with the beginning of the government of the judges. Nebuchadnezzar's death may have marked the return of the Tyrian exiles and a change in government.[179]

Of the eleven preserved texts mentioning the city of Ṣurru, six belong to the Uruk archives, four to those from Sippar and one to the ones in Nippur. They are administrative documents with various credits or debits involving several functionaries or temple dignitaries from Eanna in Uruk and Ebabbar in Sippar. The texts intimate that the city was a center of farming and exchange of agricultural products such as cattle, dates, wheat, and barley. Ṣurru thus may have been at the center of an agricultural area depending on the sanctuaries of Eanna in Uruk

---

[175] See Zadok in ed. Röllig, *Répertoire géographique*, 1974-, 8.351.
[176] Joannès, "Trois textes," 1987, 148.
[177] First suggested by Eph'al, "Western Minorities," *Orientalia* 47 (1978): 81ff.
[178] Weidner, "Jojachin," 1939, 2.923-35.
[179] Joannès, "Localisation," 1982, 149.

and Ebabbar in Sippar where the Tyrian deportees served as labor for the exploitation of estates or cattle breeding.[180]

Phoenicians also lived near Moabites in the surroundings of Babylon. This may have been the result of a Neo-Babylonian tendency to settle together deportees from adjacent countries.[181]

The reasons for the siege of Tyre evidently have to do with Egypt with whom Tyre had good relations. Nebuchadnezzar needed to establish a safe base for his ultimate goal: the conquest of Egypt. This is the motivation for the conquest of all the small states in Western Asia and of the Phoenician cities of Arwad, Sidon, and Tyre.[182] It is also probable that the new Egyptian navy could have represented a threat to Babylon as long as the Phoenician states were independent.[183] Whether the siege was due to an Egypto-Tyrian alliance, is not clear.[184] It is a matter of speculation as well whether the cause of Nebuchadnezzar's attack on Tyre was his demand that all the Phoenician town-states become Babylonian satellites and by the subsequent refusal of the Phoenician cities.[185] The thirteen-year siege may have been the occasion for Apries' naval campaign in which he fought "a battle with the king of Tyre by sea."[186]

After the siege, Tyre's power was exhausted. Tyre lost her overseas territories with the exception of her colonies in Cyprus.[187] Carthage became an independent state and took over Tyre's overseas

---

[180] Joannès, "Localisation," 1982, 150.

[181] See Zadok, "Phoenicians," 1978, 230.

[182] See Katzenstein, *History*, 1997, 335. In his *Ant.* (10.9.7 [181-82]), Josephus mentions a campaign against Moab and Ammon in Nebuchadnezzar's twenty-third year (582). Quoting the Babylonian priest Berossus, Josephus states "he [Berossus] then says, "That this Babylonian king [Nebuchadnezzar II] conquered Egypt, and Syria, and Phoenicia, and Arabia" (*Ag. Ap.*, 1.18 [133]).

[183] Katzenstein's suggestion (*History*, 1997, 335).

[184] Suggested by Freedy and Redford, "Dates," 1970, 483.

[185] Katzenstein, *History*, 1997, 329-30.

[186] Herodotus, 2.161.

[187] It is not known when Kition became independent of Tyre and was ruled by an independent king. Baal-melekh (480 BCE) is the first known king of Kition. The numismatic evidence shows that Oz-baal (Azzibaal), his son, was already king of Kition and Idalion (Katzenstein, *History*, 1997, 339; Yon, "Kition," in *DCPP*, ed. Lipiński, 1992, 248-49).

territories. However, a filial relationship between the former colony and Tyre continued until the Roman destruction of Carthage in 146 BCE.

It is generally assumed that the Phocaeans colonized Tartessus around this time.[188] If such a colonization took place, it can be related to the decline of Tyre's dominion in the Mediterranean.[189] Herodotus (1.163) refers to the beginning of the Phocaean colonization of Tartessus in the reign of Arganthonius, the legendary king of Tartessus. The account reads:

> The Phocaeans were the earliest Greeks to make long voyages by sea; they opened up the Adriatic, Tyrrhenia, Iberia, and Tartessus. [...] When they reached Tartessus they became friendly with the Tartessian king, whose name was Arganthonius. He had ruled Tartessus for eighty years, and lived to be 120 altogether. The Phocaeans got to be on such very good terms with him that he initially suggested that they leave Ionia and settle wherever they liked within his kingdom.[190]

Although the exact location of Tartessus is still unknown, the discovery of 6th century Attic pottery in Huelva City confirms the identification of the site with the city of Tartessus.[191] The excavation of an empty lot in the center of Huelva hints at Phocaean colonization. The site provided an impressive amount of Greek ware, 1400 fragments in a trench only 6 by 4 meters. Almost all of it was dated to the first half of the 6th century BCE. The findings show that two generations of potters exported their

---

[188] In his recent book *Myth and Territory* (1999), Malkin maintains that such a colonization never took place.

[189] The Phocaeans found Massalia in southern France c. 600 or c. 545 BCE (there are two divergent traditions), Emporiae (Ampurias) c. 600 (the earliest archaeological material is from c. 600-575), and Alalia on the east coast of Corsica c. 565. See Graham, "Colonial Expansion," in *CAH*, eds. Boardman et al., 1982, 3.3.139-62; Katzenstein, *History*, 1997, 337; Rouillard, "Phocéens," in *DCPP*, ed. Lipiński, 1992, 353; Lancel, *Carthage*, 1997, 79. The Phocaean colonization is related to the demand for silver in Greece (the first Greek coins were minted c. 580-570 BCE) and to the silver wealth of Tartessus (see Chamorro, "Survey," *American Journal of Archaeology* 91 [1987]: 203).

[190] This passage of Herodotus' *Histories* can just be a folk story lacking any probability.

[191] Muhly, "Search," in *Mediterranean Peoples*, eds. Gitin et al., 1998, 315.

wares to Tartessus. The pottery findings are the result of the activities of Phocaean traders active during the first half of the 6[192] century BCE.[192]

It was left to Carthage to defeat the Phocaeans in the naval battle of Alalia in 540 BCE.

---

[192] Chamorro, "Survey," 1987, 201-03, 226, 227.

3
Economic and Political Factors in Ezekiel's Condemnation of Tyre

1. Tyre's Role in the 7th-6th Centuries and our Sources

An examination of the historical sources for the second half of the 7th century and the first half of the sixth century BCE reveals how meager they are and how little we know about the period in question. In my historical reconstruction in chapter 2, I tried to stick to the historical facts as closely as possible drawing a sharp line between facts and conjectures.

In dealing with Tyrian history and assessing Tyre's role at any given time, we encounter an additional obstacle that has to do with the absence of Tyrian annals. Only a handful of Phoenician inscriptions have been preserved and very few come from Tyre itself. The data archaeology can provide is also very limited due to the impossibility of excavating Tyre itself, the modern city is built on top of the old one, and to the permanent political instability of the area.

In the absence of local sources, to evaluate Tyre's role in the 7th-6th centuries we must have resource to external sources. They are the Assyrian and Babylonian Chronicles, the Bible, classical sources (Homer, Herodotus, Strabo, Diodorus, Avienus, Pliny...), and Josephus. There are historical uncertainties inherent in using these sources. Each of them expresses the point of view of external cultures and the mentality of their authors. Each piece of evidence must undergo a critical examination and be submitted to a "decoding."[1]

The Neo-Assyrian and Neo-Babylonian Chronicles were propaganda instruments designed to show the superiority of their countries, gods, and kings. These empires required regular amounts of

---

[1] This is true for any period of Tyrian history. See, the treatment of the problem in the Achaemenid period in Elayi and Sapin, *Beyond the River* (1998), chapters 6, OF WHAT USE ARE INSCRIPTIONS? and 7, READING THE TEXTUAL SOURCES ANOTHER WAY (pp. 85-109).

tribute in precious metals and luxury products. Such products, listed in their Chronicles, are a very important source of information about the Phoenicians. In the Bible, Phoenicians and Tyrians were shrewd merchants, their business acumen and wealth were proverbial. They were portrayed as economically and politically successful and haughty and this haughtiness was the direct result of their economic success. There was a fascination with the Phoenicians in classical sources. Prejudice is also evident: Greek historians saw the Phoenicians as greedy, unscrupulous, oppressing merchants. Josephus finally, was very removed from the original events and his main concern was to corroborate the biblical account.

Each source has its own strengths and biases. The reliability of a fact stated in a given source increases when we can correlate textual sources among themselves, mainly when they represent independent traditions such as the Neo-Assyrian Chronicles and classical writers. The same is true about correlating archaeological data with textual sources. To illustrate this, all textual sources indicate that one of the reasons for the Phoenician expansion in the West was the procurement of silver and metals in general. Archaeological data from the Phoenician settlements in the Mediterranean demonstrates Phoenician participation in the metal trade. We can say therefore that Phoenician share in the Mediterranean metal trade is an established fact.

On the other hand the limits between fables, tales, and historical facts was not clearly delineated in ancient times.[2] For this reason, we have to be very careful in using them. In view of the historical uncertainties inherent in using these sources, the conclusions and suggestions made in this chapter are necessarily tentative and provisional.

By bringing together all available sources and archaeological data at our disposal, the purpose of this chapter is to demonstrate Tyre's economic superiority and political influence in the region during the

---

[2] Consider for example legends about the Oestrymnides (Avienus) or Cassiterite (Pliny the Elder) islands, the episodes of Phoenician piracy preserved in Homer's *Odyssey* and Herodotus' *Histories*, or Diodorus' and Strabo's stories about Phoenician skill for appropriating large silver cargoes in exchange for cheap goods. The same applies to the other sources as well.

period under study, and to establish the importance of economic and political factors never fully applied to the study of the Tyrian oracles.

The chapter starts with an analysis of Tyre's economic and political relations with the major empires of the second half of the 7th century and the first half of the 6th century (Assyria, Egypt, and Babylonia) in a chronological order. Tyre's economic and political relations with Judah's neighbors (the Philistines, Edom, and Arabia) come next. Then the commodities Judah needed most are determined. Metals and horses are the logical answer and Tyre had a practical monopoly over their trade and distribution. A process of extension of Tyre's influence and territorial penetration in postexilic times is examined afterwards. Finally social and religious factors are taken into account: Tyre had a share in selling Judean slaves, Tyrian products were status symbols, and there was an unmistaken link between Tyrian economic activities and her religion.

2. Tyre and the Assyrian Oppression

Assyria was the first empire to initiate a colonialist, and militarist strategy in the Near East.[3] The Bible echoes this militarist, ruthless imperial policy. As the foremost Phoenician city, to the prophets' minds, Tyre represented greed, unjust gain, dishonest practices, and the Assyrian oppression.[4] Ezekiel 27 gives us the most detailed portrait of Tyre's trade and the basis for connecting it with the Assyrian imperial power.

The Assyrian empire has been traditionally viewed as a tribute-driven empire (Diakonoff, Polanyi, Elat).[5] A growing number of authors nevertheless consider the Assyrian empire in the seventh century as a hybrid system, partly tribute-driven and also having elements of a trade-

---

[3] Heavy taxation was characteristic of the Neo-Assyrian empire as well.

[4] Phoenician greed is a commonplace in classical sources. The treatment accorded to the Phoenicians in these sources is rather negative. They are portrayed as pirates and are blamed for introducing greed and luxury into Greece. Hosea's allusion (12:8) to deceitful balances associated with "Canaanites" (=Phoenicians) stresses the same idea.

[5] See for example Diakonoff, "Features," in *Third International Conference of Economic History*, 1969, 13-32. Diakonoff uses the term "forcible exchange" to characterize the Assyrian economy.

driven economy. This seems to have contributed to the economic development of the western vassal states in the Levant.[6] The Assyrian empire followed a different policy with these states; instead of decimating them like the more economically superfluous land-based states, they were allowed to maintain their independence and even encouraged to continue and expand their existing trade networks. They were essential in providing the Assyrian empire with much needed metals and luxury goods. Phoenicians, Arabs, and Philistines are three cases in point.

Assyrian rule in Phoenicia lasted for about a century. It started with Tiglath-Pileser III (744-727 BCE) in 738 BCE and ended c. 640 BCE when Ashurbanipal's last recorded campaign took place. Assyria gave special treatment to the Phoenician states, which were virtually autonomous. In return they supplied the Assyrian empire with commodities the latter could not otherwise obtain. The Phoenician cities were subject to increasing tribute demands as time went by.

Assyrian policy in the Levant was part of a larger scheme in which Egypt was the determining factor and final goal. Assyria intended to control the southern road of Syria-Palestine with the aim of attacking Egypt. This finally happened under Esarhaddon in 671 BCE. Under these circumstances and in order to keep her autonomy and benefits, Tyre had to reorientate her trade toward Assyria.[7] Tyre herself was not incorporated into the empire and managed to maintain her political independence, trade, and intermediary status to the last days of the Assyrian empire.[8] Assyria received Tyre's tribute and was granted preferential treatment in trade making it unnecessary for her to intervene in Tyrian economic affairs or to compete with Tyre's trade. By these means, Assyria intended to reorientate economic activity and trade to Assyria herself. The position of Tyre in the Assyrian empire was so

---

[6] Allen, *Contested Peripheries*, 1997, 170-71; Oppenheim, "Comment," in *Third International Conference of Economic History*, 1969, 33-40 and specially pages 35-36; Postgate, "Economic Structure," in *Power and Propaganda*, ed. Larsen, 1979, 198-99, 205-06.

[7] See Aubet, *West*, 1993, 74.

[8] The treaty between Esarhaddon and Baal of Tyre (c. 674) after the defeat of Sidon in 676 granted the Tyrian ships freedom of trade beyond the Assyrian sphere. This and other documents seem to indicate the Assyrian kings were interested in having the Tyrian traders continuing with their own trading activities (see *ANET* 533-34).

central that in a treaty in c. 674 BCE Esarhaddon (680-669 BCE) ceded Dor to king Baal of Tyre apparently for administrative purposes.

The inscriptions of the Neo-Assyrian empire give us a glance into Tyre's prosperity and trade products. Foremost among these commodities were metals (especially silver) and luxury products. Shortly after 734 BCE, Tiglath-Pileser III received 150 talents of gold (about 4,5 tons) from Mattan II of Tyre a sum never equaled in any collection of tribute from Phoenicia.[9] The importance of metal exploitation and trade can not be overstated. Metal was indispensable in guaranteeing economic self-sufficiency in the ancient world. Metal possession meant having at one's disposal raw material for agriculture and military industry. And metal had a prestige element as well. During the first millennium, iron was the most important strategic material. Assyria and Babylonia needed large amounts of iron. The 160 tons of iron found at Sargon II's palace illustrate the quantity of metal reaching Assyria from the Levant.[10]

With the evolution of the Assyrian economic system towards a market economy, the value of things in the Near East came to be determined according to a metal standard (gold or more often silver). By the 7th century, silver came to function as a standard of value and exchange. 'Hallmarks' stabilized its weight and quality and temples functioned as "national banks" warranting its quality, and providing loans.[11] As a consequence, the demand for silver greatly increased.

---

[9] *ARAB* 1.288 (# 803). See also Aubet, *West*, 1993, 47, 70-73; Jankowska, "Some Problems," in *Ancient Mesopotamia*, ed. Diakonoff, 1969, 254-55; Bunnens, "Luxe phénicien," in *Phoenicia and its Neighbours*, eds. Gubel and Lipiński, 1985, 27-28. Assyrian tribute lists for the 8th and 7th centuries almost always start with metals followed in importance by ivory, cloth, wooden furniture, perfumes, horses, and chariots. They give us a hint as to the value attached to these commodities and their demand during the same period. See Aubet, *West*, 1993, 70; Frankenstein, "Far West," in *Power and Propaganda*, ed. Larsen, 1979, 272; Elat, "Overland Trade," in *Ah Assyria*, eds. Cogan and Eph'al, 1991, 21.

[10] Aubet, *West*, 1993, 61-62.

[11] See Lipiński, "Temples," in *State and Temple Economy*, ed. Lipiński, 1979, 2.565-88.

The combined evidence from archaeology and classical sources shows that Tyrian expansion in the West is related to the metal trade.[12] The foundation of Kition c. 820 BCE was prompted by Tyre's need to control directly Cyprus' copper resources. The establishment of Tyrian emporia in southern Spain during the early 8th century was motivated by Tyre's desire to control the silver resources. The Iberian silver trade seems to have been a Tyrian monopoly.[13] As agent of Assyrian imperialism, Tyre influenced the economy of southern Spain through Cadiz and other colonies and incorporated the Iberian Peninsula in the Mediterranean trading network.[14]

Classical sources corroborate that one of the main reasons for the Phoenician expansion in the West was the procurement of silver. They indicate the Phoenicians took advantage of native people. This fact reinforces the connection between Phoenician metal trade, irregular

---

[12] The search for new murex sources, the growing tribute demands of the Neo-Assyrian empire, population increases, and difficulties to expand inland in the Levant are additional reasons for the Phoenician colonization in the West.

[13] Aubet, *West*, 1993, 237. The Phoenicians negotiated with products, they did not exploit the mines themselves. Tyre's policy concentrated on controlling the trade routes by sea and land and securing the supply of metals and exotic materials (Aubet, *West*, 1993, 60). The archaeological evidence points to an exploitation of the mines by the local Tartessian population prior to the Phoenician arrival and to their remaining in Tartessian hands. The Phoenician role consisted in providing new markets and encouraging large-scale production (see Chamorro, "Survey," 1987, 199-200). It has been estimated that during the period of the Phoenician colonization enough silver was extracted to leave c. 20 tons of silver slag in the countryside (see Frankenstein, "Far West," 1979, 284). Classical sources maintain that the Phoenicians kept this silver trade secret for a long time. It was not until 640 BCE that Colaeus, a Samian merchant, blown beyond the Pillars of Hercules, found his way to Tartessus and brought home a fabulous cargo (Herodotus, 4.152). For the greater part of the next hundred years, the Phocaeans maintained trade relations with Tartessus. Large quantities of silver must have accumulated before the minting of the first coins in Greece (c. 580-570). Areas lacking natural metal resources such as the city of Naucratis may have been supplied with metal by trade. Tartessian silver may have been a source of such metal. (No lead isotope study of Tartessian silver has so far been conducted and the matter is a subject of controversy.) Soon after 550 BCE, Spanish silver trade became a Carthaginian monopoly (see Cary, "Sources," in *Mélanges Gustave Glotz*, 1932, 1.136-38; Chamorro, "Survey," 203).

[14] Ed. Bierling, *Phoenicians in Spain* (2002) presents a collection of essays by various authors that explore the ways in which the Phoenician colonization of the Iberian Peninsula was a function of Assyrian westward expansion.

commercial practices, and oppression. Describing Tartessus' proverbial wealth in silver,[15] Diodorus (5.35.4-5) informs us about the Phoenician exchange system: "Now the natives were ignorant of the use of [...] silver, and the Phoenicians [...] purchased the silver in exchange for other wares of little if any worth."[16] Strabo (3.2.9; 3.5.11) tells a similar story. Other classical sources stress the Phoenician skill for appropriating large silver cargoes in exchange for oil[17] and cheap goods.[18] Such lopsided exchange is characteristic of a colonial system. As part of the same colonial policy, the Phoenicians monopolized the trade and distribution of luxury items by dominating the maritime transport.

Phoenician metal extraction and trade in the Iberian Peninsula was by no means limited to silver. Tyre brought back from Spain other metals such as gold, iron, and tin. During the 7th century, the Cadiz commercial area underwent an economic expansion to control a new metal, tin. According to classical sources, the Phoenicians sailed from very remote times to the Oestrymnides islands in search of tin[19] and the Gaditanians obtained tin in the Cassiterite islands.[20] Even though the exact location of these islands remains unknown, classical authors variously locate them off the coast of Galicia, in Brittany, or even in the

---

[15] Around the year 600 BCE, Strabo (3.2.11) also referred to the huge silver resources of the Tartessus river.

[16] The case with gold is different. As the Carambolo treasure shows, the local Tartessian population had developed sophisticated techniques of gold working.

[17] The finding of amphoras related in form to "Canaanite jars" that must have served for olive oil and wine transport at the Tell of Castillo Doña Blanca (11 miles from Gadir) and other sites provide evidence for this trade. The earliest of them date to the first half of the 8th century. They are found in all Tartessian sites during the 7th century. In some sites such as Carambolo Bajo, amphora fragments represent more than 50% of all ceramics recovered (see Chamorro, "Survey," 1987, 213).

[18] Aristotle, De mirabilibus auscultationibus, 135 (= Aristotle, Minor Works, 1936, 307ff.).

[19] Avienus, 113-16.

[20] Strabo, 3.5.11. Strabo states that the inhabitants of the Cassiterite islands exchanged tin and lead for pottery, salt, and bronze tools brought by traders. At first, Phoenicians from Gadeira (Cadiz) had a monopoly of this commerce. They even kept secret the routes that lead to these islands.

British Islands.[21] Traces of Phoenician shipping have been found along the Portuguese coast in the 7th century BCE.

Beginning in the early eighth century, Phoenician groups gradually settled along the coast of Malaga, Granada, and Almeria, which experienced a spectacular growth of colonists between 720 and 700 BCE[22] and maximum economic growth during the seventh century. Population increases are documented in the Tartessian sites in the course of the 7th century.[23] The beginning of the sixth century was characterized by a deep economic crisis. Silver extraction in Riotinto was abandoned. Gadir abandoned the silver trade. All Phoenician activities came to a halt in the years 600-580 BCE. Silver was not profitable anymore. The aforementioned settlements were abandoned around 580-550 BCE. The year 550 BCE marks the transition from the Phoenician to the Punic phases in the West.[24] To some extent Phoenician trade drained the West and had negative ecological consequences such as deforestation.

Phoenician participation in the Mediterranean silver trade is well corroborated archaeologically in southern Spain. Ancient silver slag is found in the Tartessian towns of Huelva: the huge slag dumps (15 to 20 million tons) found at Riotinto (Huelva) and the smaller ones at other sites of the Huelva region such as Tharsis, Sotiel-Coronada, and 60 other smaller sites are considered to be the result of Cypriot and Phoenician

---

[21] Pliny the Elder, 4.22.119. It is possible that the location of the Cassiterite islands moved north over a period of time. First it referred to the Western coast of Galicia and its islands and then to Brittany. In Roman times, when the alluvial deposits of tin (cassiterite) in Galicia and the deposits in Brittany were exhausted and better sources were found, the term was extended to Great Britain and the Scilly Islands. See Madroñero, "Tin Trade," *Bulletin of the Metals Museum* 18 (1992): 44-88 for a detailed discussion of the problem. Madroñero supports the identification of the islands off the coast of Galicia as the Cassiterides or "Tin Islands."

[22] At the same time the *tophet* (cemetery) was established in Carthage and Motya and Toscanos became industrial centers.

[23] Chamorro, "Survey," 1987, 231. The fact that "red-slip" sherds found in southern Spain represent the largest sample of Phoenician ware outside Phoenicia gives an idea of the extent of the Phoenician activities in Spain. A single excavation season in one site, Cerro de la Mezquitilla, produced 9,000 Phoenician sherds (see Chamorro, "Survey," 1987, 213-15).

[24] Aubet, *West*, 1993, 259, 263-64, 273-75, 281.

silver smelting activities.[25] Excavations at Riotinto (Cerro Salomón) revealed the existence of a mining community from the 8th – 7th centuries BCE. A group of Phoenician structures was uncovered; the associated artifacts (granite pestles, stone mortars, and grinding implements) are typical of ancient smelting sites. Phoenician domestic pottery, amphorae, and equipment were also unearthed. Metallurgical analysis of slags revealed a high proportion of silver (600 g. per metric ton) comparable with the richest of ores.[26]

The presence of bronze luxury goods and art objects in Tartessian sites shows Phoenician metal trade as well.[27] Egyptian bronze braziers found in Tartessian orientalizing contexts of the 7th and 6th centuries were carried to the West by Phoenician traders.[28] Phoenician double-spring fibulas found in Toscanos, Frigiliana, and Trayamar during the 7th century in Iberian Phoenician contexts are connected to the Phoenician trade in iron.[29] Luxury items found in the context of Tartessian Orientalizing necropoli from the 7th and 6th centuries such as ivories, scarabs, belt-buckles are either the product of Phoenician trade or the result of local workshops with Phoenician influence.[30] The Phoenician influence is also appreciable in architecture. The San Pedro wall in Huelva City (700 BCE) belongs to the type Pritchard called "Phoenician ribbed wall" with parallels in Ras Shamra, Megiddo IV, Tyre IX and Hazor VB.[31]

---

[25] See Blanco and Luzón, "Riotinto," *Antiquity* 43 (1969): 124; Chamorro, "Survey," 1987, 199. They considered the slag dumps at Riotinto represent the largest accumulation in one site of ancient pyrometallurgical residues.

[26] Blanco and Luzón, "Riotinto," 1969, 124, 128-29. As commented earlier, the archaeological evidence from other sites (Quebrantahuesos, Tejada) points to an exploitation of the mines by the local Tartessian population prior to the Phoenician arrival and to their remaining in Tartessian hands. The Phoenician role consisted in providing new markets and encouraging large-scale production (see Chamorro, "Survey," 1987, 199-200).

[27] See summary in Chamorro, "Survey," 1987, 215-31.

[28] The braziers appeared at Sanan (Nubia) between 730 and 530 BCE and seem to have originated in Egypt (see Chamorro, "Survey," 1987, 217).

[29] The earliest well-dated iron in the Iberian Peninsula appears in the early 7th century. Iron slag is found in Phoenician settlements (see Chamorro, "Survey," 1987, 219).

[30] This is the case with the 200 ivory fragments found mainly in the necropoli of Los Alcores (Seville).

[31] See Chamorro, "Survey," 1987, 222-23.

Phoenician trade also extended inland in the Levant. After Assyria's defeat of the Syrian kingdoms in the 8th century, the Phoenicians became the main suppliers of raw materials and gained control over the overland trade routes.[32] There is evidence of Phoenician names, deities and scripts in documents in Cilicia.[33] Phoenician inscriptions and graffiti have been found in Kuntillet 'Ajrud in the Negev (8th Century)[34] and in Abu Simbel in Egypt (6th Century).[35] Oppenheim has shown that, during the Neo-Babylonian period, Tyre exercised a monopoly on the supply of products and raw materials through overland trade. Furthermore there is evidence of private trade on the part of Tyre during the Assyrian period.[36]

---

[32] See Frankenstein, "Far West," 1979, 273.

[33] See Lebrun, "L'Anatolie," in *Phoenicia and the East Mediterranean*, ed. Lipiński, 1987, 23-33; Gibson, *Textbook*, 1982, 3.30-64. The Incirli (Zincirli) Stele illustrates Phoenician penetration in Cilicia in the second half of the 8th century. This penetration continued through the end of the 7th century. See Mosca and Russell, "Phoenician Inscription," 1987, 1-28. On paleographical grounds, Mosca and Russell date this inscription to the beginning of the 7th century.

[34] Fragments of three graffiti inscriptions, written in Phoenician script but in the Hebrew language, were found in the bench room of the main building at Kuntillet 'Ajrud. The site may have served as a "wayside shrine." See Meshel, *Kuntillet 'Ajrud* (1978); Dever, "Asherah," *Bulletin of the American Schools of Oriental Research* 255 (1984): 21-37; Emerton, "New Light," *ZAW* 94 (1982): 2-20; Lémaire, "Date," *Studi epigrafici e linguistici* 1 (1984): 131-43.

[35] *CIS* I.111-12.

[36] In contrast to the situation in the second-millenium BCE, few references to privately organized trade are known during the Neo-Assyrian period. The use of papyrus by the Aramaic merchants that controlled trade is the explanation Oppenheim proposed for the lack of written evidence of private trade (see Oppenheim, *Ancient Mesopotamia*, 1977, 94). The existence of private trade is undeniable anyway (see Oppenheim, "Comment," 1969, 36). A number of documents such as the treaty between Esarhaddon and Baal of Tyre demonstrate its presence in the Neo-Assyrian empire (see Postgate, "Economic Structure," 1979, 206). Karen Radner has analyzed new cuneiform evidence for this period in two recent articles (Radner, "Traders," in *Trade and Finance*, ed. Dercksen, 1999, 101-26; idem, "Money," in *Trade and Finance*, ed. Dercksen, 1999, 127-57). She concluded that "the evidence for trade in the Neo-Assyrian period, both conducted by state agents and private entrepreneurs, is far less scanty than generally assumed" ("Money," 1999, 138). The situation is even clearer for the Neo-Babylonian period (see below, under 3.4), the Nūr-Sîn family archive of 223 cuneiform contracts and letters dating between 603 and 507 BCE demonstrates the existence of independent private traders during this period. 173 documents out of the 223 belong to the Neo-Babylonian

Between the 8th and 7th centuries, worked ivory was one of the products that brought the most prestige to Tyre's commerce. The property of a very restricted social elite and a symbol of the power and wealth of the Assyrian kings, ivory has been found in royal palaces such as Nimrud and Khorsabad outside Phoenicia.[37] Ez. 27:6 shows ivory was a social status symbol. *The Odyssey* (19.565) equates it with ostentation, power and corruption.[38] The fact that this luxury trade climaxed between the 8th and the 7th centuries shows it had the support of the Assyrian kings.[39]

Tyrian participation and share in the economic expansion that took place during the Neo-Assyrian period has been substantiated in this section. Her share in the metal trade and the amazing growth of Tyrian colonies in the West has been established as well.

3. Tyre's Alliance with Egypt

Ezekiel's oracles against Tyre are a continuation of the polemic begun by Jeremiah against relying on Egypt for support (Jer. 37:7; 46:1-12). Tyre was identified as a strategic ally of Egypt[40] and was blamed for Egypt's past and present grievances to the Judeans. Like Egypt, Tyre was also not reliable in times of crisis.

---

period. In his unpublished Ph.D. dissertation, L. B. Shiff, collected these 223 cuneiform contracts and letters and presented them in transliteration and translation, many for the first time (see Shiff, *Nur-Sin Archive*, 1987).

[37] See Cecchini, "Ivoirerie," in *CPP*, ed. Krings, 1995, 517-24.

[38] Aubet, *West*, 1993, 38-39. *The Iliad* (23.740-45) supplies additional evidence of the circulation of Phoenician products as social status symbols. This section tells how, during Patroclus' funeral, Achilles presented a large silver crater 'a masterpiece of Sidonian craftsmanship,' as a price. Luxury products such as this one passed from one hand to another becoming social status symbols at the end of the process.

[39] Baslez, "Ivoires," in *DCPP*, ed. Lipiński, 1992, 237.

[40] The Egyptian intervention in Phoenicia during the entire 7th century is by no means to be underestimated. By encouraging and actively supporting the rebel city, Egypt participated in almost every Tyrian revolt (or Phoenician for that matter) against Assyria during that century. No question that Egypt's influence in the area increased after the Assyrian decline.

The Assyrian domination in the Levant started to weaken c. 640 BCE[41] and the Assyrian state collapsed in the years 614-609 BCE (on this matter, see discussions in 2.1). After having been an Assyrian tributary under Assurbanipal, Psammetichus I (664-610 BCE) overthrew the Assyrian control of Egypt between 656 and 652 BCE. He counted upon the support of Gyges king of Lydia in this process.[42] Immediately afterwards, he started to undermine the Assyrian domination of Palestine. Herodotus (2.157) notes that he besieged the city of Azotus (Ashdod) for 29 years.[43] If this information is accurate and since the reign of Psammetichus ended in 610, the siege must have started before 639 BCE. Towards the end of his reign, according to D. B. Redford, Psammetichus' "direct control extended along the coast as far as and including Phoenicia, where he boasts that his officers supervised timber production and export."[44] According to an Egyptian stele from his 52nd year (612), the Lebanese princes were vassals under an Egyptian commissioner and paid tribute to Pharaoh.[45] Sometime prior to 616 BCE, Psammetichus made an alliance with Sin-šar(ra)-iškun. By this alliance the Egyptian army fought in the Euphrates against the Babylonians in 616 BCE.[46] It is unclear whether this Egypto-Assyrian alliance was an attempt on Psammetichus' part to maintain the balance of power in Mesopotamia, the result of his fear of losing Syria, a consequence of the unstable conditions in Mesopotamia, or part of his desire to gain a free hand in Palestine and Syria.[47]

Much of the evidence for the Egyptian domination of the Levant comes from excavations that lack precise dating. The evidence from

---

[41] The latest datable evidence of Assyrian domination in the Levant is as follows: 1) Assyrian deeds of sale found at Gezer (651-649 BCE), 2) the mention of a governor at Samaria (646 BCE), and 3) Assurbanipal's punitive expedition against Akko and Ušu (mainland Tyre) (644-643 BCE) (*ANET* 300). I am indebted in this section to Asher, *Neighbours*, 1996, 23-28.

[42] Gyges and Psammetichus made an alliance by which Greek soldiers from the area of Ionia under Lydian control entered the Egyptian service.

[43] Ashkelon may have passed into Egyptian control voluntarily (see Redford, *Egypt*, 1992, 442; Asher, *Neighbours*, 1996, 25).

[44] Redford, *Egypt*, 1992, 442.

[45] Freedy and Redford, "Dates," 1970, 477.

[46] See Wiseman, *Chronicles*, 1974, 55-56.

[47] See Asher, *Neighbours*, 1996, 34; Spalinger, "Egypt and Babylonia," 1977, 224.

written sources concentrates on the period after 620.[48] The archaeological evidence for the Egyptian presence is most clear in the coastal region from the Philistine to the Phoenician cities. This suggests that Egypt's primary goal was to control the Via Maris and the sea traffic in the East Mediterranean. The Egyptian inscriptions in the area are from the last two decades of the 7th century: the statue inscription of Hor from Psammetichus I's reign refers to "cedar from the (royal) domain," an indication of control over Phoenicia and Lebanon.[49] There is a statue of Psammetichus from Arwad and a stele of Necho II was found at Sidon.[50] Additional archaeological finds include objects found in Sidon (a bronze trinket and a sistrum handle with the name Amasis inscribed on it)[51] and objects from Tyre (a round fragment of diorite and a stone trinket fragment with a measure of capacity and an Egyptian inscription in monumental hieroglyphs).[52] When the Egyptian presence becomes tangible, the question is whether this presence implies direct political control of the area or just points to commercial contact and exchange. Redford and Spalinger support the former possibility. Katzenstein and Asher speak of commercial contacts only. Still other authors like Vanderhooft remain undecided. The question should remain open. No traces of systematic military pressure have been found in the area and the

---

[48] The written sources for the period are presented in Redford, *Egypt*, 1992, 442; Vanderhooft, *Neo-Babylonian Empire*, 1999, 70-71; Katzenstein, *History*, 1997, 299, note 24 and 313, note 100.

[49] Breasted, *Ancient Records*, 1962, 4 # 967 (p. 494, note g) and 970. See also Redford, *Egypt*, 1992, 442.

[50] See Porter and Moss, *Egyptian-Hieroglyphic Texts*, 1951, 7.384; Gardiner, *Egypt*, 1961, 358; Katzenstein, *History*, 1997, 313, note 100. For Gardiner, Necho's stele proved "Necho's control of the Phoenician coast" (p. 358). It rather illustrates the good relations existing between Egypt and the Phoenician cities at this time.

[51] According to Scandone, Renan spoke of amulets and scarabs in some tombs. They can be ascribed to the first millenium BCE. No more precise dating is possible. See Scandone, "Testimonianze egiziane," *RSF* 12 (1984): 149-63. In any event, scarabs are always datable with the greatest difficulty. For this reason one has to be very cautious in using them to date anything. Many states in the Levant and Cyprus seem to have been able to produce high-quality Egyptianizing scarabs themselves. Their presence can seldom be used to prove or disprove anything about Egyptian activity in the Phoenician territory.

[52] See Renan, *Mission*, 1864, 546-47; Scandone, "Testimonianze Egiziane," 1984, 151-52.

destruction layers are more likely to be attributed to Nebuchadnezzar's campaigns.

The Egyptian objects from Ashkelon include a hoard of bronzes, a figurine of Osiris, seven bronze situlae, fragments of an Egyptian bronze offering table, a falcon, a jackal, a frog, a figurine of Bes, Egyptian barrel jars and tripod stands, and a jewelry box made of abalone shell with nine small Egyptian amulets in an abalone box.[53] These finds led Stager to postulate the existence of an Egyptian enclave at Ashkelon with a sanctuary. For him Egyptian rule of the Levant implied more than just commercial interaction in the area.[54]

A number of Egyptian objects dated after the dissolution of the Assyrian rule in 630 BCE have been found at Tell Miqne-Ekron as well. These include a fragment of an inscribed sistrum, a 26th dynasty scarab, an Egyptian figurine, a remarkable gold uraeus, and numerous faience and shell amulets and figurines.[55] The expanded oil industry of the city may have arisen after the Egyptian takeover of the area under Egyptian sponsorship.[56] The same conclusion holds for Tel Batash-Timna where an important olive oil industry developed in the mid-7th century.

Necho II (610-595 BCE) continued with this policy in the Levant. According to Herodotus (2.159), after a battle in Magdolus (Meggido or Migdol), he conquered the city of Cadytis (Gaza). Jer. 47:1 also refers to an attack on Gaza (cf. section 2.4). The short-lived Egyptian dominion in the Levant ended with the Egyptian defeat in the battle of Carchemish (605 BCE) (on this matter, see discussions in 2.5).

The Saqqara papyrus or Adon letter (end of the 7th century) provides additional indication of Egyptian influence in Philistia. The

---

[53] See Stager, "Archaeology of Destruction," 1996, 69.

[54] See pictures in Stager, "Fury of Babylon," 1996, 61.

[55] See Gitin, "Ekron of the Philistines," 1990, 41-42.

[56] Thus Stager, "Archaeology of Destruction," 1996, 26; idem, "Fury of Babylon," 1996, 66; Vanderhooft, Neo-Babylonian Empire, 1999, 74. According to S. Gitin, the excavator of the site, the phenomenal physical and economic growth of the site took place in the first half of the 7th century. T. Dothan and S. Gitin consider that "the oil industry was probably created as a direct result of the stability produced by the Pax Assyriaca and the commercial interests of the expanding Assyrian empire" (Dothan and Gitin, "Ekron," ABD, 2.420). See also Gitin's article "Ekron of the Philistines," 1990, 33-42, 59.

sender, Adon king of Ekron,[57] asked his overlord in Egypt for military aid in the face of the Babylonian invasion that had taken Aphek.

The fact that Herodotus (2.112) mentions the existence of the camp of the Tyrians in Memphis around a sacred precinct established by a king who apparently was Psammetichus I, indicates that there were well-established trade connections between Tyre and Egypt.[58] A fragmentary inscription on a statue of Hor, an army commander at Heracleopolis, refers to the use of "cedar from the (royal) domain." The inscription, according to D. B. Redford, belongs to the days of Psammetichus I.[59] Katzenstein speculates about the possibility of the existence of a trade-agreement between Egypt and Tyre between 635 and 610 BCE.[60] Genuine Egyptian amulets and trinkets were found in Carthage during the period of the 26th dynasty. A sharp decrease in their number took place towards the end of the 6th century.[61]

Discoveries from Tell el-Maskhuta substantiate the idea of a Phoenician share in Necho II's enterprises. According to Herodotus (2.158), Necho built a canal linking the Pelusiac branch of the Nile River to the Red Sea by way of Wadi Tumilat. Apparently, Necho's purpose in building the canal was to capture the spice and incense trade with the Mediterranean world.[62] Evidence for the Phoenician presence in Tell el-

---

[57] The identification of the city is disputed. I follow Porten's opinion. According to him, the reverse of the letter contains a line in Demotic with the name Ekron (see Porten, "King Adon," 1981, 36-52).

[58] See Katzenstein, *History*, 1997, 298-99. Culican supposes that since Necho II invited the Phoenicians to circumnavigate Africa (Herodotus, 4.42), the Tyrians shipbuilding activities were carried out in the Tyrian Camp (Culican, "Phoenician Colonization," 1991, 471). Inside the Camp there was a temple of Proteus (Baal ?) and a another of "foreign Aphrodite" (Astarte).

[59] See Redford, *Egypt*, 1992, 442. The inscription was first assigned to Psammetichus I's reign by Breasted in *Ancient Records*, 4 # 967 (p. 494, note g) and 970 (cf. section 2.2).

[60] Katzenstein, *History*, 1997, 300-01.

[61] See Harden, *The Phoenicians*, 1962, 162; Katzenstein, *History*, 1997, 300. Lancel indicates that "certain amulets peculiar to the XXVIth dynasty [...] are to be found in plenty at Carthage in tombs dated between the middle of the seventh and the sixth century, contemporary with that dynasty" (Lancel, *Carthage*, 1997, 68). See also Vercoutter, *Mobilier*, 1945, 282.

[62] Most of this trade does not leave traces in the archaeological record (see Holladay, "Maskhuta," *ABD*, 4.591).

Maskhuta is plentiful (see below, under 3.7): vast numbers of Phoenician amphoras beginning with the earliest 7th century levels, a Phoenician terra-cotta figurine found in a small limestone shrine suggesting the existence of a Phoenician sanctuary, and a few Phoenician ostraca or "jar labels" written in Demotic.[63] Phoenician merchants had a leading role in the canal-related Mediterranean trade entering through the site. It seems that this Phoenician domination of trade between the Mediterranean and the Red Sea continued during the Persian period until Alexander's destruction of Tyre (332 BCE) and the foundation of Alexandria.[64]

A list of commodities and trading partners illustrates the scope, variety, and wealth of Egyptian trade during Necho II's reign. In his time Egypt enjoyed free access to wine and alum from Phoenicia, medical herbs from Palestine, aromatic substances and bitumen from Transjordan, and exotic products from south Arabia.[65]

Joel 4:6[66] provides important information relating Tyre to Judah and the Ionians. Joel 4:6 says that "the sons of Judah and the sons of Jerusalem you [Tyre, Sidon, and Philistia] have sold to the Ionians. It is my opinion that "Ionian"[67] here conveys an indirect reference to the

---

[63] See Holladay, "Maskhuta," 1992, 590. Large amounts of Greek amphorae showing Greek involvement in trade in the area have been found on the site.

[64] See Lemaire, "Commerce," in *Phoenicia and the East Mediterranean*, ed. Lipiński, 1987, 59.

[65] See Redford, *Egypt*, 1992, 435; Drioton and Vandier, *L'Égypte*, 1938, 583-84.

[66] Estimates about the date of Joel have ranged widely from the 9th to the middle of the 4th century BCE. This is due to the fact that only internal evidence can be used for dating the book (see Myers, "Date," *ZAW* 74 [1962]: 177). Most scholars, however, now place Joel in the postexilic period, somewhere between the late 6th (Myers, "Date," 1962, 195 [c. 520 BCE]; Ahlström, *Joel*, 1971, 129) and the early 4th centuries (Wolff, *Joel and Amos*, 1977, 4-6). Wolff concludes that Joel 4:4-8 "must be dated between 400 and 343" (p. 78). As it has been noticed, "References in Joel 3-4 [...] to the fall of Judah, the dispersion of the Jews, and the return of the exiles (4:2, 7 [...]) all point to a postexilic political scene" (Hiebert, "Joel," *ABD*, 3.879). In any event, it is my opinion that the book echoes events that took place around the destruction of Jerusalem in 586 BCE.

[67] The term יון is used with the meaning "Ionian" in the Bible. The ancient Near East sources make no distinction between different Greek tribes at this time. The Egyptians themselves seem to have called the Greeks generically "Ionians." They were both land soldiers and comprised a large part of the Egyptian navy and merchant marine at this period. יון came to designate all Greeks in general at a later time.

Egyptians, who were Tyre's trading partners. It is a recognized fact that, during this period the Greeks, Carians, and Ionians predominantly, came to the Levant as traders or mercenaries under Egyptian sponsorship.

As said before, Psammetichus I (664-610 BCE) was able to unify Egypt and throw off the Assyrian domination around 654 BCE. A pact with king Gyges of Lydia was instrumental in this endeavor. By this pact a group of Greek soldiers from Ionia under Lydian auspices entered Egyptian service. Psammetichus considered these Ionian hoplites the best available warriors.[68]

Between 616 and 605, both Psammetichus I and Necho II used their Greek mercenaries against the Babylonians. First of all, an increase of Greek pottery in the Levant during the second half of the 7th century has been detected. This increase is especially important in the southern Levant. East Greek ceramics had been reaching the Levant since the 8th century in places such as Al Mina and Tel Sukas but the Greek ceramics from the second half of the 7th century are more numerous, are distributed more widely, and include more forms than previously.[69]

As a reward for their help, Psammetichus I established Greek trading colonies in the Delta region. Naucratis was the most important of them. These settlements boosted the Greek penetration in the eastern Mediterranean. Although the exact date for the foundation of Naucratis is not known, the Corinthian pottery at the site dates from c. 630-620 BCE.[70] The Greeks exported wine, olive oil, and silver to Egypt. In addition to this, Psammetichus established garrisons with Greek soldiers in three places: Elephantine on the Nubian desert; Marea against the

---

[68] Herodotus (2.154) informs us that Psammetichus had both Ionian and Carian mercenaries. Psammetichus realized that the Egyptian army was inferior to the armies of Western Asia at this time. Scarcity of iron and modern weaponry and a negative attitude toward soldiering seem to have been the determining factors for this inferiority (see Redford, *Egypt*, 1992, 443). As a result, Saïte Egypt became an employer of Greeks and Asiatics. Most scholars recognize the important role Greek mercenaries played in Psammetichus' quick ascent to power. These mercenaries were likely to have been in Egypt early in Psammetichus' reign.

[69] See Waldbaum, "Contacts," BASOR 293 (1994): 59-61; Stager, "Archaeology of Destruction," 1996, 21-22. For this section in general, see Vanderhooft, *Neo-Babylonian Empire*, 1999, 76-81.

[70] See Braun, "Greeks in Egypt," in *CAH*, eds. Boardman et al., 1982, 3.3.38.

Lybians; and Daphnae in the east.[71] Jeremiah fled to Daphnae with a Jewish contingent to escape the Babylonian captivity in 582 BCE and predicted Egypt's imminent conquest (Jer. 46:6-7).

Egypt may have employed Greek mercenaries for the protection and administration of the coastal route and sea traffic.[72] Meṣad Ḥashavyahu constitutes the clearest evidence of Greek presence in the Levant during this period. Greek pottery of the last third of the seventh century and a workshop for making iron implements has been discovered there. The fort may have been an Egyptian garrison with East Greek, Judean, and other mercenaries and clients of Egypt.[73] Since a Hebrew letter seems to imply that the garrison had a Jewish governor,[74] the inhabitants may have been in the service of Josiah and forced to abandon the post during the Egyptian invasion of 609 BCE.[75] Subsequently, Greeks were employed as mercenaries by the Judeans. A Hebrew letter from Tell Arad addressed to one Eliashib, gives instructions to supply wine, bread, and oil "to the Kittim" (*lktym*). Greek mercenaries from the island of Lesbos took part in the Babylonian siege of Ashkelon in 604 BCE as well.[76] There, a Greek shield decorated with Gorgon's head, fine Egyptian objects, and Necho II's sealings were found. These finds corroborate the presence of Greek mercenaries in the battle of Carchemish in 605 BCE.[77]

Necho II (610-595 BCE) continued with the same policy. Greek and Phoenician influence went hand in hand during his reign. Egypt

---

[71] Herodotus, 2.30.

[72] The Greek penetration in the Levant is due to Egyptian influence in the area, friendly relations between the Egyptians and Greeks, and demographic pressures in the East Greek states.

[73] I follow Na'aman's interpretation of the site (see Na'aman, "Judah," 1991, 3-66). For a discussion of different interpretations of the site, see Vanderhooft, *Neo-Babylonian Empire*, 1999, 78-79.

[74] See Naveh, "Hebrew Letter," 1960, 129-39; idem, "More Hebrew Inscriptions," *IEJ* 12 (1962): 27-32.

[75] Braun's suggestion in "Greeks in the Near East," in *CAH*, eds. Boardman et al., 1982, 3.3.21-22. Wiseman's alternative interpretation is that Meṣad Ḥasahvyahu was a Greek settlement under Egyptian control which, after 604 BCE, changed sides to be under a Jewish governor (see Wiseman, *Nebuchadnezzar*, 1985, 24).

[76] See Braun, "Greeks in the Near East," 1982, 22.

[77] C. L. Woolley's suggestion as presented in Wiseman, *Nebuchadnezzar*, 1985, 15-16.

developed a navy of triremes under a joint Greek-Phoenician supervision.[78] According to Herodotus (4.42) at the same time, Necho employed Phoenician sailors for his circumnavigation of Africa at the same time.[79]

During the reign of Psammetichus II (595-589 BCE), the same philhellene and philphoenician policy continued. The Saïte navy was manned by Greeks.[80] In his 3rd year, he campaigned against Nubia with Greek and Phoenician mercenaries. The graffiti from Abu Simbel (591) document the presence of Greek mercenaries in his army. They are written in an East Greek Doric and Ionian dialect. Phoenician graffiti are also attested.[81] The last two pharaohs of the Saïte dynasty Apries (589-570 BCE) and Amasis (570-526 BCE), continued with the same philhellene policy.

The Babylonian hegemony marked an almost complete cessation of Greek imports in the Levant.[82] It seems that Babylonian policy gave priority to eradication of the Egyptian influence in the Levant and the destruction of its client cities, not to the economic exploitation of the area (see below, under 3.4). The destruction of Ashkelon (604 BCE), Ekron (603 BCE), Gaza (601 BCE), Ashdod (c. 600 BCE), Tel Batash-Timnah, and perhaps Tel Sera' and other sites supports this conclusion.[83] Nebuchadnezzar disrupted the Greek trade that shifted toward Egypt

---

[78] Braun ("Greeks in the Near East," 1982, 49) observes that "Herodotus does not say who built Necho's ships for him, and recent controversy has pitted the claims of Greek shipbuilders against Phoenician. But it would be strange if Necho did not employ both." Braun gives a detailed bibliography on the polemic about who (Greeks or Phoenicians) supervised the construction of Necho's navy.

[79] A useful article on the Egyptian navy and merchant marine during this period is Darnell, "*Knb.wt* Vessels," in *Life in a Multi-Cultural Society*, ed. Johnson, 1992, 67-89.

[80] In Braun's opinion, this was due to the impossibility of recruiting sailors in large numbers from Babylonian occupied Phoenicia. Hor, the admiral of Psammetichus' navy, received the title of "commander of the Greeks" (Braun, "Greeks in the Near East," 1982, 50).

[81] *CIS* I.111-12.

[82] Dor may be an exception to this cessation of Greek imports. Stern found a number of Greek pottery sherds that began to arrive in the early 6th century. In any event, he acknowledges that there is no real stratum for the Neo-Babylonian period (see Stern, "Masters," *BAR* 19 [1993]: 42-44).

[83] See Vanderhooft, *Neo-Babylonian Empire*, 1999, 81-89.

proper. Increasing numbers of "Ionians" were deported to Babylon as craftsmen and mercenaries in the early 6th century. Finally Nebuchadnezzar attacked Egypt in 601 BCE.[84] The attack was a failure.

Greek involvement in slave trade is known from *The Odyssey* (17.425-39). Private documents confirm such involvement. A certain man named Yamani sold a slave woman to another officer at Nineveh c. 661 BCE. He is presumably identical with the Yamani who witnessed a similar sale in 659 and 654.[85]

This section has shown that Tyre was a strategic ally of Egypt during the end of the 7th century BCE. Due to the fact that Egypt's primary goal was to control the Via Maris and the sea traffic in the East Mediterranean, contacts between Tyre and Egypt were mainly commercial but they had a political dimension as well. Archaeological data shows contacts between Tyre and Egypt through the Philistine ports. Herodotus mentions the presence of a Tyrian colony in Memphis, and Phoenician participation in Necho II's enterprises such as developing a navy of triremes and building a canal linking the Pelusiac branch of the Nile River to the Red Sea. Archaeological discoveries at Tell el-Maskhuta confirm Phoenician participation in these projects. Phoenician and Greek influence went hand in hand during the Saïte dynasty. Joel 4:6 accuses Tyre of selling Judeans to the "Ionians." The text echoes events that took place around the destruction of Jerusalem and might convey an indirect reference to Egypt as well.

4. Tyre and Babylon

Babylon was a land-based empire with huge tribute demands. Nebuchadnezzar, as we have seen, was not interested in the economic exploitation of the Levant,[86] yet the Phoenicians assisted Babylon in the procurement of a number of commodities the empire could not otherwise obtain. These products came in form of tribute. A number of studies have

---

[84] See Spalinger, "Egypt and Babylonia," 1977, 237-42.

[85] See Kohler and Ungnad, *Assyrische Rechtsurkunden*, 1913, 73, 60. The name Yamani means "Ionian," "Greek."

[86] This applies especially to Judah and the Philistine ports.

dealt with the economic relations between the Neo-Babylonian empire and the Phoenician cities.[87]

The first biblical mention of the Phoenician kingdoms in the Neo-Babylonian period is in Jer. 27-28, which tells of a conspiracy of the kings of Judah, Tyre, Edom, Moab and Sidon against Babylonian rule in 594 BCE (on this matter, see discussions in 2.7).

D. S. Vanderhooft's conclusions on the character of Nebuchadnezzar's imperialist policy and administration in the Levant point to the absence of a policy of systematic economic exploitation of the conquered territories in the Levant.[88] Nebuchadnezzar, in sharp contrast with the Neo-Assyrian kings, sought to eradicate the Egyptian clients in the region and control the area by means of military campaigns and the delivery of tribute. The extensive destruction of Philistia and Judah,[89] the meager material remains of Babylonian origin in Judea,[90]

---

[87] See Diakonoff, "Naval Power," 1992, 168-93; Elat, "Overland Trade," 1991, 21-35; Oppenheim, "Essay," *JCS* 21 (1967): 236-54; Vanderhooft, *Neo-Babylonian Empire*, 1999, 112-14.

[88] Vanderhooft deals with the nature of the Neo-Babylonian imperialism in the Levant and examines the characteristics of the Neo-Babylonian economy as presented in the royal inscriptions (see Vanderhooft, *Neo-Babylonian Empire*, 1999, 45-49, 56-57, 82-83, 97-98, 104-12). In a recent study, Stern corroborates Vanderhooft's conclusions (see Stern, *Archaeology*, 2001, 303-09). Stern considers the Neo-Babylonian empire as a highly centralized regime that concentrated entirely on the welfare of Babylon and neglected completely the periphery.

[89] Evidence of Babylonian destruction in Judah and adjacent areas is overwhelming. Among the cities destroyed and devastated in the late 7th century are Jerusalem, Ramat Raḥel, Lachish, Beth-shemesh, Ein Gedi, Arad, Kadesh Barnea, Ashkelon, Ekron, Timnah, Ashdod, and Tell Seraʻ. The material culture suffered a sharp contraction in demographic terms during the late 7th century-early 6th century as well. Signs of continuity between the Babylonian and Persian periods exists only in the territory of Benjamin to the north of Jerusalem. Tell en-Naṣbeh, Gibeah (Tell el-Ful), Bethel, and other places have yielded material for this period. But very little material can be certainly labeled as Babylonian and all of it comes from Tell en-Naṣbeh, which must have been the biblical Mizpah, the site of Gedaliah's governorship (see Stern, *Archaeology*, 2001, 321-26 and section 2.8). For the destruction of the Philistine cities, see Stern, *Archaeology*, 2001, 316-19. During the Persian period, a new Phoenician population repopulated the Philistine cities.

[90] The Assyrians constructed and used administrative buildings. Neo-Assyrian tablets were found in Tel Jemmeh and Gezer. Assyrian ware is also common in Judah. Unlike

and the decrease in East Greek trade in the Levant back up this conclusion.

The Neo-Babylonian Chronicles demonstrate the existence of yearly campaigns in which Nebuchadnezzar collected tribute and booty.[91] The picture presented in these inscriptions is one of one-way delivery of goods from the tributary states to the Babylonian core.[92] They emphasize the supply of raw materials, workmen, and precious and manufactured items for Babylon and the Babylonian cities. The emphasis on goods flowing into Babylon corresponds with Nebuchadnezzar's building projects. He attempted to make Babylon the most splendid, cultic center in the world.[93] The inscriptions list the different goods brought as tribute but do not convey any information about the origin of the products. Nebuchadnezzar's Istanbul prism-fragment is outstanding among these inscriptions for the information it supplies about the economic background of Nebuchadnezzar's reign.[94] The last seven lines begin with "king of the land of X" and a list of toponyms which include Tyre, Gaza, Sidon, Arwad, and Ashdod. It is assumed that these western kings participated in the construction of the palace since they contributed either raw materials or workmen.

In his "Essay on overland trade in the first millenium," A. L. Oppenheim published two economic texts, YOS 6 168 and TCL 12 84.[95] The texts, dated to the early years of Nabonidus' reign (551-550 BCE), demonstrate the one-sidedness of the Chaldean Chronicles and provide

---

the Assyrians, the Babylonians had no interventionist intentions in the area (see Stern, *Archaeology*, 2001, 12-31, 36-39, 309).

[91] See Wiseman, *Chronicles*, 1974, 69-75.

[92] Nebuchadnezzar's main purpose was to make Babylon the economic center of the world. He considered the delivery of tribute and goods to Babylon from vassal kingdoms an expression of imperial hegemony. One-way delivery of goods was very important during the Neo-Assyrian empire but not as an expression of imperial hegemony and is absent from the inscriptions of the Persian empire.

[93] Babylon was the physical justification of Nebuchadnezzar's imperial policy and its splendor legitimated him in his role as ruler of the world divinely sanctioned by Marduk.

[94] Nebuchadnezzar's Istanbul-prism fragment is a building inscription commemorating the completion of Nebuchadnezzar's royal palace in Babylon and dating to his 7th year (599). The text is published in Unger, *Babylon*, 1970, 282-94.

[95] Oppenheim, "Essay," 1967, 236-54.

evidence for bilateral trade[96] during the early part of Nabonidus reign.[97] They list a number of commodities imported together with their amounts. Among the commodities listed are metals (copper, iron from Yamana and Labnanu, and tin); foodstuffs (wine, honey…); and fibers (blue-purple wool and fabrics).[98]

Oppenheim's main conclusions are as follows:[99]

1) The texts illustrate Mesopotamian trade concerned with the distribution of large-scale imports furnished by overland trade.

2) The tablets demonstrate the existence of a long-standing private merchant venture with an official or semiofficial status.

3) The commodities imported coincide with those listed in the Assyrian inscriptions as tribute or booty.

4) No economic motivation for the importation of fine linen from Syria and Egypt into Babylon exists. Prestige value was the determinant reason for its importation.

5) The reference to the exportation of purple-dyed wool, a Tyrian monopoly suggests that Tyrian merchants directed this trade. The fact that the chief-merchant of Nebuchadnezzar II (604-562 BCE) *Ḥanūnu* (Phoenician Hanno), had a well attested Phoenician name is an additional indication that Phoenician trade was in Tyrian hands or controlled by them.

The above economic documents, in Elat's opinion, only prove at best the existence of limited bilateral trade during Nabonidus' reign between the Phoenician cities and Babylon. For him one-way forced

---

[96] Scholars use the expression "bilateral trade" in opposition to "force delivery of goods" or "tribute" to Babylon. In context it refers to "commercial trade" (see Oppenheim, "Essay," 1967, 241, 246; Elat, "Overland Trade," 1991, 22ff.; Vanderhooft, *Neo-Babylonian Empire*, 1999, 50, 123-24).

[97] Nabonidus sojourn in the Arabian oasis of Teima may be related to the king's desire to control trade routes.

[98] Oppenheim, "Essay," 1967, 238.

[99] See Oppenheim, "Essay," 1967, 246, 251, 253. Oppenheim's article is a most important one and remains our main source for reconstructing trade between Babylon and the West during the Neo-Babylonian period. The two texts published in the article refer to trading agents commissioned by the temple to carry precious metals and to purchase a list of products. It is likely that representatives of western trading houses operated in Babylon as well. If this is the case, the texts hint at the existence of trade from Babylon to the exterior and vice versa (see Joannès, "Structures," in *Trade and Finance*, ed. Dercksen, 1999, 175-94).

exchange was characteristic of the Neo-Assyrian and Neo-Babylonian periods before the fall of Tyre. During Nebuchadnezzar's first years, his overarching concern was Egypt.[100] Elat argued that the extant documents support the conclusion that only after the pacifying of relations with Egypt,[101] did Nebuchadnezzar switch his policy toward Phoenicia and other countries of the West and favor bilateral trade.[102] The same policy was followed by Nebuchadnezzar's successors and by the Persian empire.[103]

S. W. Cole's publication of the mid-eighth century Governor's Archive from Nippur[104] provides evidence for the bilateral trade identified by Oppenheim for the early part of Nabonidus's reign. The documents show how merchants sent traders along established routes with capital in the form of silver or goods to obtain desired items for import.[105] They show that, even if there is little evidence for the 7th and 6th centuries, such trade was probably characteristic of the period.

---

[100] The destruction of Ashkelon in 604 BCE and the 13-year siege of Tyre (588/7-573 BCE) were the direct result of this concern with Egypt. By destroying the Philistine and Phoenician cities of the coast, Nebuchadnezzar weakened Egypt's economic and political position.

[101] The siege of Tyre ended c. 572 BCE. Both Jeremiah (Jer. 43:8-13; 46:13-26) and Ezekiel (29:17-19) refer to a second campaign against Egypt (c. 570). No extrabiblical reference to such campaign has been found.

[102] Elat states that "only in the latter part of Nebuchadnezzar's reign do documents appear dealing with the shipment of commodities from Babylonian cities to Tyre or testifying to Babylonian commercial activity in Tyre" (Elat, "Overland Trade," 1991, 32-34). The evidence he refers to is as follows:

1) A contract recorded in Tyre in Nebuchadnezzar's 40th (565 BCE) year reporting on the delivery of cows by Qadesh's governor.
2) A document from Uruk (GCCI I 169:4) dated to Nebuchadnezzar's 42nd year (563 BCE) dealing with the marketing of dates from Uruk for military officials in Tyre.
3) Documents YOS 6 168 and TCL 12, 84 dated to the early part of Nabonidus reign (551-550 BCE) and studied by Oppenheim.
4) Document YOS 6 63:5-9 dated to Cyrus' seventh year (552 BCE) reporting on the import of white honey, wine, iron, tin, copper, and purple wool from Syria.
5) Document BIN 1 4 from an official at the Eanna temple in Uruk listing commodities such as silver, cedar, and red purple wool dated to 533-32 BCE in the reign of Cyrus II or Cambyses II.

[103] Elat, "Overland Trade," 1991, 35.

[104] Cole, *Nippur* (1996).

[105] Cole, *Nippur*, 1996, 82 indicates that the governors of Nippur were involved in trade: "One of them, Kudurru, was a prominent Babylonian businessman, like his

In his reconstruction of the economic life of the Nūr-Sîn family, L. B. Shiff has demonstrated the existence of independent private traders during the Neo-Babylonian period.[106] Shiff studied an archive of 223 cuneiform contracts and letters dating between 603 and 507 BCE.[107] The archive contains promissory notes and receipts for obligations of silver, gold, building materials, fabrics, clothing, oil, wool, grains, and other naturalia and fungibles. The information about Iddin-Marduk, the best-known member of the family, shows his ability to adapt his business activities to obtain maximization of profits. This is indicated by his concentration on wholesale trading commodities and on money-lending at a later time. As a wholesaler, he incurs considerable potential losses to obtain substantial gains. He was not a representative of the government or the temples but was willing to participate in business with governmental authorities.

This section dealing with Tyre under the Neo-Babylonian empire has shown the existence of bilateral trade (international and local) from the beginning of the Neo-Babylonian period, the presence of private traders, and a significant Tyrian participation in this international trade.

5. Tyre's Economic Relations and Trade Alliance with the Philistines

The Philistines were one of Judah's traditional enemies. During the early part of the 8th century, this enmity was exacerbated by the rebellion of Hezekiah (715-687 BCE) against Sennacherib (704-681 BCE). The rebellion took place in 701 BCE and ended with the siege and subsequent surrender of Jerusalem. Hezekiah paid a huge tribute and

---

predecessors, was involved in the slave-trade; but unlike them, he also traded in wool, purple textiles, iron, and mules. [...] The letters reveal that Nippur had trade contacts with Babylon, the middle Euphrates, Kalḫu, Dēr, the high Zagros, and Bīt-Dakkūri."

[106] The Nūr-Sîn family specialized in large-scale money lending and in the importation and exportation of large amounts of produce. It had no apparent affiliation with the central authorities dominating the economy at the time (see Shiff, *Nur-Sin Archive*, 1987, v, 4, 31, 115-16).

[107] There are a number of letters from the Persian period dated to Cyrus', Cambyses', and Darius' reigns. Out of the total of 223 letters, 173 belong to the Neo-Babylonian period and 52 to Nebuchadnezzar's reign.

Sennacherib gave part of the Judean territory to the main Philistine cities. The Assyrian Chronicle reads as follows:

> As for Hezekiah, the Jew, who had not submitted to my yoke, 46 of his strong walled cities and the cities of their environs, which were numberless, I besieged, I captured, I plundered as booty I counted them. Him, like a caged bird, in Jerusalem, his royal city, I shut up. Earthworks I threw up about it. His cities, which I plundered, I cut off from his land and gave to the kings of Ashdod, Ashkelon, Ekron, and Gaza; I diminished his land.[108]

It is evident that this action exacerbated the enmity between Judah and the Philistines and resulted in Judah's impoverishment.[109] In addition, a number of Bible references and archaeological finds link the Phoenicians and especially Tyre to the Philistines. The most important of these references are as follows:

a) Jer. 47:1-5. Jer. 47:1-5 is an oracle against the Philistines "before Pharaoh attacked and captured Gaza."[110] Verse 4 reads:

"Because of the day that is coming to devastate the Philistines, to cut off from Tyre and Sidon every helper that remains."

According to the Babylonian Chronicle, Nebuchadnezzar destroyed Ashkelon in 604 BCE.[111] Among the other main Philistine cities, Ekron was destroyed in 603 BCE, Gaza in 601 BCE, and Ashdod c. 600 BCE. Jer. 47:1-5 may allude to a trade agreement between

---

[108] *ARAB* 2.143 (# 312).

[109] By this action, Sennacherib may have intended to preserve the balance of power between the four cities of Philistia. As a result "Philistia was consolidated as a semi-neutral buffer area between Assyria and Egypt" (see Tadmor, "Philistia," 1966, 87). This action together with the heavy taxation of the Neo-Assyrian empire had a devastating economic effect on Judah. The Shephelah was spared from Sennacherib's devastation. Isserlin (*The Israelites*, 1998, 96) comments that "during the reign of Manasseh the Judean hill country recovered well and population even expanded into the Judean desert and the Beersheba region."

[110] In section 2.5 we saw three possible scenarios for this oracle: 1) A campaign by Psammetichus I before 610. 2) An attack against Gaza by Necho II just before the battle of Meggido in 609. 3) Necho II's siege of Gaza in 601 BCE as an aftermath to the battle with the Babylonians.

[111] Wiseman, *Chronicles*, 1974, 69.

Phoenicia and Philistia similar to the *ḫubūr* from the 11th-century BCE Egyptian "Tale of Wenamon."[112]
b) *Joel 4:4-8.*[113] Verses 4-6 of Joel 4 read in part as follows:

> Furthermore, what are you to me, O Tyre and Sidon, and all the districts of Philistia? [...] 5 For you have taken my silver and gold, and have carried my most valuable things into your palaces. 6 The sons of Judah and the sons of Jerusalem you have sold to the Ionians in order to remove them far from their own territory.

Greek involvement in slave trade is documented in *The Odyssey* (17.425-39). In antiquity, according to it, trade and piracy went hand in hand among Greeks.[114]
c) *Zech. 9:2b-8.*[115] Zech. 9:2b-6 supplies the following information:

---

[112] See Stager, "Fury of Babylon," 1996, 59. The *ḫubūr* was a trade agreement, mainly between two head of states by which they shared both profits and losses. For a thorough study of the term, see Hoch, *Semitic Words*, 1994, 240-41. For a discussion of trade practices during the 11th century, see Egberts, "Chronology," *Journal of Egyptian Archaeology* 77 (1991): 57-67; idem, "Chronology Revised," *ZÄS* 125 (1998): 93-108; Green, "Wenamun's Demand," *ZÄS* 106 (1979): 116-20; idem, "*m-k-m-r* und *w-r-k-t-r*," *ZÄS* 113 (1986): 115-19; Liverani, "Wen-Amun," in *Prestige and Interest*, ed. Liverani, 1990, 247-54; De Spens, "Analyse juridique," in *Le commerce en Égypte ancienne*, eds. Grimal and Menu, 1998, 105-26.

[113] For a discussion of the dating of Joel 4:4-8, see note 66 above.

[114] For Greek trade in the Levant, see Braun, "Greeks in the Near East," 1982, 7-14.

[115] Estimates on the date of Zec 9:1-8, the section constituting the beginning of "Deutero-Zechariah," have ranged widely from preexilic to postexilic times. Authors dating it to the 8th century are Winckler, Kraeling, Horst, Jepsen, Bright, Katzenstein, and Malamat. Otzen prefers the 7th century and Josiah's time. Numerous scholars envision a postexilic setting at the beginning of the Achaemenid period (Lamarche); during Alexander's conquest in 332 BCE (Stade, Mitchell, Smith, Bewer, Nowack, Delcor, Chary); or in the Maccabbean period (Martin, Sellin, Treves). Briquel-Chatonnet (*Relations*, 1992, 176-79) presents a full discussion of the issue. Meyers and Meyers (*Zechariah 9-14*, 1993, 26) date the collection of oracles and utterances that constitute Zechariah 9-14 to the end of the period beginning with the dedication of the Second Temple in 515 BCE and ending with the Mission of Nehemiah 445 BCE (p. 26). They make a good case for linking Zechariah 9-14 to the Greco-Egyptian rebellion (ending in 455) and its aftermath and to the extension of the Persian control on their Levantine holdings, especially Yehud (pp.18-28). They admit the existence of close links between Zech. 9:1-8 and Ezekiel 26-28 (p. 41). In their comment on the first part of verse 3, which they translate "Tyre has built herself a bulwark," they recognize that

Tyre and Sidon, for they are shrewd indeed
Tyre has built a rampart for herself,
and heaped up silver like dust,
and gold like the mud of the streets.
Behold! The Lord will dispossess her
and into the sea he will hurl her wealth,
and fire will consume her.
Ashkelon will see it and fear;
Gaza too, and will agonize greatly;
Ekron also, because her expectations are withered.
And the king of Gaza will perish;
Ashkelon will not be inhabited;
a hybrid (or bastard) population will dwell in Ashdod,
and I will cut off the pride of Philistia.

These texts suggest that (1) the prophets Jeremiah, Joel, and Zechariah saw Tyre as a power oppressing Judah. (2) The oppression hinted at seems to be of an economic and trading nature. (3) Tyre aligned herself with other traditional enemies of Judah such as the Philistine cities.

There is additional historical evidence linking the Philistine cities with Tyre and the Phoenician cities. As commented earlier, the Egyptian "Tale of Wenamon" from the 11th century shows that there was a trade agreement (*ḫubūr*) between Phoenician and Philistine cities.[116] In his treaty with Tyrian king Baal I (c. 674 BCE), Assyrian king Esarhaddon granted Baal ports of trade and trade roads "toward Akko, Dor, in the district of the Philistines."[117] The expression "in the district of the Philistines" seems to refer to the hinterland connected to Akko and

---

the section evokes and reworks Ezekiel 26-28. While acknowledging the possibility that the allusion to Tyre's fortifications could refer to one of the Assyrian or Babylonian sieges, they conclude that the text transcends a narrow historical focus (pp. 98-99). In my opinion, the text could be postexilic and at the same time take the perspective of a time when the cities and states it mentions existed. In support of this idea, notice that, during the Persian period, Sidon, not Tyre, was the leading Phoenician city and that the Philistine city states had ceased to exist.

[116] *ANET* 29. See also Goedicke, *Wenamun* (1975); Bunnens, "Ounamon," *RSF* 6 (1978): 1-16; and bibliography in note 112 above.

[117] *ANET* 534.

Dor.[118] Phoenician Red-Slipped Ware, "Samaria ware," and Red and Cream-Polished Phoenician ware have been found in large quantities in Ashkelon (604 BCE destruction debris) and Ashdod (c. 600 BCE destruction debris). These finds demonstrate the existence of important trade connections between Phoenician and Philistine cities during the 7th century.[119] A Phoenician inscription written in the late 7th century script was found in Ashkelon as well[120] and a Phoenician (?) royal dedicatory inscription in Philistine script at Ekron (7th century).[121]

During the Achaemenid period (538-332 BCE), Sidon and Tyre had an intense influence on the Philistine coast (see below, under 3.9).[122] According to the sarcophagus inscription of the Sidonian King Eshmun'ezer (465-451 BCE), Sidon was the ruler of "Dor and Jaffa."[123] The Periplus of Pseudo-Scylax (338-335 BCE) indicates that, during the Achaemenid Period, the coast from Sarepta to Carmel and the Philistine city of Ashkelon were under Tyrian control.[124]

This section has demonstrated the existence of important trade connections between the Phoenician and Philistine cities during the 7th century. The evidence can be interpreted as hinting at the existence of a trade agreement (ḥubūr) between Tyre and Philistia during the 7th

---

[118] At least this is Katzenstein's interpretation (*History*, 1997, 273).

[119] Stager, "Fury of Babylon," 1996, 58-59; idem, "Archaeology of Destruction," 1996, 66-67. Much smaller amounts of Red-Slipped ware were found in Ekron and Timnah located in the interior. In the 7th century, Ashkelon was producing Red-Slipped wares. Notice that during Solomon's reign (end of 10th century BCE) Israel was Tyre's main provider of wine and oil. In the late 7th century the Philistines were exporting these products to Tyre and Egypt. The Philistine coast was good for viticulture and the interior produced cereals and oils.

[120] Stager, "Fury of Babylon," 1996, 65. The ostracon was found outside what is considered a wine shop. It lists units of "red wine" and "strong drink."

[121] See Demsky, "Name of Goddess," *JANES* 25 (1997): 1-5; idem, "Discovering a Goddess," *BAR* 24 (1998): 53-58; Gitin, "Temple Inscription," *BA* 59 (1996): 101-2; Gitin, Dothan, and Naveh, "Dedicatory Inscription," *IEJ* 48 (1997): 1-18.

[122] Soon after Nebuchadnezzar's destruction of the main Philistine cities, the Philistines faded away from history. At that time, the kingdom of Judah also ceased to exist. Afterwards, under the Persian administration, the province of Yehud was created. From a geographical point of view, Yehud was much smaller than the former kingdom of Judah and a much less significant player in the politics of the area.

[123] Xella, "Eshmunazor," in *DCPP*, ed. Lipiński, 1992, 160; Stern, *Dor*, 1994, 149.

[124] Marcotte, "Pseudo-Skylax," in *DCPP*, ed. Lipiński, 1992, 418-19.

century similar to the one linking them in the 11th century. This trade agreement resulted in the exclusion of Judah from international trade. Intense commercial and political relations between Tyre, Sidon, and the Philistine coast continued during the Persian empire. By that time, the Philistine city states had ceased to exist. In place of the once important kingdom of Judah, destroyed by Nebuchadnezzar, the Persians created the tiny, insignificant province of Yehud.

6. Tyre's Economic Relations with Edom

Relations between Judah and the Edomites during the second half of the 8th century and the first half of the 6th century were difficult. The Edomites seized Elat (c. 735 BCE) which remained in their control till the end of the 6th century and gave them control of the major trade routes with the Red Sea via Gaza and Transjordan.[125] The combined evidence from the Bible and archaeology (Edomite pottery and ostraca) "suggests the presence of an Edomite element in the population of the region between Beer-sheba and the S[outh] end of the Dead Sea in the 7th century B.C."[126] Additional evidence of Edomite presence in the Negeb has been found in Arad, Tell Meshash, Ḥorvat Qitmit, and Ḥorvat 'Uza.[127]

During the 7th century Edom together with Ammon and Moab experienced a prosperity which must be related to trade through the King's Highway. The discovery of a Phoenician inscription on a pitcher of the end of the 7th century in Tell es-Sa'idiyeh,[128] may indicate a Phoenician role in this international trade.[129] So it seems that in the last decade of the 7th century and in spite of not having common borders, Tyre and Edom developed strong commercial links. Tyre's selling of Judean captured prisoners as slaves to Edom (Am. 1:9) is an additional argument in favor of the existence of extensive trade relations between Tyre and Edom (on this matter, see discussions in 3.11). Ez. 27:16 also

---

[125] See Bartlett, "Edom," *ABD*, 2.292-93; Myers, "Edom and Judah," 387-88; Lemaire "Edom," in *DCPP,* ed. Lipiński, 1992, 143-44.

[126] Bartlett, "Edom," 1992, 292.

[127] Bartlett, "Edom," 1992, 292.

[128] See Lemaire, "Inscription phénicienne," *RSF* 10 (1982): 11-12.

[129] Lemaire's conclusion in Lemaire, "Commerce," 1987, 53.

mentions Edom[130] as one of Tyre's trade partners providing turquoise, purple embroidery, byssus, coral, and agate in exchange for Tyrian exports. None of these commodities seems to originate in Edom. They represent rather South Arabian trade.[131]

7. Tyre and the Arabian Trade

The Arabian Peninsula was known in ancient times for its prized spices and aromatic resins such as frankincense and myrrh (Is. 60:6). Camel caravans carried gold, precious wood from Ophir (1 Kgs. 9:28; 10:11), and precious gems as did the Queen of Sheba on her visit to King Solomon (1 Kgs. 10:1-10; 2 Chr. 9:1-9, 14). Such caravans moved along the desert routes that ran parallel to the Red Sea until reaching the Sinai Peninsula from which they could branch off to Egypt or continue up into Palestine to Gaza and Ashkelon or to Damascus through the King's Highway in Transjordan. Assyrian documents show that gold, silver, copper, camels, and other livestock were Arabian tribute products.[132]

Circumstantial evidence points to Tyrian participation in this Arabian trade. This evidence is as follows:

a) Arab tribes, together with Phoenicians and Philistines received a differential treatment from the Assyrian empire and were able to maintain their independence as well as to expand their economic sphere of influence. As we have seen, Tyre and the Philistine cities had close economic and trade relations. This might be the result of the growing demand for incense from the 8th century onward that brought increased political and economic power to those controlling the incense trade.[133]

---

[130] An emendation from Aram to Edom proposed by many scholars (Diakonoff for example) is accepted here.

[131] See Diakonoff, "Naval Power," 1992, 190. In the 10th century Solomon profited from this South Arabian trade by making an alliance with king Hiram of Tyre. At that time Israel controlled the caravan route between the Red Sea and Damascus which passed through Edomite territory (see below, under 3.8.g).

[132] See Edens and Bawden, "Tayma'," *Journal of the Economic and Social History of the Orient* 32 (1989): 85; Eph'al, *Ancient Arabs*, 1982, 106.

[133] Knauf, "Ishmaelites," *ABD*, 1992, 3.517. The Assyrian difficulty to deal with this heterogeneous, unstable group of tribes is certainly an additional reason for such a lenient policy (Knauf, "Ishmaelites," 1992, 518).

b) As commented in the previous section and provided that we accept the necessary emendation from Aram to Edom, the Edomite commodities listed in Ez. 27:16 (turquoise, purple, embroidery, byssus, coral, and agate) originated in South Arabia and seem to reflect South Arabian trade with Tyre.[134]

c) Archaeological finds from isolated caravan cult places such as Kuntillet 'Ajrud and Ḥorvat Qitmit (7th century) reveal a Phoenician presence in the area. The Kuntillet 'Ajrud drawings (776-750 BCE) show Phoenician influences mixed with Midianite motifs. Their style has been labeled as syncretistic Phoenico Arabian.[135] Two Phoenician ostraca (# 2070 and 8058) and one Aramaic ostracon with Phoenician names found at Tell el-Kheleifeh and dating back to the Achaemenid period (5th century) confirm the importance of the Arabian route for Phoenician trade.[136]

d) The Egyptian takeover of Philistia during the reign of Psammetichus I, after the Assyrian collapse, gave Egypt control of the trade termini, enabling it to control the southern trade and to entrust it to the Arab tribes and the Edomites. Tyrian merchants benefited from the Arabian trade as trade partners of Saïte Egypt.

e) The discoveries at Wadi Tumilat (Tell el-Maskhuta), located in the route of Necho II's canal, linking the Pelusianic branch of the Nile river to the Red Sea which was built early in the last decade of the 7th century, show Phoenician involvement in the project.[137] The findings include Phoenician amphoras beginning with the earliest 7th century levels, a Phoenician terra-cotta figurine found in a limestone shrine suggesting the resident status of ethnic Phoenicians and a few Phoenician ostraca or "jar labels" in Demotic. In the opinion of J. S. Holladay, one of the excavators, the discoveries show "heavy Phoenician involvement, probably amounting to a monopoly of the canal-related Mediterranean trade entering the Pelusiac branch of the

---

[134] Section 6 showed that there were strong commercial links between Edom and Tyre.

[135] See Van Beek, "Drawings," *TA* 9 (1982): 46.

[136] See Lemaire, "Commerce," 1987, 50, 56; Delavault and Lemaire, "Inscriptions phéniciennes," *RSF* 3 (1976): 28-30; Briquel-Chatonnet, "Syro-Palestine et Jordanie," in *CPP*, ed. Krings, 1995, 595.

[137] In Herodotus' words, "It was Necho who made the original attempt to dig a canal through to the Red Sea" (2.158) (cf. sections 2.6 and 3.3).

Nile."[138] They also demonstrate Phoenician participation in Necho's endeavor to put an end to the Arabian domination of the overland caravan routes of the lucrative spice and incense trade.[139]

The data presented in this section shows that Tyre had an important share in the Arabian trade that was the result of a network of political alliances. Phoenician presence in isolated caravan cult places hint at such participation. But it is the Phoenician intense involvement in Necho II's canal-related Mediterranean amounting to a monopoly of this trade what proves Tyre's participation in this Arabian trade.

8. Judah's Lack of Metal Resources and its Consequences

Considering the commodities listed in Ezekiel 27, the question arises as to what products were most indispensable to Judah's economy. Metals provide the logical answer. Horses, a Tyrian import from Cappadocia and Egypt, can be considered as very important as well and will be discussed in section 10.

The importance of metals justifies a survey of the availability of metal resources in Judah in this section. The metals surveyed are gold, silver, copper, tin, and iron. The study demonstrates the inadequacy and insufficiency of Judah's metal resources. As in Solomon's time, only trade could supply the metals so badly needed by the Judean economy.

An analysis of the Judean economy in the late 7th-early 6th century is a difficult endeavor. There is a lack of quantitative data and only a limited number of studies on economy and trade in ancient Judah.[140]

---

[138] Holladay, "Maskhuta," 1992, 590.

[139] According to Holladay, monopoly of this trade or tribute was the driving force behind the Neo-Assyrian and Neo-Babylonian effort in the West. In his opinion, Nabuchadnezzar's campaigns against Egypt (the site experienced two massive destructions, in 601 and 568 BCE) were also related to the spice and incense trade with the Mediterranean (Holladay, "Maskhuta," 1992, 591). The relation of the site to the incense trade is reinforced by the discovery of miniature incense altars and of Himyaritic (South Arabian) silver coinage usually related to overland incense trade.

[140] Studies dealing at any length with the economy of ancient Judah are as follows: Buhl, *Verhältnisse*, 1890, 68-128; Gowen, "Trade Terms," *Journal of the Society of Oriental Research* 6 (1922): 1-16; Neufeld, "Emergence," *Hebrew Union College Annual* 31 (1960): 31-53; Elat, *Economic Relations*, 1977, 182-86; idem, "Trade and

There is no question that Judah is poor in mineral resources. There is no gold, silver, or tin, a vital element in bronze production, in Palestine.[141]

a. Gold

The largest gold deposits in the Near East are located in the Egyptian side of the Red Sea, Nubia, the West Coast of Arabia, Midian, Persia, and Armenia. The biblical account says that King Solomon imported gold from Ophir,[142] which scholars have variously located in southern Arabia, India, East Africa, or on either coast of the Red Sea.[143] Solomon also imported gold from the kingdom of Sheba (2 Chr. 9:1; Ps. 72:15), which was located in South Arabia.

b. Silver

Silver, known in the Near East from ancient times, was the most valued metal until the Persian period. It was used in jewelry and as the standard for business transactions. Before the invention of coinage in Lydia (Asia Minor) in the 7th century, silver ingots or pieces of metals were used for business transactions in North Syria and Mesopotamia. Some Neo-Assyrian temples such as the Ishtar of Arbeles warranted silver quality and weight by means of a hallmark. They served as a kind of "Federal Reserve" lending money, collecting debts and warranting silver quality. Their assets were both the king's and the gods' property. The practice continued during the Neo-Babylonian period.[144]

Commerce," in *World History of the Jewish People*, ed. Malamat, 1979, 4.2.173-86; idem, "Monarchy and Trade," in *State and Temple Economy*, ed. Lipiński, 1979, 2.527-46; Briquel-Chatonnet, *Relations*, 1992, 229-85.

[141] Most of the data presented in the sections that follow appears in Forbes, *Ancient Technology*, vols. 8 (1971), 157-64, 202-05 and 9 (1972), 10-16, 130-36, 181-83.

[142] 1 Kgs. 9:28; 10:11; 22:48; 1 Chr. 29:4; Job 22:24; 23:16; Ps. 45:9; Is. 13:12.

[143] See Elat, "Trade and Commerce," 1979, 4.2.180; Baker, "Ophir," *ABD*, 5.26-27. An inscribed sherd dating from the 8th century and discovered at Tell Qasile, near Jaffa, provides the only extrabiblical reference to Ophir but sheds no light on its geographical location. The inscription on the sherd says "gold of Ophir to Beth-horon. 30 shekels" (see Maisler, "Hebrew Ostraca," *JNES* 10 [1951]: 265-67).

[144] Lipiński, "Temples," 1979, 567-69, 571-74, 587-88.

Palestine and Syria are very poor in silver ores. The only two sources worth mentioning are located in Gebel Akra (Mount Tasios) and the area southeast of the Dead Sea.[145] Silver remains were found in Gezer, Ta'anach, and Tell el-Ajjul. Silver appears prominently in the account of Solomon's times. 1 Kings 10:27 says that Solomon "made silver as abundant in Jerusalem as stones" (compare to 2 Chr. 9:27). This silver was the result of Phoenician trade (2 Chr. 9:21). Phoenicians brought silver from Tarshish and served as local silver distributors (cf. section 3.2). 2 Chr. 9:14 mentions Arabia as another silver distributor.[146]

c. Tin

There were no tin mines in Palestine. Tin's main usefulness was as a hardening agent. Alloyed with copper, tin makes the metal harder and more resistant to corrosion and lowers the melting point of copper.[147] In the ancient Near East, tin was much more expensive than copper and was used in much smaller quantities. This fact made economically profitable to transport tin over large distances to the copper sources.[148]

Tin ores existed in Asia Minor,[149] the Caucasus,[150] Southwestern Iran, Spain, Central France, Central Germany, and Cornwall.[151] During the Bronze Age, Byblos imported tin into the Near East by overland route.[152] In the Iron Age, the Phoenicians imported it from the Far West Mediterranean.

---

[145] Forbes, *Ancient Technology*, 1971, 8.210.

[146] The historicity of Solomon's account is discussed in section 3.8.g on Judah and the metal trade.

[147] Copper with 2-18% tin has been found in ancient Times.

[148] See Muhly, *Copper and Tin*, 1973, 239.

[149] Darmanlar, Eshkishehir, Central Anatolia, Ushak, Kastamuni, Ak Dagh, Tillek, Karasheikh, Erzeroum, and Erganimadeni.

[150] The Belaia river, central Caucasus, Sharopani, Gori, Phorzom, Allaverdi, Gandza, the Kara Dagh and Karabakh mountains, and the Araxes bank near Migri.

[151] Forbes, *Ancient Technology*, 1972, 9.130-37.

[152] Muhly, *Copper and Tin*, 1973, 337.

d. Copper

Copper mines have been located in Edom near Khirbet en Nahas and Umm el 'Ama.[153] In Forbes' opinion, these mines go back "to Solomonic date."[154] No evidence for their exploitation during the late 7th-early 6th century has been found.[155] There are important copper deposits in Egypt,[156] North Africa,[157] Tyre, Sidon, Sarepta, Aleppo, Arabia,[158] Baluchistan,[159] Afghanistan, Persia, Caucasia and Transcaucasia, Asia Minor, ancient Greece, Italy, and other places of Europe.

e. Iron

Iron ores are the most widespread ores on earth.[160] Iron is widely distributed throughout the Near East. It would be impossible to

---

[153] N. Glueck identified a large industrial center at Tell el-Kheleifeh with biblical Ezion Geber. He called it a "Pittsburgh of Palestine" and went on to say that "for its day and age, [it was] one of the largest, if not the largest of metallurgical centers in existence" built to refine copper and iron (Glueck, *Other Side*, 1970, 92-93). See also Glueck, *Negev* (1959).

[154] Forbes, *Ancient Technology*, 1972, 9.11-12.

[155] Glueck suggested an earlier date for their establishment and thought their exploitation continued down to the 6th century (*Negev*, 1959, 155). Against this opinion, Rothenberg has shown that the mines did not exist before Solomon and were not in use at any other period afterwards. No sign of exploitation of the copper mines or smelting camps has been found between the 8th and 6th centuries BCE ("Copper Industries," *PEQ* 94 [1962]: 40). The fact that no slag was found in the industrial complex prompted Rothenberg to challenge Glueck's assumption according to which Tell el-Kheleifeh was a metallurgical center. Rothenberg suggested the site was a large store complex built by Solomon for storing grain and other supplies for the trade caravans and soldiers and the mining enterprises in the Arabah, and a caravanserai for the incense route from Arabia to Egypt and Syria (pp. 49-56). During the late 7th-early 6th centuries the area where the mines are located was under Edomite not Judean control.

[156] The most important copper mines are located in the Sinai. There are copper deposits in Wadi Magharah, Serabit el-Khadim, Gebel Um Rinna, Wadi Malha, Wadi Kharig, Wadi Nasb, She Baba, the plain of Senned, Wadi 'Arabah, and Gebel Atawi.

[157] More than 60 mines have been found.

[158] Around Madina in Midian and Bahrein islands.

[159] Merwara Ajmer, Rohira in Sirohi state.

[160] Forbes, *Ancient Technology*, 1972, 9.177. According to Forbes, "no less than 4.2% of our earth is formed by iron or its compounds" (9.177).

enumerate all the deposits of iron ores in the ancient Near East. Only the most important of them are mentioned here.[161]

There are minor iron deposits in Egypt in Wadi Baba and other valleys of the Sinai Peninsula but no iron mine of Egypt can be said with certainty to have been worked in antiquity. Richer sources exist in Syria in places such as Alexandria and Germanicia located near the Taurus Mountains. Deposits in Cyprus are to be found in Soli, Paphos, and Tamassos where there are traces of ancient mines. Iron ores also abound in the Aegean (Syros, Cythnos, Ceos, Seriphos, Siphnos, Gyaros, Andros, Skyros Samothrake, Samos, Rhodes, and Cos).

In Asia Minor, important deposits are present in Mons Ida near Andeira, Bythinia, Magnesia, Caria, Cibyra, Phrygia, and Lycia. Major sources are located in the Taurus and anti-Taurus region of southeastern Asia Minor (Alaya, Silinti, Amaxia, and near Junik Tepessi). Important iron ores exist in Pontus, near Amasia, Tokat, and Sivas. Cappadocian iron was famous in antiquity.

Caucasia, Transcaucasia, and Armenia are particularly rich in iron ores. Major deposits are located in Kuban on the banks of the Kotscharka river, Damyrtash on the river Bolnis, near Tamblut, Tshatash, near Sizimadani, along the Dyblaki pass near Miskan, in the Bojan valley, near Elisavetpol, in the eastern Karabagh district, near Talori, Karadagh, near Lake Urmia, north of Tabriz, in the Tiyari mountains and near Chorsabad.

In Iran there are major sources in the mountains to the northeast of Nineveh and in the neighboring area of Kurdistan, in northern Iran near Persepolis and in the Karadagh district. Other sources exist near Tabriz, in the Elburz mountains near Resht and Massula, near Kazwin (west of Teheran), near Firuzkuh, in Mount Demawend, near Damghan, Semnan, Sharud, near Kashan, Kohrud, Kuh-i Benan, in the plain of Persepolis, between Kerman and Shiraz and the islands of the Persian gulf, Carmania, in Chorassan near Semendeh and Ilak and in Afghanistan near Juwain, Heart and Bamian.

The Bible describes Palestine as a "land whose stones are iron" (Deut. 8:9) and there are a few deposits of rich iron but the poorer ones

---

[161] What follows is a summary of Forbes section on the deposits of iron ore in the ancient Near East (see Forbes, *Ancient Technology*, 9.193-96; McNutt, *Forging of Israel*, 1990, 114-15).

are quite common. The deposits located in southern Lebanon are poor and there is no evidence for their exploitation in biblical times. Deposits and some evidence for their exploitation in biblical times exist in Nahr el Kelb, Beirut, and near Merdjiba in Northern Lebanon and in Ikzim on Mount Carmel. When Nelson Glueck published the results of his extensive survey in eastern Palestine in 1935, he identified many copper mining and smelting centers but only a few deposits of iron ore. Deposits were located in the vicinity of Wadi es-Sabrah south of Petra.[162] Large heaps of iron have been noted near the town of Ajlun north of the Jabock River.[163] Mugharat el Wardeh in the Ajlun hills is recognized today as containing the major deposits of iron ore in Palestine.[164] Minor deposits have been identified in the Maktesh southwest of the Dead Sea, in Galilee, in the Negev along the Wadi Arabah, in Transjordan (Ain Tab and Resheya north of the Hermon mountains), and in the Moab-north Edom area, El Kura, near Pheinan, Midian and Usala and Sana (Yemen).[165] As it is evident, most of the aforementioned iron sources are located in areas beyond Judah's control.

It is very difficult to determine if these iron sources were exploited in antiquity and if so, to what extent they were used. Iron deposits are more available locally and are more easily exploited than those of copper but there is no definitive evidence of mining and the existing ambiguous evidence is difficult to date.[166] Two main reasons have been suggested to account for this situation: 1) continuous mining in a given location may eliminate traces of previous workings[167] and 2)

---

[162] See Glueck, *Eastern Palestine*, 1935, 49, 90.

[163] Har-El, "Valley of Craftsmen," *PEQ* 109 (1977): 76.

[164] See Stech-Wheeler, Muhly, Maxwell-Hyslop, and Maddin, "Iron at Taanach," *American Journal of Archaeology* 85 (1981): 259; Muhly, "Iron Technology," *BAR* 8 (1982): 45.

[165] See Har-El, "Valley of Craftsmen," 1977, 76; Waldbaum, *From Bronze to Iron*, 1978, 59; Stech-Wheeler et al., "Iron at Taanach," 1981, 259; Muhly, "Iron Technology," 1982, 45.

[166] See McNutt, *Forging of Israel*, 1990, 115-16. Moorey emphasizes the same idea with words as follows: "So far there is neither documentary nor archaeological evidence to indicate exploitation of local iron ores in antiquity, though it is a possibility in Assyria" (Moorey, *Mesopotamian Materials*, 1994, 280).

[167] Waldbaum, *From Bronze to Iron*, 1978, 59.

many iron deposits are found on the earth's surface and evidence of surface mining is difficult to spot.[168]

No scientific work on tracing the provenance of the iron used for manufacture in Mesopotamia has been done. Our knowledge depends on the known deposits supplemented by meager textual sources.[169]

Iron is not mentioned as booty or tribute until the Neo-Assyrian period where it is listed as a raw material. N. B. Jankowska studied the evidence from Neo-Assyrian inscriptions.[170] Jankowska shows that iron is recorded in the tribute of Asia Minor, Syria, and the Mediterranean coast (1.772, 801); Damascus (1.740 [150 tons]); Ḫattina (1.585, 1.477 [3 tons]); Carchemish (1.601 [3 tons]; 1.476 [7.5 tons]), Qūe (1.583); Bīt-Ḫalūpē (1.443); Bīt-Zamāni (1.405, 466, and 501 [9 tons]); Šubria (1.502); the Chaldean area (1.625); and the land of the Laqē of Hamath (1.412 [30 kg]). One may assume that the lack of data on iron is due to the nature of the sources at our disposal that, for the most part, refer to treasuries.

Most of the iron came from the west and northwest (Modern Anatolia and Syria) and north (Urartu).[171] Oppenheim published two texts of the mid-sixth century mentioning iron from "Yamana" and from "Lebanon."[172] Spain was also a major supplier of iron.

The importance of iron as "the main strategic material" during this period[173] can not be overstated. The introduction of iron tools and

---

[168] Muhly, "Iron Technology," 1982, 44. Copper mining requires underground shafts and galleries. Iron deposits are found on the earth's surface (compare to Deut. 8:9).

[169] Moorey, *Mesopotamian Materials*, 1994, 280.

[170] Jankowska, "Some Problems," 1969, 263. The references in parenthesis are to *ARAB*.

[171] See Moorey, *Mesopotamian Materials*, 1994, 281.

[172] The same two texts already mentioned. On this matter, see Oppenheim, "Essay," 1967, 240ff. and discussions in section 3.4.

[173] See Diakonoff, "Features," 1969, 28. The introduction of iron tools and weapons c. 1,200 BCE had important implications for the economy of the family in ancient Israel. At that time, the use of iron tools and weapons enabled the Israelites to live in the formerly uninhabited areas of the Hill Country. Iron axes allowed them to clear large tracts of woodland, iron plows to increase agricultural production, and iron quarrying tools to cut tunnels for irrigation and cisterns for water storage (see Stager, "Archaeology of the Family," *BASOR* 260 [1985]: 9-10). Iron had also important applications in trade. Its widespread use beginning at the end of the 10th century enabled the Phoenicians to perfect their ship building techniques and to build larger,

weapons c. 1,200 BCE enabled the Israelites to take control and live in the formerly uninhabited areas of the hill country. During the first millennium BCE, iron was the basic and most widespread component used in the fabrication of weapons and in the making of household appliances or tools such as axes, awls, picks, blades, plowshares, razors, knifes, sickles, chisels… The 160 tons of iron found at Sargon II's palace give us an idea of the extent of the Neo-Assyrian iron demand. The Neo-Babylonian empire and Judah needed iron ore as well.

P. M. McNutt's study and a number of other surveys of the iron objects retrieved in Palestine during the Iron Age I[174] show that by the late 10th century iron was adopted as the primary material for manufacturing utilitarian metal objects.[175] The process was related to the development and diffusion of carburized iron, which was superior to bronze for manufacturing utilitarian tools and weapons.[176] In McNutt's inventory of iron objects from Iron Age I levels, which she groups in four categories (tools, weapons, jewelry, and other), the total number of iron objects from "Non-Philistine"[177] settlements in the 10th century is 167, out of which 65 are tools, 54 weapons, 40 jewelry, and 11 other.[178] She concludes that "carburized iron was consistently produced in Northern [sic] Palestine by the end of the tenth century."[179] This interpretation is valid even with all the limitations and inadequacies of the artifactual evidence available to us. Some of these limitations are as follows: 1) the tendency of terrestrial iron to rust away and of

---

stronger ships that were able to sail greater distances (see Katzenstein, "Tarshish Ship," in *Alle soglie della classicità*, ed. Aquaro, 1996, 1.239).

[174] McNutt, *Forging of Israel*, 1990, 143-211; Waldbaum, *From Bronze to Iron* (1978).

[175] McNutt, *Forging of Israel*, 1990, 146, 205. See also the studies by Waldbaum (1978, 1980); Stech-Wheeler, Muhly, Maxwell-Hyslop, and Maddin (1981).

[176] Carburization is achieved by heating iron in contact with carbon at a high temperature. When 0.2 to 0.7% carbon is present, it is called steeled iron and it is hardened when reheated and quenched. The process of carburization was first made between 1200 and 1000 BCE. By the late 10th century BCE Palestinian smiths produced carburized iron on a fairly consistent basis (see McNutt, *Forging of Israel*, 1990, 138, 146, 148-51, 203).

[177] McNutt distinguishes between "Philistine" and "Non-Philistine" settlements.

[178] See chart in McNutt, *Forging of Israel*, 1990, 202. The figures for "Philistine" sites are as follows: total 41, tools 23, weapons 7, jewelry 9, other 2.

[179] McNutt, *Forging of Israel*, 1990, 203. No statistical analysis of the iron objects retrieved in Israel during the 9th to 6th centuries is available.

archaeologists in the past not to record deposits of rust; 2) the little attention paid to iron objects in excavations; and 3) the random, aleatory character of the discoveries.[180]

Not all areas of the ancient Near East adopted iron technology at the same time. The approximate and tentative dates for the adoption of iron-based economies in the different areas of the ancient Near East are as follows: Greece, Crete and Palestine in the 10th century;[181] Syria some time between 925 and 800 BCE;[182] Anatolia c. 850-600.[183] Mesopotamia seems to have been a latecomer in the adoption of iron-based technology. By the 9th century iron was widely used but had not yet replaced bronze in the manufacture of most tools and weapons. This did not take place until the 8th to 7th centuries.[184] Clear evidence for the acceptance of the iron technology in Egypt comes from the 7th century and later.[185]

Both textual sources and archaeological data provide information about the size of the Israelite army and its weaponry. As in many other areas of the ancient Near East, textual sources and archaeological data do not coincide on the size of the Israelite army. The Bible provides some data on this question. According to Judg. 5:8, the Israelite army totaled 40,000 warriors.[186] The Monolith Inscription of Shalmaneser III states that Ahab was able to supply 2,000 chariots and 10,000 foot soldiers to join the allied forces that fought Shalmaneser III at Qarqar in 853 BCE.[187] After the first siege of Jerusalem in Jehoiachin 's time (597), Nebuchadnezzar deported the ruling classes of Judah a total of 10,000

---

[180] See McNutt, *Forging of Israel*, 1990, 100-01; Moorey, *Mesopotamian Materials*, 1994, 289. For this reason, arguments based on statistical evidence have to be handle with special care.

[181] McNutt, *Forging of Israel*, 1990, 146-47; Waldbaum, *From Bronze to Iron*, 1978, 34.

[182] Waldbaum, *From Bronze to Iron*, 1978, 27-29; Snodgrass, "Early Metallurgy," in *The Age of Iron*, eds. Wertime and Muhly, 1980, 356-57.

[183] McNutt, *Forging of Israel*, 1990, 147; Snodgrass, "Early Metallurgy," 1980, 357.

[184] McNutt, *Forging of Israel*, 1990, 147-48; Moorey, *Mesopotamian Materials*, 1994, 290; Waldbaum, "Appearance of Iron," in *The Age of Iron*, eds. Wertime and Muhly, 1980, 82.

[185] McNutt, *Forging of Israel*, 1990, 148.

[186] One can not take this figure as verifiable or more than literary. As Isserlin has noted (*The Israelites*, 1998, 192), "Numbers actually involved in combat tended to be much smaller."

[187] *ANET* 279.

men together with their families (2 Kgs. 24:14) (cf. section 2.6). Among the deportees were the warriors, artisans, and the smiths. 2 Kgs. 24:16 indicates that the Judean regular army ("the mighty men," "man of valor," or "soldiers" (אנשי החיל in Hebrew), at the time numbered 7,000 men and the auxiliary troops ("craftsmen and artisans") 1,000.[188]

We get a different picture from the archaeological data that, to a certain extent, is at cross-purposes with the information provided by textual sources. The only comprehensive study on the use of iron in Iron Age II Israel is a recent dissertation by A. C. Emery, *Weapons of the Israelite Monarchy: A Catalogue with Its Linguistic and Cross-Cultural Implication* (Harvard, December 1998). Emery presented a catalogue of the artifacts of hand-held weapons excavated in southern Levant in Iron Age II (1000 to 586 BCE). Only the hand-held weaponry published with at least an illustration or photograph and its dimensions was included in the study. Arrowheads, metal points of lances and spears, blades of daggers and swords, knives, armor scales, helmets, sling stones, mace heads, tridents, and one standard were included in the catalogue.[189] Emery provided a database[190] and noticed that "most artifacts are made of iron, many of bronze, and a few of bone or stone."[191]

Emery's catalogue included a total of 947 artifacts. The classification of the items according to the materials of which they were made is as follows:

---

[188] See Asher, *Neighbours*, 1996, 188-90. Jer. 52:28 gives a different figure. It indicates that 3,025 "Judeans" were deported at this time.

[189] The artifacts found above the 586 BCE destruction level were excluded. The catalogue did not include axes (according to the author they were used as tools), larger machines of war, and artifacts associated with cavalry and chariots (see Emery, *Weapons*, 1998, 1-20).

[190] In the database (pp. 174-229) he supplied information as follows: the archaeological site where the object was found, date of the artifact, a description of the location where the artifact was found, the material from which it was made if different from iron, and some unusual features if any.

[191] Emery, *Weapons*, 1998, 15. Emery's remarks together with the chart I made using Emery's database corroborate the importance of iron and bronze as strategic materials for the Israelite army during the Iron Age II period. 97.14% of all weapons were made of iron (73.02%) or bronze (23.12%). This fact, rather than the total of weapons or the actual size of Israelite army, is the most relevant part of Emery's study to the present discussion. The chart shows also that almost three fourths of all weapons were made of iron.

MATERIAL	NUMBER OF ARTIFACTS	PERCENTAGE
Iron	701	74.02
Bronze	219	23.12
Bone	15	1.59
Stone	9	0.95
Copper	3	0.32
Total	947	100

Emery offers a number of possible explanations to account for the small number of finds:[192] 1) No citizen militia existed and the weapons were in the hands of a small professional army that exercised a strong control over them. 2) The culture was too poor to produce many weapons. 3) The times were peaceful enough in certain areas so that there was no need to maintain stores of weapons. 4) Civilians' only weapons were cutting tools used normally about the home. 5) The weapons used were made of materials other than metals and flint such as wood that leave no material remains.

Emery's study has its limitations: 1) the catalogue includes only hand-held weapons. 2) The weapons must have been published with at least an illustration or photograph and their dimensions. 3) Axes are not included in the catalogue. 4) The artifacts found above the 586 BCE destruction level are also excluded from the catalogue. To these self-imposed limitations of Emery's study one has to add the tendency of terrestrial iron to rust, the little attention paid to iron objects in early excavations, and the random, aleatory character of the discoveries. Some or even many of the weapons might have been recycled over time and passed from generation to generation as well.

In spite of these limitations, Emery's conclusions are accurate and indisputable. The size of the Israelite/Judean army must have been very small. The archaeological data suggests that the figures given in the written sources must have been highly exaggerated.[193]

---

[192] Emery, *Weapons*, 1998, 168-69.
[193] Out of the 947 artifacts 145 are dated to the 7th-6th centuries. 20 of them proceed from places beyond the territory of Judah (Meggido, Abu Salim, Her). Most of the remaining 125 artifacts (a 13% of the total) come from Jerusalem, Lachish, Jemmmeh,

The comparison between textual and archaeological data on weapons during the Israelite monarchy illustrates that textual and artifactual remains sometimes present incompatible evidence. When this is the case, most experts on ancient metallurgy consider that material evidence reflects more accurately the actual situation than textual information.[194]

By using the Bible, archaeology, and the Assyrian pictorical representations,[195] we can get a sense, although incomplete and deficient, of the equipment of the Judean army, the weapons they used, and the materials they employed for the fabrication of such weapons.[196] Among the offensive weapons, lances, or pikes, were dominant at first. Shafts were 4-6 ft long and heads were of iron or bronze. Swords and dirks were standard army equipment according to the Bible.[197] Among weapons for long distance fighting, bows and arrows were very important. No bows have been found but arrowheads are plentiful. They were more often made from iron than bronze with variations in time and location. The 'Scythian' type of arrowhead came in about 600 BCE. As defensive weapons, the Israelite soldiers used helmets and body armor. None of the helmets survived but the reliefs of Sennacherib's attack on Lachish show the Judean defenders wearing conical helmets of leather or bronze. Chariots were very important among non-personal army equipment. The information we have on them comes from the Lachish reliefs. There is a depiction of a large chariot with eight-spoke wheels and four horses, which might have been the governor's personal chariot.

---

and Naṣbeh. Since the catalogue covers some 310 years, we would expect every century to yield some 316 artifacts. The 125 hand-held weapons found in Judah during the 7th-6th centuries represent a 35.5% of this amount. The destruction of the Northern Kingdom in 722 BCE is undoubtedly related to this decrease but Tyre's curbing of Judah's access to metals may also have something to do with it.

[194] See McNutt, *Forging of Israel*, 1990, 101.

[195] See Yadin's study *Warfare* (1963).

[196] In this section I rely on Isserlin, *The Israelites*, 1998, 195-98.

[197] Finds have been few. The best example known is a straight iron sword, 3 ft 4 in, from Vered Jericho, found in a 7th century context. A slightly curved iron slashing sword, 24.6 in long, found in Tell Beit Mirsim (c. 588) belongs to a different fighting tradition which, after having been used in Assyria, was developed as infantry equipment in Greece. See Eitan, "Rare Sword," *Israel Museum Journal* 12 (1994): 61-62; Isserlin, *The Israelites*, 1998, 197.

Smaller six-spoked wheel chariots are being thrown down on the attacking Assyrians. They are probably the Judean chariots stationed at Lachish. Only a few armour remains or horse trappings have been found.[198]

The above cursory survey illustrates the importance of iron and bronze as strategic materials for the Judean army.

f. The Origin of Judah's Metals

In spite of Judah's lack of metal resources and according to the Assyrian Chronicle, in 701 BCE, Hezekiah (c. 715-687 BCE) paid 900 kg of gold and 24 tons of silver to the Assyrian king Sennacherib (704-681 BCE). The Chronicle reads: "With 30 talents of gold, 800 talents of silver and all kinds of treasure from his palace, he sent his daughters, his palace women, his male and female singers, to Nineveh, and he dispatched his messengers to pay the tribute."[199]

The record in 2 Kings 23:33 indicates that Jehoiakim paid a tribute of a hundred silver talents (3 tons) and a gold talent (30 kg) to pharaoh Necho II in 609 BCE.[200] Furthermore, the Babylonian Chronicle for the year 597 BCE states that, after besieging Jerusalem and deposing king Jehoiakim, Nebuchadnezzar "received his [Jehoiakim's] heavy tribute." As 2 Kgs. 24:13 states, Nebuchadnezzar "carried off from there all the treasures of YHWH's Temple and the treasures of the King's Palace. He cut in pieces all the gold vessels that Solomon the king of Israel had made in YHWH's Temple." It is clear that precious metals were part of both the "tribute" mentioned in the Chronicle and of the "Palace and Temple treasures" of the biblical account.

---

[198] An iron armour scale (10th century) from an iron chariot was found at Tell el-Far'ah and a cheek-piece for a chariot or cavalry horse at Lachish.

[199] *ARAB* 2.143 (# 312). The figure could have been inflated.

[200] Between 604-601 Nebuchadnezzar marched every year to the Ḫatti-land to collect and dispatch the annual tribute. One would assume that part of this tribute included metals from the kingdom of Judah. Furthermore, in the siege of Jerusalem mentioned in Dan. 1:1-4 (604 BCE), if it ever took place, Nebuchadnezzar is said to have taken the vessels of the temple. This vessels could be part of the tribute referred to in the Babylonian Chronicle.

Judah paid no tribute in copper, iron, or tin.[201] Since there were no sizable natural silver or gold deposits in Judah, Judah must have obtained these resources through trade and barter. Judah exchanged agricultural products such as "wheat, millet, honey, oil, and balm"[202] for metals.[203]

Joel 4:5[204] gives us additional information linking Tyre and Judah's metal resources. It accuses Tyre of having taken Judah's silver and gold and having carried them into Tyre's palaces. It is not clear whether this refers to a literal action of looting or happened as part of Tyre's economic activities.[205] These actions seem to suggest that Tyre was taking advantage of Judah's weakness and depriving her of her limited metal resources.

g. Judah and the Metal Trade (10th-6th Centuries)

A comparison between the 10th century and the late 7th-early 6th centuries illuminates the circumstances favoring or hindering trade in ancient Israel.

During the reigns of David (c. 1010-970 BCE) and Solomon (c. 970-930 BCE) the kingdom of Israel reached its maximum geographical extension. Israel included most of Northern Transjordan, Edom, and Philistia. Israel's privileged geopolitical position between Egypt in the South and Syria, Anatolia, and Mesopotamia in the North made possible her involvement in international trade. This expansion allowed Israel to gain control of two main roads: the Via Maris connecting Egypt and Damascus through the coast and the King's Highway passing through Transjordan and connecting the Red Sea and Damascus. It seems that

---

[201] See Jankowska, "Some Problems," 1969, 260-65. Judah's absence in the grain and fodder tribute lists is not surprising. Grain and fodder were exacted by a taxation system not included in the tribute lists.

[202] Ez. 27:17. Solomon provided king Hiram with wheat and fine oil (1 Kgs. 5:24).

[203] The same situation continued throughout Israel's history (10th century, 7th-6th centuries, the Persian period, the Seleucid period...) (cf. section 3.9).

[204] See note 66 above for a discussion of the dating of Joel.

[205] A despoiling of the Temple (2 Kgs. 24:13) or a carrying away of the sacred implements on the part of Tyre are not attested.

Solomon received transit dues for the products circulating in these two roads (1 Kgs. 10:15).[206]

According to the biblical sources, King Solomon established a trade alliance with Hiram of Tyre (1 Kgs. 5:26). By this alliance, Tyre supplied building materials, gold, and craftsmen for the Temple (1 Kgs. 5:22-24). In exchange Israel provided wheat, barley, wine, and oil (1 Kgs. 5:2-6; 2 Chr. 2:11-16). Solomon and Hiram also organized a common naval expedition from Ezion-geber in the Red Sea which was formerly an Egyptian and South Arabian monopoly. They brought back gold, silver, alum wood, precious stones, ivory, and rarities like apes and peacocks (1 Kgs. 9:26-28; 10:11, 12).[207]

---

[206] Ishida, "Solomon," *ABD* 6.109. Ishida recognizes the historical uncertainties resulting from using the biblical account on Solomon for historical purposes. Evidently, we can not take the figures about Solomon's mercantile activities and revenues given in the account at face value. They must have been fabulously exaggerated. The account of Solomon's mercantile ventures aimed at showing Solomon's prosperity under God's blessing. It was not meant to be a historical report of Solomon's financial affairs. Nevertheless, in Ishida's assessment, which I share, "We can hardly deny the substantial historicity comprised in them" (p. 109). A number of authors have cast doubts on this whole scenario. They doubt any 10th century finds of Solomon's wealth. Finkelstein has consistently done so in a number of books. In *Israelite Settlement* (1988), he estimates the Israelite population on the eve of the Monarchy "in the tens of thousands, many times fewer than any of the figures bandied about by scholars in the past" (p. 355). In *Shiloh* (1993), he concludes that "it is now clear that the site [Shiloh] was not occupied in the early phases of the Iron Age II. [...] The ceramic evidence that Shiloh was already abandoned at the end of the 11th century B.C.E. also rules out the theory that the site emerged as a sanctuary of national importance only in the days of Saul" (p. 389). Finkelstein has maintained similar positions in the book coedited with Lederman, *Highlands of Many Cultures* (1997). In his extensive archaeological survey, Mazar acknowledges that "unfortunately, the archaeological evidence for the period of the United Monarchy is sparse, often controversial, and it does not provide unequivocal answers to these questions [on the existence of a mighty kingdom as described in the biblical sources]." On Solomon's building activities in Jerusalem, Mazar comments that "the intensive building activity of Solomon [...] in Jerusalem [...] [is] illuminated only by indirect sources" (*Archaeology*, 1990, 371, 375). He also dates the largest group of public buildings, found at Meggido Stratum IVA and identified as royal stables or storehouses, to the time of Ahab in the 9th century. Mazar has expressed similar opinions in his recent book *David* (1997).

[207] For an extensive discussion of Solomon's maritime ventures and alliance with Hiram, see Stieglitz, *Maritime Activity*, 1971, 147-60. Stieglitz sees in this Phoenician-

The visit of the Queen of Sheba is also related to the Red Sea and Transjordan trade.[208] The Queen of Sheba brought gold, precious stones, and spices (1 Kgs. 10:10; 2 Chr. 9:8) Solomon's merchants also imported horses from Egypt and Que in South-East Anatolia and chariots from Egypt and exported them to Hittite and Aramean kingdoms (1 Kgs. 10:28-29).

What made possible this trade activity in the 10th century, provided that we accept the historical reliability of the Bible account, was: 1) Israel's control of international trade routes (the King's Highway and the Via Maris). 2) Tyre's and Israel's economies complemented each other. Israel was rich in agricultural products and had an agricultural surplus and Tyre had expertise in shipbuilding, craftsmanship, and trade.

Neither of these two circumstances was true in the late 7th early 6th century. Edom controlled the two major trade routes: King's Highway and the overland route to Gaza (cf. section 3.5). Tyre did not need Judah's agricultural surpluses since the Philistine cities became Tyre's main providers of agricultural products. The largest oil production complex with more than 100 olive presses dating to the last half of the 7th century has been found at Tel Miqneh (Ekron) and an olive oil industry developed in Tell-Batash Timna in the mid 7th century as well. A royal winery found at Ashkelon and similar Iron II winepresses found near Ashdod suggest that coastal Philistia was a producer and exporter of wine.[209] The presence of many Phoenician amphorae in the Philistine coast off Ashkelon and Ashdod during the same period suggests that the Philistines were Tyre's main oil suppliers at this time.[210] Tyre could even

---

Israelite alliance an attempt to challenge "Egypt's monopoly of the Red Sea trade" (158).

[208] Goods coming from the Red Sea were transported by caravan through Transjordan. Solomon controlled this caravan road (the King's Highway).

[209] A large building (400 square meters) destroyed in 604 BCE and identified by Stager as a winery was excavated in Ashkelon. The building contained three winepresses, numerous dipper jugglets and wine jars, and dozens of unbaked tablets, thought to be jar stoppers used in the fermentation process (see Stager, "Archaeology of Destruction," 1996, 62-65). In his study of Ashkelon, Allen found "only minimal evidence for grape cultivation in the area outside the mound" (*Contested Peripheries*, 1997, 231, 233-38).

[210] See Stager, "Archaeology of Destruction," 1996, 64, 70; Eitam and Shomroni, "Oil Industry," in *Olive Oil in Antiquity*, eds. Heltzer and Eitam, 1987, 37-56; Gitin,

have imported oil from Carthage, which managed to control an extensive peripheral territory and succeeded in filling North Africa with olives and producing tons of oil for local consumption and export. Carthage culminated this expansion process from at least the 6th century.[211]

h. Judah's Deprivation of Basic Vital Metals

As a result of the above facts, it is possible to say that Tyre was in a position to oppress Judah economically. It is not farfetched to imagine that Tyre could have easily curbed Judah's access to international trade routes and experienced a shortage of metals such as copper, tin, and iron. Potentially this could have had a very negative impact on the Judean economy since, as we have seen, Judah is poor in metal resources, which she could only acquired through trade. On the other hand, it is a recognized fact that during the Neo-Assyrian empire Tyre exercised a monopoly on trade and trade routes in tin from the Atlantic coast and silver, lead, and iron from Spain (cf. section 3.2).[212] Tyre may also have had a preferential trade agreement with the Neo-Assyrian empire.[213] During the Neo-Babylonian domination, the chief-merchant of Nebuchadnezzar II (604-562 BCE) was a Phoenician named *Ḥanūnu*

"Miqne-Ekron," in *Olive Oil in Antiquity*, eds. Helzer and Eitan, 1987, 81-97; Dothan and Gitin, "Ekron," 1992, 419-20.

[211] The exact date in which this process ended is disputed. Aubet suggests the 6th century (*West*, 1993, 199). Lancel proposes a much later date (*Carthage*, 1997, 276-77).

[212] See Casson, *Ancient Mariners*, 1959, 70, 72, 82. Aubet states that "the exploitation of the Iberian silver seems to have been the prerogative of the state of Tyre" (*West*, 1993, 237). The first lead isotope analysis on objects from Israel has been done on a number of silver pieces from six silver caches found at Ekron. A total of 604 pieces were in the caches. They were tested in Oxford, England. Dr. Seymour Gitin announced the results in a lecture at the 1999 Annual Meeting of the Society of Biblical Literature. They are as follows: the lead isotope analysis showed that many of the samples came from Greece and some from Riotinto (Spain), and Iran. The results are presented in ed. Balmuth, *Hacksilver* (2001). If Tyre had a monopoly on the silver trade and controlled the maritime and overland routes and the only lead isotope analysis done on objects from Israel shows that they came from Greece, Riotinto, and Iran, it is only logical to conclude that they got there as a result of Tyrian trade. On the technique of lead isotope analyses applied to provenance studies, see Gale's article "Lead Isotope," in *Archaeometry*, ed. Maniatis, 1989, 469-503.

[213] Aubet, *West*, 1993, 72-73.

(Hanno in Phoenician), and the overland trade routes during the Neo-Babylonian empire might have been controlled by Tyre as well.[214]

Since Tyre was in a dominant position, she could easily take advantage of Judah's weakness. She may have charged high dues for commercializing Judah's products, paid very little for them, charged Judah high prices for metals, and imposed tariffs on their distribution, or even curbed Judah's access to international markets.

9. Tyre's Extended Commercial Influence

There is textual and archaeological evidence of Tyrian economic penetration and extension of her influence in the interior of Galilee, Samaria, and even Jerusalem in exilic and postexilic times.[215] In the Achaemenid Period (539-332 BCE), coastal cities in the two sides of the Carmel range were placed under Phoenician control and their economies flourished. Their material culture continued to be Phoenician until the Hellenistic times. One may assume that this expansion started soon after the destruction of Jerusalem and perhaps even earlier.

Written sources (Phoenician inscriptions and classical authors) and the archaeological record confirm the idea of a Phoenician territorial expansion in the Levant during the Achaemenid period. The inscription of the Sidonian king Eshmun'ezer II (c. 465-451 BCE) shows that the Persian king had placed the area of the Carmel and Sharon coasts under Sidonian administration. The inscription says that the Persian king had ceded Eshmun'ezer "Dor and Joppa, the rich lands of Dagon which are in the plain of Sharon, as a reward for the striking deeds which I performed."[216] Another fragmentary Phoenician ostracon mentions one "Melekna[tan]...son of Esh[mun]"[217] and in an inscription from the mid-

---

[214] Oppenheim, "Essay," 1967, 253.

[215] See Lipiński, "Israel et Judah," in *DCPP*, ed. Lipiński, 1992, 231-32; Müller, "Phönizien in Juda," *Welt des Orients* 6 (1971): 189-204. This penetration process may be the result of Tyre's desire to open new markets after loosing her colonies in the Mediterranean in the wake of Nebuchadnezzar's thirteen-year siege of the city.

[216] Gibson, *Textbook*, 1982, 3.109 (inscription # 28).

[217] See Stern, "Masters," 1993, 46. Stern dates both this inscription and Eshmune'ezer's to the late 6th century and suggests that Dor was under Sidonian administration from the late 6th century.

fourth century BCE, Dor is still described as a "Sidonian city."[218] Dor continued under Sidonian administration until its conquest by Alexander the Great in 332 BCE. Pseudo-Scylax in his Periplus (338-335 BCE) corroborates the Tyrian and Sidonian territorial expansion in the Levantine coast. Tyre occupied the littoral from Sarepta to Mount Carmel and the city of Ashkelon. Sidon possessed Ornithopolis and Dor.[219] Epigraphic material shows Ashkelonites bearing Phoenician names (CIS I.115; KAI 54) during the Achaemenid Period. The excavations at the site have unearthed monumental constructions in carved stone of the Phoenician type, Phoenician transport jugs, Phoenician inscriptions, Tanit shaped small objects, Phoenician coins of the 4th century, and a huge dog cemetery from the 5th century which may be related to Phoenician healing cults.[220] From Ashkelon, Tyrian commerce might have easily stretched to reach the caravan trade that existed between the Red Sea and the Mediterranean Sea linking Gaza and Elat. Two inscriptions from Tell el-Kheleifeh, incision[221] # 8058 (5th century) and ostracon # 2070 (c. 400 BCE) written in Phoenician cursive suggest such participation.[222]

Coins found throughout Galilee[223] and the old territory of Judah supply additional proof of an extended Tyrian influence.[224] Their presence in Galilee in relative large numbers beginning in the Seleucid Period has been explained as reflecting the prevalence of Tyrian import from Galilee and the result of payment of Tyrian merchants for Galilean

---

[218] Stern, "Masters," 1993, 44.

[219] See Stern, Authors, 1984, vol. 3.10; Peretti, Periplo (1979).

[220] See Stager, "Hundreds of Dogs," BAR 17 (1991): 27-42.

[221] It seems to me that Lemaire uses the terms "incision" and "inscription" as synonymous (see Lemaire, "Commerce," 1987, 56).

[222] Ostracon # 2070 contains a list of theophoric Phoenician names written in cursive. Eshmoun, Baal, and Resheph are among the Phoenician deities mentioned (see Lemaire, "Commerce," 1987, 56; Delavault and Lemaire, "Inscriptions phéniciennes," 1979, 28-30).

[223] See Barag, "Tyrian Currency," Israel Numismatic Journal 6-7 (1982-83): 7-13.

[224] Almost all the Phoenician coins found in Palestine are from Tyre and Sidon. According to Stern, the presence of Phoenician and Greek coins (most of them from Athens) provide evidence "for the rapid growth of international commerce" in the Achaemenid period (Stern, "Between Persia and Greece," in Archaeology of Society, ed. Levy, 1995, 435. See also Kindler, "Mint of Tyre," Eretz-Israel 8 (1967): 318-24.

goods (wheat, oil, wine, fruits, and the like).[225] Some ethnic and/or demographic infiltration may have taken place as well.[226] During the Hellenistic and perhaps even the Persian period, a Sidonian community settled at Mareshah a city located in the south foothills of Judah, and in Shechem (Samaria) as well. Tyrian influence is also present in Samaria, where a postexilic Phoenician bronze workshop has been found.[227] Epigraphic material, mainly coming from Hazor, indicates a Phoenician presence in Galilee and other areas as far as Tell el-Kheleifeh (5th century).[228]

Bible references to such a Tyrian penetration include Ne. 13:16, which mentions the presence in Jerusalem of Tyrian merchants trading in fish and in all kinds of merchandise during the Achaemenid period.[229]

---

[225] See Hanson, *Tyrian Influence*, 1980, 53. Only one coin is from the Achaemenid period. Coinage started in Tyre at the end of the 5th century (see Hanson, *Tyrian Influence*, 1980, 19-20).

[226] See Rappaport, "Phoenicia and Galilee," in *Numismatique*, eds. Hackens and Moucharte, 1992, 264. Rosh Zayit provides an example of Phoenician penetration in Galilee in an earlier period.

[227] See Lemaire, "Samarie," in *DCPP*, ed. Lipiński, 1992, 386; Stern, *Material Culture* (1982); idem, "Art Center," in *Atti del I Congresso di studi fenici e punici*, 1983, 1.211-12.

[228] See Delavault and Lemaire, "Inscriptions phéniciennes," 1979, 1-39; Naveh, "Phoenician Inscriptions," *IEJ* 37 (1987): 25-35; and below, under section 3.7.

[229] The Achaemenid empire created the province of Yehud (*Yehud Medineta'*) in what had been the territory of the old kingdom of Judah. The size of this province was very small in comparison with the territory of the former Judean kingdom. No scholarly consensus has been achieved on the boundaries of the province. Stern, nevertheless, determined its limits by studying the distribution of a type of seal impression and a group of coins bearing the legend of Yehud. Seal impressions and coins are connected with the administration of the province. He compared their geographical distribution with the rosters of returnees from Babylon in Ezra 2:21-35 and Neh. 7:25-35. The result was that the boundaries of the impressions correspond with the furthest limits of the borders contained in the rosters. These borders are as follows: Tell en-Naṣbeh (Mizpah) in the north, Beth-Zur in the south, Jericho and En-Gedi in the east, and Azekah and Gezer in the West. The entire province had some 60 kilometers from north to south and about the same from east to west (see Stern, *Material Culture*, 1982, 245-47) (In a recent book, *Yehud* [1999], Carter maintains that the province of Yehud was even smaller.) The reduced size of Yehud's territory may be due in part to Edomite encroachments. During the 6th century, Arab tribes began to expel the Edomites from their "traditional dwelling places in Transjordan and forced them to migrate north and west, to the northern Negev and southern Judaean hills." There is evidence for Edomite

The "Canaanites" lodging in the Maktesh quarter of Jerusalem (Zeph. 1:11) may have been such.[230] Tyrian and Sidonian merchants were suppliers of wood for the rebuilding of the temple according to Ezra 3:7. They were paid with wheat, oil, and wine. Finally 1 Macc. 5:22 and other passages show Phoenician interference in the Judean affairs. In view of the economic interests of the Phoenician cities in Galilee, which included the provision of foodstuffs at low prices, such interference may have been an attempt to "avoid unfriendly influence or rule in Galilee."[231]

In summary, textual sources and the archaeological evidence show an extension of Tyre's influence during the Persian and Hellenistic periods. The process itself may have started earlier during the Neo-Babylonian period. This economic and political penetration was especially important in inland areas close to Tyre and on the Philistine coast but affected areas as far inland as Jerusalem.

10. Horses

As commented earlier, horses were one of the most indispensable products from the list of commodities listed in Ezekiel 27. They were

---

encroachment in the northern Negev during the Persian period as well (Stern, *Material Culture*, 1982, 249). Meyers and Meyers (*Zechariah 9-14*, 1993, 16-26) present an excellent survey of the history of Yehud in the 6th and 5th centuries together with a section on economic and demographic conditions (pp. 22-26). They think that, during the first century of the Persian period (538-440 BCE), Yehud was much less populated than in the period taken as a whole. A dramatic population decrease characterized this century (p. 23). The situation in Jerusalem was even more dramatic. The total figures they give for the population of Yehud are as follows: 10,850 for Persian I (538-440 BCE) and 17,000 for Persian II (439-332 BCE). For Jerusalem the figures are 475-500 for Persian I and 1,750 for Period II (pp. 24-25). Comparing the type of sites in Yehud with those in the adjacent areas, very few sites in Yehud could be characterized as urban settlements. This is in sharp contrast with the situation in the areas bordering on Yehud, the coastal plain and, to a lesser extent, the Shephelah, where sizable, well-planned urban centers, linked to the Phoenician centers to the north, flourished (pp. 24-25). These conclusions confirm the importance of the Phoenician presence in the Levantine coast during the Achaemenid period.

[230] Zephaniah was written in Josiah's time. It is possible though that the "Canaanites" referred to in Zeph. 1:11 continued living in Jerusalem during the Achaemenid period.

[231] Rappaport, "Phoenicia and Galilee," 1992, 264-65.

very extensively used in ancient warfare. Introduced in the ancient Near East in the early part of the second millennium BCE, the domestic horse was harnessed to chariots.[232] Chariotry was a very prestigious and highly expensive part of any army. The prerogative of rich and powerful kingdoms (horse breeding, raising, and feeding were very expensive), chariotry was used to disperse the enemy, prevent an orderly retreat and maximize losses of men and equipment. Ancient Egypt,[233] the Hittites, Israel, Judah, Assyria, Persia, and other states of the ancient Near East used chariots drawn by two, three, and even four horses.

The Assyrian army relied heavily on the horse and had a remount service unrivalled in the ancient world. In the military use of horses, the Assyrian emphasis was upon chariots, cavalry took a second place.[234] The chariots represented the principal strength of the Assyrian army in open battle. As a result, the Assyrian empire needed to insure a steady horse supply and horse dealings were a state monopoly.

Horses were part of the chariotry and cavalry in the standing army, the reserves, in provincial billets, posting stations, and the provincial standing force.[235] War-horses were kept at Nineveh were they were cared for and trained. Cavalry units were stationed at each of the capital cities. Horses, chariots, and cavalrymen were sent to border regions where they were ready to intervene at any time.[236]

The Assyrian empire faced an endemic insufficiency of horse supplies. Its ever-increasing demands meant that ever larger number of horses had to be found to be used with chariots and horsemen. During the 7th century, horses "continue to be used extensively in harness, and there is evidence of their use as mounts."[237]

Few horses were used for agricultural purposes in Assyria and they were noted in census returns. The central administration had to organize a constant supply of horses. Fine horses coming from Egypt, Anatolia,

---

[232] See Watkins, "Beginnings," in *Warfare*, ed. Hackett, 1989, 27-28.
[233] The first chariots mentioned in the Bible in Gen. 41:46; 46:29; and Exodus 14 are Egyptian.
[234] Hackett, *Warfare*, 1989, 11.
[235] Postgate, *Taxation*, 1974, 211.
[236] Malbran-Labat, *L'armée*, 1982, 70. No reference is made to draft donkeys or camels.
[237] Littauer and Crowel, *Wheeled Vehicles*, 1979, 110.

and other foreign courts were noted when received as tribute and added to the royal stables.

Esarhaddon overcame the shortage of horses by collecting tribute (*maddattu*) in horses in Media and by raiding the Iranian plateau. He encouraged his officials to do the same. Esarhadon's primary means of recruitment consisted in the appointment of one official (the *mušarkisu*) in charge of collecting horses for the central administration to each province.

The officials' "horse reports"[238] are letters to the king detailing the numbers and places they were held, their condition, and whether they were suitable for or already trained to the yoke. The horses are classed in two broad categories: riding (*ša pēthalli*) and draft horses (*ša nīri*). Draft horses included Kusean horses (from Nubia and Ethiopia by import via Philistia)[239] and Mesu horses (from a region East of Assyria and the Iranian up-lands in general). The riding horses (*ša pēthalli*) are less common than draft horses and of a finer quality. Horse trade played an important part in supplying the Assyrian military needs. The horses were coming from Egypt via the Philistine cities.[240]

The total of horses and mules in the 'horse reports' is 2911, 2725 horses and 136 mules. They come from Arpad, Damascus, Hatarikka, Kullania, Mantsuate, and Guzana, in the West; Lahiru, (Mat)Zamua, and Parsua, in the East; and the Assyrian homeland.[241] The largest contingents come from Arpad (192), Barhalza (122), and Arrapha (83).[242] The deliveries included large numbers of draught horses, which must have been used for wars. The dates of the deliveries range from the

---

[238] The so-called 'Horse Reports' are twenty-seven letters of Kouyunjik written during Esarhaddon's and perhaps Assurbanipal's reigns. See Malbran-Labat, *L'armée*, 1982, 60-75; Postgate, *Taxation*, 1974, 7-18; Wiseman, "The Assyrians," in *Warfare*, ed. Hackett, 1989, 43-44.

[239] See Allen, *Contested Peripheries*, 1997, 291. Some scholars identify "Kushu" with another country located to the East of Assyria (see Malbran-Labat, *L'armée*, 1982, 64).

[240] Allen, *Contested Peripheries*, 1993, 322.

[241] Postgate, *Taxation*, 1974, 15.

[242] Malbran-Labat, *L'armée*, 1982, 66. A. Salonen distinguishes 6 large centers of horse collection and breeding: 1) Persia and Elam: Kusa, Mesa, Parsua. 2) Assyria and North-Mesopotamia: Ashur, Kalhu, Arrapha, Barhalza, Lahiru. 3) Urmiah and the Van region. 4) Syria and Palestine: Qarnie, Dana, Kullania, Arpad, Isana, Manṣuate. 5) Asia Minor: Melitene. 6) Arabia: Muṣaṣir (Salonen, *Hippologica accadica*, 1956, 36).

first to the third month of the same year. This would allow the assembly of animals for the summer campaign in Nineveh.[243]

The few existing animals in private hands were not enough to supply the army. There were larger numbers in corrals in the heart of the empire and in the provinces where they were billeted for the winter under the governors' personal responsibility.[244] Internal levies were practiced.[245]

During the 7th century, when Assyria's control over Egypt and the northeastern parts of the empire diminished, Assyria suffered a shortage of horses, which affected the whole country's military potential.[246] In this situation control of horse trade was vital for the empire.

During the Neo-Babylonian empire, horses and chariots continued to occupy a special place in military strategy. According to the Babylonian Chronicle, after marching against Egypt in 601 in an unsuccessful campaign, Nebuchadnezzar "turned back and returned to Babylon" to gather together "his chariots and horses in great numbers."[247]

An overview of Israelite history and the biblical material demonstrates that the Israelites did not have chariots before David's period.[248] Solomon built a sizeable chariotry of 1,400 chariots and 12,000 horses (1 Kgs. 10:26) and stables (1 Kgs. 9:19) which denoted considerable strength for this period.[249] He also imported horses from Egypt and Que (Cilicia) and exported them to the Hittite and Aramean kings (1 Kgs. 10:28-29). Phoenician intervention in Solomon's horse trade is likely in view of the fact that Solomon made contacts with

---

[243] Postgate, *Taxation*, 1974, 18. It is an open question whether horse deliveries were due to tribute or the result of an extensive strategic distribution of the Assyrian cavalry.

[244] Postgate, *Taxation*, 1974, 210. This was part of their taxation responsibilities. A number of governors complained that they did not have enough straw to feed the horses and mules assigned to them (see Postgate, *Taxation*, 1974, 117).

[245] Postgate, *Taxation*, 1974, 61.

[246] Postgate, "Economic Structure," 1979, 218. Several demand oracles on the collection of tribute in horses in Media dating back to Esarhaddon's reign testify to the king's concern for assuring a steady horse supply

[247] Wiseman, *Chronicles*, 1974, 71.

[248] Littauer and Crowel, "Chariots," *ABD*, 1.891.

[249] Herzog and Gichon, *Battles*, 1997, 119. It is very likely that the figures have been considerably exaggerated.

Cappadocia via the Cilician coast. This coast, controlled by the kingdom of Que, entertained close contacts with the Phoenicians as the Karatepe, Incirli (Zincirli), and Cebel Ires Daki inscriptions show. It is an open question whether the consignment of horses took place by ship from the Cilician coast to the ports of Syria and Palestine as Elat suggests.[250]

The annals of the Assyrian king Shalmaneser III (858-824 BCE) mention that in the battle of Qarqar (853 BCE) king Ahab (c. 870-851 BCE) of Israel brought "2,000 chariots."[251] If this number has not been inflated, Ahab's alliance with Tyre may explain part of his capability to maintain such an extensive force.[252] Chariots were located in major cities, called "chariot cities," controlling important roads. Some scholars consider a group of buildings at Meggido IVA as stables for chariot horses dating from either Solomon's or Ahab's reigns.[253] If they are real stables, they were capable of accommodating 150 chariots. Horses were also used to carry intelligence reports and letters. The size of the chariot forces declined later and by the end of the 9th century during the reign of Jehoahaz (c. 815-802 BCE), they numbered only fifty horsemen and ten chariots (2 Kgs. 13:7). Yet, after the fall of Samaria in 721 BCE by Sargon II (721-705 BCE), Israelite chariotry was still prestigious enough for Sargon to incorporate a unit in his army.

In the kingdom of Judah, the emphasis was on the infantry. Her hilly terrain was unsuited for chariots. This made foot soldiers indispensable. Horsemen were employed mainly for scouting, the conveyance of news, and harassment.[254] Isaiah's words (Is. 31:1, 3) uttered in the wake of Sennacherib's siege of Jerusalem in 701 BCE, show Judah's limited resources for military expenditures and her dependency on foreign chariot forces:

> Woe to those that go down to Egypt for help,
> who rely on horses,
> and who trust in chariots, because they are many

---

[250] Elat, "Monarchy and Trade," 1979, 541.
[251] *ANET* 273. The figure may include chariots from the kingdom of Judah. A minimum of 6,000 horses was needed for such a force.
[252] Herzog and Gichon, *Battles*, 1997, 163-64.
[253] Yadin, Holladay, Isserlin, among others (see Isserlin, *The Israelites*, 1998, 139).
[254] Yadin, *Warfare*, 1963, 2.302-03.

and on horsemen, because they are very mighty,[255]
but do not look to the Holy One of Israel,
nor seek YHWH! [...]
The Egyptians, though, are human, and not God;
their horses are flesh, and not spirit.

Our information about chariots in Judah comes mainly from the Lachish reliefs. These give a detailed representation of a large chariot with high, eight-spoked wheels and a square body, fitted for four horses. The chariot was probably the governor's personal vehicle. There are pictures of smaller six-spoked chariots as well. They were probably the Judean battle chariots stationed at Lachish.[256] After Sennacherib's invasion, there are no more representations of chariots in Judah.[257]

The Bible contains a number of references to horses, horsemen, cavalry and chariots in the contexts of the Assyrian, Babylonian, and Egyptian empires.

Horses were not native to Palestine and during the Old Testament times were neither bred nor kept by the inhabitants of Palestine.[258] Cappadocia was a major horse-breeding center. Documents and inscriptions show that horses were exported from Cappadocia to most regions of the ancient Near East in the Neo-Assyrian empire.[259] Ez. 27:14 shows that Tyre imported horses and mules from Beth-Togarma which is Cappadocia or western Armenia.[260] Redford points to an understanding of some sort between Josiah and Psammetichus I (664-

---

[255] Or "very numerous" (עְצְמוּ מֵאֹד) (see *BDB*, 782b [עצם2]).
[256] Few actual remains of chariots or horse trappings have been found. They are an iron scale with particles of wood found at Tell el-Far'ah (10th century) that must come from an armored chariot, a cheek-piece for a chariot or cavalry horse found in Lachish, and a doubtful one found at Meggido (see Isserlin, *The Israelites*, 1998, 198).
[257] Only textual evidence suggests the existence of chariots in Judah in later periods. The account in 2 Chr. 35:21-24 indicates that, after been mortally wounded at Meggido, Josiah was transferred by his servants from his chariot to a second war chariot.
[258] Elat, "Monarchy and Trade," 1979, 542.
[259] Elat gives a full bibliography on the subject (see Elat, "Monarchy and Trade," 1979, 540-41).
[260] Diakonoff, "Naval Power," 1992, 187. The Akkadian term for Beth-Togarma is *Til-garimmu*. Diakonoff states that "*Tilgarimmu* [...] is rather to be read *Til-Garimme*, 'The mound of Garimmu,' apparently present-day Görün" ("Naval Power," 1992, 178, note 48).

610 BCE) by which Judeans performed military service in Egypt in return for horses and Greek garrison troops.[261]

In Israel, during the campaign of King Jehoram (c. 848-841 BCE) against Mesha of Moab, King Jehoshaphat of Judah (873-849 BCE) offered his horses to help Israel (2 Kgs. 3:7). As symbols of the Assyrian military might, horses and chariots are mentioned in prophecies announcing the end of the Assyrian empire and Nineveh's destruction (Nah. 3:2, 3). During Sennacherib's siege of Jerusalem (701 BCE), horses represent diplomatic gifts and illustrate Hezekiah's foolishness in relying on Egypt for chariots and horses (Is. 30:16; 31:1-3; 36:8-9; 2 Kgs. 18:21, 23-24).[262] Horses symbolize political alliances as well (Ez. 23:12). During the kingdom of Hezekiah, God promised to put an end to chariots and horses in Israel in an ideal future time (Mic. 5:10). In the account of Josiah's encounter with Pharaoh Necho II in Meggido in 609 BCE, after been mortally wounded, Josiah's servants transferred him from his chariot to a second war chariot (2 Chr. 35:21-24; 2 Kgs. 23:29-30).[263] The account hints at the existence of war chariots in Judah in the late 7th century.

At the twilight of the Egyptian domination in the Levant in 605 BCE, Pharaoh Necho II is depicted as harnessing horses and mounting steeds in preparation for the battle in Carchemish (Jer. 46:2, 9).

During the Neo-Babylonian period once again Ezekiel warns Zedekiah against breaking his covenant with Nebuchadnezzar and sending ambassadors to Egypt to look for horses (Ez. 17:15). Horses and chariots epitomize the terror caused by Babylon the "enemy from the north" (Jer. 1:13, 14; 4:13-18, 29; 5:15-17; 6:1-5, 23; 50:42) and the Chaldeans (Hab. 1:8). Babylonian stallions make the land quake (Jer. 8:16). They are an integral part of Nebuchadnezzar's assault on Tyre (Ez. 26:7, 11, 14). God announces his forthcoming destruction of Babylon, her chariots and horses (Is. 43:17; 50:37; Jer. 51:21) and Gog (Ez. 38:4, 15). In the exilic time, Zechariah prophesied the coming of the messianic era represented by the destruction of weapons of war, chariots from Ephraim and war horses from Jerusalem (Zech. 9:14).

---

[261] Redford, *Egypt*, 1992, 445.

[262] In this context, Sennacherib promised to provide two thousand horses to Hezekiah.

[263] 2 Kgs. 23:29-30 just mentions that Josiah's servants carried him dead in a chariot from Megiddo.

This section illustrates the importance of horses for war purposes during the end of the 7th century and the beginning of the 6th century, Judah's lack of horses or chariotry, and Tyre's participation in the horse trade.

11. Slave Trade

Ezekiel's oracles against Tyre contain a reference to Tyre's participation in the slave trade. Ez. 27:13 reads as follows: "Javan, Tubal, and Meshech were your traders (רכליך). They sold slaves and copper implements for your imports."

Phoenicians were linked to slave trade in antiquity. Classical, biblical, and other ancient Near East sources are unanimous on this. Traces of Phoenician slave trade exist as early as the 13th century (*KTU* 3.4). The Ugaritic texts provide evidence of slave possession by the Phoenicians as well. Text 16.191 + 272, for example, deals with the redemption of seven persons from the *birtym* (inhabitants of Beirut) by one Iwrk[l] and the obligations imposed on them vis-à-vis their redemptor.[264] The Egyptian Papyrus Bologna 1086 (early 12th century) mentions a certain Knr, a Phoenician merchant who carried on sea trade between Phoenicia and Egypt. The Papyrus names a "Syrian from the land of Arwad," Nkdj, who was part of Knr's slave crew.[265]

Phoenician slave trade during the first millennium BCE is documented almost everywhere in the ancient Near East, in Greece, in Palestine (Am. 1:9; Joel 4:6), in Northern Mesopotamia...[266]

Classical authors consider the Phoenicians frightful pirates (Homer, *The Odyssey* 14.288-90; 15.415-16; Herodotus, 1.1; 2.54). In *The Odyssey*, piracy as a way of life was taken for granted. Slaves obtained by means of kidnapping or raiding were a commodity the Greeks traded in and the Phoenicians of Sidon were very successful in combining trade with kidnapping (14.287-98; 15.403-84).[267] Herodotus

---

[264] See Yaron, "Document of Redemption," *Vetus Testamentum* 10 (1960): 83-90.

[265] See, Wolf, "Papyrus Bologna 1086," *ZÄS* 65 (1930): 89, 92-93. A more up-to-date treatment is presented in Kaplony, "Papyrus Bologna 1086,'" in *Intellectual Heritage*, ed. Luft, 1992, 309-22.

[266] Lipiński, "Phoenicians," *Orientalia lovaniensia periodica* 16 (1985): 84-89.

[267] See Braun, "Greeks in the Near East," 1982, 6, 14.

confirms the same image of the Phoenicians. He relates two different episodes of Phoenician piracy. The first one (1.1) involves piracy and kidnapping. It reads as follows:

> Once, then, the Phoenicians came to Argos and began to dispose of their cargo. Five or six days after they had arrived, when they had sold almost everything, a number of women came down to the shore, including the king's daughter, whose name (as the Greeks agree too) was Io, the daughter of Inachus. These women were standing around the stern of the ship, buying any items which particularly caught their fancy, when the Phoenicians gave the word and suddenly charged at them. Most of the women got away, but Io and some others were captured. The Phoenicians took them on to their ship and sailed away for Egypt.

The second one (2.54) adds slave trade to piracy and kidnapping. Herodotus states as follows:

> Here is a tale the Egyptians tell about the oracle in Greece and the one in Libya. According to the priests of Theban Zeus, two women-priestesses, in fact-were abducted from Thebes by some Phoenicians. The priests found out that one of the women had been sold in Libya and the other to Greeks, and they claimed that these women were the original founders of the two oracles in those two countries.[268]

Further evidence of Phoenician slave trade is provided by a document deed from Kouyunjik (Northern Mesopotamia) dated to 709 BCE.[269] The document deals with a slave sale by a certain Dagan-milki. The seller (Dagan-milki), the scribe (Tabnî), and two of the witnesses (Aḫîram, Bin-Dikir) and slaves (*Mil-ki-ú-ri*) seem to bear Phoenician names. Two other witnesses, Paqaḫ and Nabdiyahû, are Israelites.

---

[268] As mentioned already (cf. section 3.1), the specific details and circumstances of these two texts can be fictional. Their importance is that both of them point to Phoenician participation in slave trade.

[269] The document (K 383) is a tablet in the Kouyunjik collection of the British Museum (see discussion in Lipiński, "Phoenicians," 1985, 84-90).

Dagan-milki and Tabnî are known from other documents dated to 687 and 680 respectively. They suggest the existence of slave traffic from the Mediterranean coast to Assyria proper. These slaves might be skilled craftsmen who were to exercise their profession in Assyria.[270] The document nicely supplements Ez. 27:13.

In addition to Ez. 27:13, other biblical passages refer to Phoenician slave trade in more specific terms. After the destruction of Jerusalem, Tyrian merchants were selling Judean exiles to Edom and the Greeks. The books of Amos and Joel contain this accusation. Am. 1:9 indicts Tyre of trading Judean captured prisoners as slaves to the Edomites.[271] His words are as follows: "Thus speaks YHWH: On account of Tyre's three crimes, and for four, I will not turn it back, because they delivered up[272] a complete deportation[273] to Edom, and did not remember the

---

[270] One of them seems to be a "Greek" or "Ionian." Other two bear West Semitic names and may have been Israelites (see Lipiński, "Phoenicians," 1985, 89).

[271] Estimates on the date of Amos 1-2 have ranged widely from preexilic to postexilic times. Cazelles ("L'arrière-plan," in *VIth Congress of Jewish Studies*, 1977, 1.71-76), followed by Briquel-Chatonnet (*Relations*, 1992, 134-35), considers that Amos 1-2 dates to the end of Amos' ministry after Jeroboam II's death (c. 746 BCE). Both of them argue that the word גלות ("deportation") does not refer to slaves. They relate it to the Assyrian practice of displacing conquered populations and to the Assyrian term *šallat gimri*. Andersen and Freedman conclude that "there are no compelling reasons against accepting most if not all of the book as possibly, indeed probably (we can never say 'certainly') Amos'" (*Amos*, 1989, 144). For them, the text hints at Tyrian collaboration with the Neo-Assyrian empire in its conquest of the Levant during the second half of the 8th century. Other commentators reject the authenticity of Amos 1-2 on the basis of vocabulary (presence of late words such as אח, ברית, חק, תורה, זכר ברית, אף, רחמים) and historical criteria (Edomite profiting by Judah's defeat, Phoenician penetration in Palestine, similarity to Joel 4:6). They consider it the work of a Deuteronomic redactor during Josiah's reform or the Exile. Soggin (*Prophet Amos* [1987]); Schmidt ("Deuteronomistische Redaktion," *ZAW* 77 [1965]: 174-78); Barton (*Amos's Oracles* [1980], 22-24) defend this position, among others. On the basis of Ezekiel's parallels, H. W. Wolff assigns Amos' oracles against Tyre and Edom to the period after 587 BCE. He notices that "the redactor of Amos has not introduced an oracle against Babylon, just as there is none in Ezekiel, where Babylon is the executor of Yahweh's will" (Wolff, *Joel and Amos*, 1977, 151-52). Whatever the case, Amos 1:9 refers to a real grievance with Tyre for selling Judean slaves to the Edomites.

[272] The verb הסגיר as a technical term for "handing over" slaves, prisoners, escapees, and for forced deportation appears also in the Phoenician inscription of Ešmunʿazōr, the king of Sidon (see Paul, *Amos*, 1991, 60). Paul considers the oracle a late interpolation

covenant of kinship." Amos might refer here to the practice of using slave labor in the copper mines located in Edom. Joel 4:6[274] accuses Tyre of selling Judean slaves to the Ionians. It reads: "And the sons of Judah and the sons of Jerusalem you [Tyre, Sidon, and Philistia] have sold to the Ionians, removing them far from their own border."

According to classical sources (Diodorus, 20.13.2; 20.69), "The most powerful citizens of Carthage had extensive lands and farms in which slaves and prisoners of war from the period of the Punic wars worked."[275] They had a share in the slave trade as well.[276] Prisoners of war were one of the main sources of slaves in the ancient Near East.[277]

12. Tyre and the Trade Routes

The reference to Phoenician monopoly of trade routes is a commonplace among different sources at different periods (cf. Herodotus, 4.152 for example). Beginning in the early 10th century and coinciding with the weakening of the Egyptian hold in the Levant, Tyre started a policy that was intended to benefit from and take advantage of the changing geopolitical conditions of western Asia. By the middle of the 10th century, Tyre may have achieved a trade monopoly in the sea transport (2 Chr. 8:18).[278] This primacy in sea trade allowed Hiram I of

---

on, among other grounds, the fact that "Tyre's guilt is engaging in slave trade, and this accusation reappears only in exilic or postexilic texts (Ezek 27:13; Joel 4:6-7)" (p. 18).

[273] According to Wolff, an exilic author modified "the phrase 'to deport into exile' (הגלה גלות), which in 1:6 was used to refer to the carrying off of people into slavery, because in the meantime the expression had come to refer exclusively to the deportation policies of the Babylonian empire. The Phoenicians themselves did not practice deportation of subject peoples; they merely delivered up (refugees of) the "exile" (גלות) (Wolff, Joel and Amos, 1977, 158-59).

[274] For the dating of the book of Joel, see note 66 above. Even though most scholars place Joel in the postexilic period, it is my opinion that the book echoes events that took place around the destruction of Jerusalem in 586 BCE. Alternatively, it is the reduced and impoverished territory of Judah during the Neo-Babylonian period (586-539 BCE) or the tiny Persian province of Yehud which the prophet had in mind.

[275] Aubet, West, 1993, 199.

[276] See Van Gucht, "Esclaves," in DCPP, ed. Lipiński, 1992, 157.

[277] 1 Macc. 3:41 and 2 Macc. 8:11 indicate that slave trade merchants were in the vicinity of places where prisoners of war could be bought.

[278] Aubet, West, 1993, 35.

Tyre to enter on a joint trade venture into the Red Sea with King Solomon who, at the time, controlled the overland trade routes (the Via Maris and the King's Highway leading to the Euphrates, Syria, Mesopotamia, and Arabia) (on this matter, see discussions in 3.8.g). Hiram I's commercial policy consisted in controlling the trade routes of the Asian continent.[279]

During the Assyrian empire, Tyre exercised a quasi-monopoly on the tin trade from the Atlantic coast and on the silver, lead, and iron trade from Spain (cf. section 3.2). Finally in the Neo-Babylonian empire, Tyre may have continued her supremacy in trade by controlling the overland trade routes that linked the Levantine states with Mesopotamia[280] (cf. section 3.4).

13. Tyrian Products as Status Symbols

Textual and archaeological evidence demonstrates that Tyrian trade concentrated on a number of products that can be labeled as "status symbols." Ivory, ebony, furniture, balsam, precious stones, turquoise, coral, rubies, jewelry, gold, silver, purple, myrrh and, frankincense[281] are noticeable among them. Tyrian craftsmen specialized in the manufacture of luxury and prestige articles destined for international trade. Tyre's trade satisfied the desires of a restricted elite in the east for prestige, authority, and dominion. For their intrinsic value, luxury goods required materials not readily accessible. Highly specialized techniques of craftsmanship were needed as well. Phoenician workshops became famous for their production of articles of carved ivory, gold, silver, and bronze objects and gold jewelry skillfully decorated. As a researcher has said, "The dignity of the Assyrian monarchy required its palaces, temples and capital city to display its power and wealth."[282] We encounter the

---

[279] For historical uncertainties about Solomon's wealth, see note 206 above. According to Casson, the Phoenicians had a trade monopoly, which lasted for three centuries (1100-800 BCE) and extended through Asia Minor, Cyprus, Rhodes, and Crete (see Casson, *Ancient Mariners*, 1959, 70).

[280] This is Oppenheim's opinion.

[281] Aromatic spices were used in religious rites, personal adornment, medicine, and embalming. They were status goods as well (see Allen, *Contested Peripheries*, 1997, 163-64; Van Beek, "Myrrh and Frankincense," *BA* 23 [1960]: 70-95).

[282] See Aubet, *West*, 1993, 59.

same situation in the West where luxury products (craters, cauldrons, tripods...) passed from hand to hand as prizes and ceremonial gifts to local kings ending up as social status symbols.[283]

a. Ivory

The Phoenicians had an important share in the ivory trade during the 8th - 7th centuries. Phoenician workshops "became famous for the production of sumptuous articles of carved ivory,"[284] and, as commented earlier, worked ivory was one of the products that brought the most prestige to Tyre's commerce. The excavations at Samaria have uncovered some 500 fragments of ivory of which at least 200 of them were carved. The excavators have connected them to Ahab's "Ivory House" (1 Kgs. 22:39). As a synonym of luxury, ivory became the object of social criticism in the 8th century. The prophet Amos used the "houses of ivory" and their richness as examples of uncontrolled luxury, immorality, and social injustice (Am. 3:15; 6:4).[285] Amos announced God's destruction of these houses. "And the houses of ivory shall perish, and the splendid houses shall come to an end," he said (Am. 3:15). He condemned the Israelites' false sense of security and the self-indulgence of those who "lay on beds of ivory." In Am. 6:4-6 he stated: "(4) [Woe to] those who lie on beds of ivory, and sprawl upon their couches, and eat lambs from the flock, and calves out of the stall; (5) who chant idly to the sound of the harp, [...] (6) who drink wine out of bowls and anoint themselves with the choicest oils."

The luxury trade in ivory products of the 8th and 7th centuries was continued in less expensive products. The scarcity of ivory sources during the late 7th and early 6th centuries (or other undetermined reasons) prompted the Phoenician carvers to work with different materials often less expensive and more readily available such as stone, alabaster, shell, and metals. A rich assemblage of Phoenician stone, alabaster, shell, and metal vases flooded the Italian Peninsula during the short period between

---

[283] See Aubet, *West*, 1993, 106.

[284] Aubet, *West*, 1993, 59.

[285] See Cecchini, "Ivoirerie," 1995, 517; Winter, "Ivory Carving," *Syria* 38 (1976): 1-22; Gubel, *Phoenician Furniture* (1987); Barnett, "Ivory Trade," *BASOR* 229 (1978): 92-97.

the collapse of the Assyrian empire (c. 640 BCE) and the Babylonian reconquest of Phoenicia (c. 580 BCE).[286]

b. Purple Dye

Purple dye was another valued Tyrian commodity and a very well known Tyrian product over which Tyre had a monopoly. Even the Greek term for red purple (phoenix) might be cognate with the name Phoenicia. Large accumulations of shells of the purple-producing murex found in the neighborhood of Tyre illustrate the extent of the Tyrian purple dye production and trade. In fact, Phoenician colonization in the Mediterranean was prompted in part by the search of murex sources.[287]

Purple dye was obtained from shellfish or mollusks such as the *Murex trunculus*, found in the shell mounds of Sidon and along the entire Mediterranean coast, and the *Murex brandaris*, found chiefly in the mounds of Tyre.[288] The Phoenician coastland from Mt. Carmel to Sidon was the habitat of these murex varieties "but the very best sources of fast brilliant dyes were processed from the gatherings between Haifa and the Ladder of Tyre."[289] The neck of these animals contains a small gland with but a single drop of fluid called the flower.[290] Thus accumulating a large amount was a costly process involving many patient people and purple dye very expensive.[291] Garments dyed purple became the mark of wealthy persons or those in high position.

The prestige value of purple garments is attested almost everywhere. The high commercial value of purple is illustrated by the

---

[286] See Stern, "Phoenician Finds," in *Immigration and Emigration*, eds. van Leberghe and Schoors, 1995, 325, 334,

[287] According to Pliny the Elder, sources of murex were what the Phoenicians searched for the most (see Jensen, "Royal Purple," *JSS* 7 [1963]: 107).

[288] Ancient Tyre became famous for a purple or deep-crimson dye known as Tyrian or Imperial purple.

[289] Jensen, "Royal Purple," 1963, 106. According to Jensen, Hellenistic writers understood purple to mean several colors: "dull red, magenta, blue, and violet-purple. The most expensive dye was Tyrian dull red" (114).

[290] For a description of the process of purple production, see Bartoloni, "Commerce and Industry," in *The Phoenicians*, ed. Moscati, 1988, 81-82.

[291] An experiment made in 1954 using 12,000 *murex brandaris* yielded 1.5 grams of crude dye (see Jensen, "Royal Purple," 1963, 109).

fact that the Hebrew term for purple (ארגמן) had the meaning of "tribute" in both Ugaritic and Hittite. In the Hittite texts, tribute was paid in the form of purple garments to the king. Already the Ugaritic texts of the 14th century BCE point to the importance of purple for international relations.[292] Agamemnon in *The Iliad* is depicted in a purple cloak (8.221) and Hector's ashes are deposited in an urn covered with purple garments (24.796).

The Bible contains several references to purple and purple garments. Hiram I of Tyre sent a Tyrian craftsman trained to work purple, blue, and crimson fabrics and fine linen to help in the construction of Solomon's Temple (2 Chr. 2:13). The vestments of the priesthood (Ex. 38; 39) and the aristocracy (Jgs. 8:26; Prov. 31:22) were made of purple.[293] Ez. 23:6 depicts Assyrian governors and commanders wearing purple clothes for their military operations.[294] Solomon's litter had a seat of purple (Cant. 3:10). King Belshazzar promised to clothe in purple and make third in his kingdom anyone that could interpret the writing on the wall (Dan. 5:7).

Persian, Macedonian, and Hellenistic monarchs used to honor a restricted entourage of advisers with distinctive purple clothes. When Alexander the Great conquered Persia (c. 332 BCE), he found large amounts of Tyrian purple-dyed textiles of all sorts in the royal treasury of Susa and Persepolis.[295]

Josephus notes that in 47 B.C.E. Herod wore purple (*Ant.*, 14.9.4 [173]).[296] In *The Wars of the Jews* (6.8.3 [390]), he mentions that one of the priests delivered great quantity of purple and scarlet together with other treasures from the Temple to Titus in exchange for his security. After the destruction of the Temple and the triumph celebration in Rome,

---

[292] See Danker, "Purple," *ABD*, 5.558. I rely on his article for this section.

[293] This custom may have a Phoenician origin. It continued during Roman Times (see Luke 16:19; Lipiński, "Jérusalem," in *DCPP*, ed. Lipiński, 1992, 238-39).

[294] The "foreign vestment" to which Zephaniah, who prophesized in Josiah's reign (640-609 BCE), refers in Zeph. 1:8 may hint at the multicolored garments the Phoenicians gave the Assyrian kings.

[295] Jensen, "Royal Purple," 1963, 109.

[296] See Jensen, "Royal Purple," 104-18; Reinhold, *History of Purple* (1970).

Vespasian ordered that "they should lay up their Law, and the purple veils of the holy place, in the royal palace itself, and keep them there."[297]

Greeks bought and copied Phoenician garments of woven, dyed wool called *ketons* and later called them *chiton*. The use of togas of purple was restricted to governmental and ecclesiastical uses in ancient Rome. "With the ascendency of the Caesars and subsequent Roman rulers, purple became the symbol of authority and finally the color of religion."[298]

At a later time, the Byzantine rulers held a trade monopoly on many articles of commerce. Purple-dyed cloth and threads were among them. The Byzantine emperors were born in the purple room at the royal palace in Constantinople and had the title *Porphyrogenitus* or born to purple.[299]

As a symbol of wealth and luxury, purple became to be associated in the popular mind with tyranny and decadence. It became the object of social criticism across centuries and cultures.[300]

The two economic tablets published by Oppenheim and previously discussed (cf. section 3.4), contain the only direct evidence from the Neo-Babylonian period for the importation of wool from the West (14 mines of blue-purple wool). The tablets also list 153 mines of linen (*ṭumânu*) another Tyrian specialty (2 Chr. 2:14).[301] Ez. 27:24 corroborates such trade.[302] It seems that the Assyrians when demanding tribute or taking booty were more interested in garments than raw materials. Royal inscriptions mention *lubulti birmi u kitê* ("multicolored decorated garments of linen"). From Carchemish to the Mediterranean coast, all the conquered kingdoms had to deliver large quantities of such garments to the Assyrian kings who distributed them among his

---

[297] *The Wars of the Jews*, 7.5.7 (162).

[298] Jensen, "Royal Purple," 1963, 115.

[299] Jensen, "Royal Purple," 1963, 117.

[300] See references in Danker, "Purple," 1992, 559.

[301] Other references are known from the Assyrian archives. Thus, letter 347 in ed. Harper, *Letters* (1892-1914), lists 4,800 pounds of red-purple wool and 420 pounds of dark purple wool. Oppenheim lists additional examples (see discussion in Oppenheim, "Essay," 1967, 244-53).

[302] Egypt was an important source of fine cloth in the ancient Near East. "Fine embroidered linen" from Egypt (Ez. 27:7) is one of the luxury products used in the construction of the superb ship Tyre (Ez. 27:5-7).

officials.[303] These garments made of linen and decorated with colored wool threads (the *riqmāh* work, Hebrew רקמה) were used in cultic events. The finest imported linen was called *būṣu* (בוץ in Hebrew), byssus in Mesopotamia and Syria. According to Oppenheim, the reason for importing fine linen (*būṣu*) into Assyria and Babylonia was not economic. The rare fine byssus linen was imported for its prestige value.

The reference in Ez. 27:7 to "blue and red purple" from מאיי אלישה usually interpreted as "the coasts of Elishah," the 2nd millennium term for Cyprus, is explained by Diakonoff as referring to Carthage with its dependencies in Sicily and Sardinia. For him, purple was not bought but extracted and processed there by Tyrians.[304] If he is right, this would reinforce the idea that purple was a Tyrian monopoly.

c. Cedar

Among the precious woods that existed in the Phoenician area, cedar had a symbolic value. For its prestige, durability, fragrance, and fungi resistance, cedar was used in construction for temples, palaces, and boats. Cedar products had both religious and magical applications: sacred offerings, brick fabrication for temples, statuettes, amulets, purification by mastication, and fumigation. Cedar products in the form of wood, oil, powder, or ash were used for the treatment of the hair (baldness, dyeing), head, ears, eyes, nose (cough), lungs, stomach, and hands (chilblain). Cedar resin and oil were used for embalming and perfume.[305]

Cedar's sacred character, it has been suggested, would explain its utilization in temple construction, sacred offerings, and rituals. The fact that Assyrian and Neo-Babylonian kings mention that the gods commanded them to go in search of cedar wood would reinforce such sacred nature.[306] Cedar's precious nature accounts better for these applications though.

---

[303] See Oppenheim, "Essay," 1967, 246.

[304] See Diakonoff, "Naval Power," 1992, 175-76.

[305] See Elayi, "L'exploitation," *Journal of the Economic and Social History of the Orient* 31 (1988): 41.

[306] Lackenbacher, *Roi batisseur*, 1982, 66-67, 87, 130-31.

Assyrian and Babylonian Annals and the Bible show the precious nature and high esteem in which cedar was held. The choicest cedar logs were exported to Egypt and Mesopotamia from the earliest times.[307] King Solomon obtained from Hiram I of Tyre cedar for the construction of the Temple in Jerusalem (1 Kgs. 9:11; 1 Chr. 22:4; 2 Chr. 2:2-15). The Assyrian kings had cedars cut down and essences of cedar were among the tribute they imposed on the Phoenician cities.[308] Adad-Nirari II (911-891 BCE) built a cedar palace in the city of Assur.[309] Aššur-nāṣir-apli II (883-859 BCE) cut down cedars during a military campaign to Lebanon (876) and used cedar for the construction of the temple of Mahir in Imgur-Bel (Balawat) and for the roof of his palace at Kahlu (880).[310] Shalmaneser III (858-824 BCE) imposed the Ḫatti kings tribute (*maddattu*) in the form of cedar logs (between 200 and 300) and cedar resin.[311] Tiglath-Pileser III used cedars from Lebanon for the roof and doors of his palace at Kalhu.[312] King Sennacherib (704-681 BCE) cut cedars from Lebanon (Is. 37:24; 2 Kgs. 19:23) and used cedar in the construction of the roof and columns of his palace at Nineveh. Esarhaddon (680-669 BCE) used cedars from Lebanon, Amanus, and Mount Sirara in the restoration of his palace at Nineveh and for the temple of Esagil at Babylon.[313] Assurbanipal (669-627 BCE) used cedars from the same mountains for the roof of his palace at Nineveh, for the restoration of the temple of Sin at Harran, and for the completion of the temple of Esagil at Babylon.[314]

---

[307] The earliest traces of cedar trade go back to the 3rd millennium BCE. A bas-relief from Karnak from the 13th Century BCE shows the princes of Canaan cutting down cedars from Lebanon as a sign of submission. Wenamon in the 11th century goes to Byblos to acquire wood (see Elayi and Bunnens, "Bois," in *DCPP*, ed. Lipiński, 1992, 76).

[308] The first mention of tribute and taxes on cedars dates back to Tiglat-Pileser I's reign (1114-1076 BCE). For cedar exploitation and trade, see Bunnens, "Luxe phénicien," 1985, 121-33; Elayi, "L'exploitation," 1988: 14-41.

[309] *ARAB* 1.123 (# 394).

[310] *ARAB* 1.195 (# 538); Elayi, "L'exploitation," 1988, 20.

[311] Mentioned for the first and only time in the Annals of the Assyrian kings (see *ARAB* 1.217 [# 601]).

[312] *ARAB* 1.288 (# 804).

[313] *ARAB* 2.252 (# 659D); 268 (# 697-98).

[314] *ARAB* 2.322 (# 837); 353 (# 914); 376 (# 979).

Assyrian governors regulated the exploitation of the Lebanese forest. A letter from Nimrud[315] written by Qurdi-aššur-lamur, the Assyrian governor at *Ušu* to an unspecified Assyrian king (Tiglath-Pileser III?) shows the Assyrians imposed taxes on wood porters. It is probable that cedar was among such wood. Another letter from Nimrud[316] dating to Tiglath-Pileser III's reign (744-727 BCE) shows the governor's opposition to the exportation of wood from Lebanon to Philistia and Egypt. It is not unlikely that the forest of Lebanon or part of it was a royal forest reserve and that the Assyrian king had the authority to grant access to it after payment of a fee as is documented in Achaemenid times (see Neh. 2:8).[317] The fact that the Assyrians imposed trade restrictions on the exportation of wood from Lebanon to Egypt and Philistia shows that there was a trade in wood with these two areas and is significant because wood trade generally does not leave traces in the archaeological record.[318]

The exploitation of the cedars from Lebanon continued during the Neo-Babylonian period. The Wadi Brisa inscriptions describe Nebuchadnezzar's rooting out of a foreign enemy traditionally identified with Egypt or alternatively with an unspecified Phoenician city. In the inscriptions Nebuchadnezzar boasted of having cut cedars and constructed a road for their transportation.[319]

In the Persian period, when the Jews reconstructed the Temple in Jerusalem, Tyrians and Sidonians provided the necessary wood for the construction (Ezra 3:7).

For propaganda reasons, the Assyrian and Neo-Babylonian Annals magnified the image of the kings cutting cedars in Lebanon. In the Bible cedars became a symbol of the dreadful Assyrian and Neo-Babylonian oppression.[320]

---

[315] Saggs, "Nimrud Letters," *Iraq* 17 (1955): 127.

[316] Saggs, "Nimrud Letters," 1955, 127.

[317] A fragmentary inscription from Psammetichus I's time mentioning "cedar from the (royal) domain" may refer to a similar arrangement.

[318] For some evidence of this cedar trade in general, see Bikai, *Cedar of Lebanon* (1991). For Phoenician-Israelite cedar trade, see Liphschitz and Waisel, "Dendroarchaeological Investigations," *IEJ* 23 (1973): 30-36.

[319] *ANET* 307.

[320] See Elayi, "L'exploitation," 1988, 41.

d. Wine, Fine Oils, Perfumes

A number of other products such as wine, fine oils, and perfumes can rather be considered "luxury products." Recent discoveries in the Mediterranean substantiate Phoenician involvement in this luxury trade. On June 22nd 1999 the discovery of two ancient Phoenician ships wrecked 30 miles off Ashkelon was announced.[321] The two shipwrecks date between 750 and 700 BCE. The larger ship was about 58 feet long and the smaller 48 feet. The artifacts retrieved included 12 'torpedo' type amphorae (there are hundreds of them), crockery for food preparation, an incense burner, and a typically Phoenician wine decanter. L. Stager identified the ships as Phoenician and maintains that they were probably shipping wine from Phoenicia to Egypt or Carthage.

e. Architecture and Art

Architecture and art are "imports or luxury items that denote wealth and status."[322] Phoenician influences on the art an architecture of monarchic Israel are an acknowledged fact.[323] It is generally thought, for example, that ashlar masonry which was characteristic of the Israelite royal architecture from the 10th century to the destruction of Jerusalem was introduced in Israel by Phoenician artisans and architects.[324] Ashlar

---

[321] L. E. Stager, in an oral communication, mentioned to me the discovery in March of 1999. The formal announcement was made in the internet in two different web-sites: www.nationalgeographic.com/events/releases//pr9906.htm and www.ngnews.com/news/1999//06/062399/Ballard 3926. A short review of the finds was presented by Sudilovsky in her article "Phoenician Shipwrecks," *BAR* 25 (1999): 16 (for additional information, see note 54 in the introduction).

[322] Dever, "Social Structure," in *Archaeology of Society,* ed. Levy, 1995, 422.

[323] See eds. Kempinski and Reich, *Architecture* (1992).

[324] Mazar, *Archaeology*, 1990, 472, 474; Dever, "Social Structure," 1995, 423; Stern, *Archaeology*, 2001, 69-70. As commented in section 3.8.g, a number of scholars doubt any 10th century finds of such wealth. See the references to Finkelstein's books, not to speak of the "minimalist school" (Thompson, Davies…) that sees no historical value in the Bible writings. One has to admit that the evidence is sometimes puzzling (see for example Isserlin, *The Israelites*, 1998, 120). Even among those scholars who admit a general period of prosperity or some degree of wealth during Solomon's reign, there is disagreement in dating particular buildings or structures. A case in point is the dating of the largest group of public buildings found at Meggido Stratum IVA and identified as

masonry was used in the royal palaces of Samaria, Jerusalem, Ramat Rahel, Megiddo, and Dan. Some of the finest city gates of the 9th –8th centuries throughout Israel were also built using this technique.[325] Close connections between Israel and Tyre during Solomon's reign and the presence of Phoenician artisans in his building activities (1 Kgs. 5:17, 18; 6:7; 7:9-11) together with the fact that the earliest examples of ashlar masonry are preserved in the Solomonic and Omride architecture suggest the Phoenicians introduced the technique in Israel.[326]

The so-called proto-Aeolic capitals were often used in connection with the ashlar masonry in royal buildings in Iron Age II Israel. Proto-aeolic capitals have been found in Megiddo, Samaria, Hazor, Jerusalem, Ramat Rahel, and Medeibiyeh (10th to 7th centuries).[327] The volutes in these capitals are a stylized form of the palmette a characteristic element of the Canaanite and Phoenician art represented in miniature works of art in ivory, stone, and metal.[328] The close links between the stone balustrade from Ramat Rahel and Phoenician ivory depictions of window balustrades indicate a connection between ashlar masonry and Phoenician formal architecture.[329]

Other luxury items such as the carved ivory inlays of Samaria (9th – 8th centuries BCE) and engraved seals and seal impressions (9th to 6th centuries BCE) are "regarded as of Phoenician inspiration, if not

---

royal stables or storehouses. Some scholars dated them to Solomon's time (Aharoni, Herzog) others to Ahab's reign (Crowfoot, Yadin, and Mazar). The important thing for present study is not so much the exact dating of the archaeological data but the fact that Phoenician architecture had an influence on the Israelite architecture.

[325] Ashlar masonry is documented in Philistia (Ekron, Ashdod, Tel Sera'); Moab (Medeibiyeh); and Phoenicia where a few structures and tombs have been found in Sarepta, Tyre, and Achzib.

[326] Although no Phoenician royal architecture is known, ashlar masonry was common in Phoenicia, Cyprus, and the Phoenician colonies during the Iron Age (see Mazar, *Archaeology*, 1990, 474-75).

[327] The capitals have been studied in Shiloh, *Proto-Aeolic Capital* (1979).

[328] The palmette represented the sacred or cosmic tree. Using the account in Ezekiel 28, Stager suggested the influence from northern Levant extended beyond the realm of physical geography to the mythological realities of sacred space (sanctuaries, gardens, and mountains) (Stager, "Garden of Eden," *Eretz-Israel* 28 [1999]: 183-94; idem, "Jerusalem as Eden," *BAR* [2000]: 36-47). Shiloh suggested that stone capitals in Israel were an adaptation of Phoenician wooden prototypes.

[329] Mazar, *Archaeology*, 1990, 475.

manufacture" although this vision is not unanimous.[330] The rock cut tombs found in Judah and specially in and around Jerusalem (8th –7th centuries) may also be related to Phoenician trade. Some of the contents of these elite rock-cut tombs are imports from Egypt and Cyprus.[331] This section has highlighted the role of Tyrian products as "status symbols" and focussed on the social dimensions of the Tyrian oracles.

14. Tyre's Religion and her Economic Activities

The present discussion concentrates on the economic and political dimensions of Ezekiel's condemnation of Tyre. Evidently the oracles have an unquestionable religious and theological dimension that has been discussed in a number of commentaries of Ezekiel. It is possible though to find a point where theological and religious issues, on the one hand, and economic and political issues, on the other, intersect. This section deals with such a point of intersection.

Ezekiel 27 presents an imposing picture of Tyre's economic activities. Tyre, Ezekiel seems to tell us, is an unbelievable history of economic and political success. By presenting this most impressive picture of Tyre's economic activities, was Ezekiel making a further point? Ezekiel was aware of the fact that Nebuchadnezzar's siege of Tyre did not end in the destruction of the city which Ezekiel had anticipated. This fact placed Tyre in a unique category.[332] Since Jerusalem and the Kingdom of Judah together with the rest of the nations around it had been utterly destroyed, was Tyre's god, Melkart, superior to YHWH, the god of Judah? Had YHWH failed Judah? The entire oracle may be interpreted as an attempt to answer these questions.

Two explicit references to religious reasons for Tyre's condemnation are listed in chapter 28. Ez. 28:2 condemns the "prince of Tyre" as follows: "Thus said the Lord YHWH: Because your heart is haughty and you have said: 'I am a god, I dwell in the seat of the gods, in the heart of seas,' but you are a human, and not god, and you have

---

[330] See Dever, "Social Structure," 1995, 423-25.

[331] See Bloch-Smith's exhaustive analysis of the material in *Judahite Burial Practices* (1992).

[332] The other nations Ezekiel referred to in his oracles were destroyed or defeated by Nebuchadnezzar. Egypt is the only other exception.

considered your mind the mind of gods." For its part, Ez. 28:18a hints at a connection between Tyre's economic activities and her religion. The text reads as follows: "By all your iniquities, in the wickedness of your trade, you profaned your sanctuary."[333]

Phoenician trade in the West began under the aegis of Melkart. Tyrian kings, as Ez. 28:2b seems to indicate, made themselves equal to the city god.[334] We have also seen the role of temples in warranting silver quality and in loan provision (cf. section 3.2). Most ancient Tyrian foundations in the Mediterranean were linked to a temple,[335] which, in most cases was dedicated to Melkart and in some instances –as in Cadiz, preceded the founding of the city. Melkart is also present in Gadir's and Carthage's foundations stories. The sanctuary had an unmistaken legitimization role. The settlement was viewed as an extension of Tyre and her king.

The economic role of the temple was related to the fact that the transactions made there were placed under the protection of the god installed in the temple whose presence warranted the honesty of the operations and monitored the dealings that took place in the temple itself. Records of such trade agreements may have been kept at the temple as well.[336]

The temple seemed to have had a share in the benefits of Tyrian maritime trade. This share came in the form of a tenth part of the profits of trade. Classical authors inform us that the Carthaginians sent a tribute representing the tenth part of the public treasure to the god Melkart of Tyre every year. This practice continued until Hellenistic times

---

[333] Verses 5 and 16 point to a connection between trade/commercial policies (רכלתך) and violence. Chapter 5, offers a full discussion of this verse and its translation (cf. section 4.1.c).

[334] Most scholars accept this interpretation and many take this statement as the reason for the oracle (Bonnet, *Melqart*, 1988, 42-47). Against this interpretation Callender suggested in his Ph.D. dissertation (*Primal Man*, 1995, 104-06) that the above words are not the Phoenician king's but the words of the speaker in the underlying myth "placed into the mouth of the *city personified*." Callender's dissertation has been published as *Adam in Myth and History* (2000). The object of the oracle thus is a political, collective entity whose character the king embodies. I find the two interpretations compatible, they complement each other.

[335] This is the case in Gadir, Utica, Paphos, Cythere, Thasos, Ialysos, and Memphis (see Bunnens, *L'expansion*, 1979, 282).

[336] See Bunnens, *L'expansion*, 1979, 284.

(Diodorus, 20.14.2; Polybius, 31.12.10-12; Arrian, 2.24.5).[337] The tribute was in reality a tenth part of the profits of western trade, which Melkart received "in exchange for seeing that all was well with shipping and trade."[338] The temple thus had an economic, political, and religious function. It worked as a protector of trade in the diaspora and may have served as an instrument of political and economic penetration.

---

[337] This practice may explain why in the 6th century a Carthaginian general sent the tenth part of the booty he had taken in Sicily to Phoenicia (Justinus, 18.7.7).
[338] Aubet, *West*, 1993, 126-28, 130-31, 222, 232, 234-36; Bunnens, *L'expansion*, 1979, 285.

Partial Commentary on Ezekiel 26:1-28:19 with Special Attention to Historical Implications and Economic and Political Considerations

1. The Economic Focus of Ezekiel 26:1-28:19: A Contextual Approach

Ezekiel 26:1-28:19 is made up of a series of four oracles against the city of Tyre. The first one (Ez. 26:1-21) depicts Nebuchadnezzar's siege and destruction of Tyre and its consequences. The second one (Ezekiel 27) is a lamentation over Tyre depicting the city as a mighty ship and presenting an impressive picture of her commercial empire, trading partners, and commodities traded. It contains a cluster of *hapax legomena* and Phoenician technical terms of an economic nature not found elsewhere in the Bible. The third one (Ez. 28:1-10) is directed against the haughty prince of Tyre and the fourth and last one (Ez. 28:11-19) against the king of Tyre. Each of the four oracles points to the importance of economic considerations as factors in the Tyrian oracles.

Chapter 3 has explored the motivations for the Tyrian oracles and established the importance of economic and political reasons as the primary causes for them. The present section concentrates on the core economic focus of each of these four oracles and on their individual contribution to the overall economic content and nature of the Tyrian oracles.

a. The First Oracle (Ez. 26:1-21)

The economic underpinnings of the first oracle against Tyre in Ezekiel 26 appear already in verse 2 that, as we are going to see, is the *crux* of the whole series of Tyrian oracles. Ez. 26:2 presents an indictment against Tyre accusing the city of seeking her own economic advantage and wanting only to enrich herself. The verse reads, "Because

Tyre said against Jerusalem (=Judah)[1] 'Aha! The peoples' ports are destroyed,[2] they have come round to me,[3] I will be filled, they are laid waste."[4]

The economic focus of the verse comes to the fore in the unusual expression "the peoples' ports" (דלתות העמים). The expression is instrumental for determining the precise nature of Tyre's economic

---

[1] In my opinion, "Jerusalem" (ירושלם) here designates a geographical unit that includes the whole territory of Judah together with the capital city. As embodiment of the remaining of the Judean people and territory, Jerusalem is an appropriate term for the whole territory of the Southern Kingdom. The reasons for my conclusion are as follows:

1) In the Bible Jerusalem (ירושלם) can stand for or represent a geographic reality larger than the city itself just as Zion (ציון), originally a mountain of Jerusalem where the Jebusite stronghold was located, can represent the entire city of Jerusalem (see Is. 1:8; 8:18; 35:10; 51:3; 52:1-2, 8; Jer. 50:5, 28; 51:10, 24, 35; Lam. 2:1, 4, 6, 8, 10, 13…). In the same way אשור and בבל can refer to the capital city, the land, the empire, and the people of that empire.

2) Only a few chapters before in Ez. 23:4, Ezekiel speaks of two rebellious sisters, Oholah and Oholibah. Oholah, he says, is Samaria and Oholibah Jerusalem. Since Ezekiel appears to offer an intentional exposition of Jer. 3:6-11 where the two sisters are called "faithless Israel" and "treacherous Judah," the term "Jerusalem" in Ez. 23:4 must represent both Jerusalem and Judah (see Zimmerli, *Ezekiel 1*, 1979, 482-84; Block, *Ezekiel 1-24*, 1997, 731-32).

3) The insignificant economic importance of Jerusalem, situated in a hilly country far from any major trade routes, precludes the possibility of considering her the subject of the following verbs (נשברה, נסבה, and החרבה) as many scholars do (see Greenberg, *Ezekiel 21-37*, 1997, 530 and following three footnotes).

4) The Neo-Babylonian Chronicles refer to Jerusalem as "the city of Judah" (see Wiseman, *Chronicles*, 1974, 73 and section 2.6).

[2] I interpret נשברה as a perfect *niph'al* 3rd person feminine plural with an old ending in ā (ה‚) (see GKC, # 44m [pp. 121-22]) whose subject is "the peoples' ports" (דלתות העמים). Morphologically it can be an active future *qal* 1st person plural with paragogic ה (cohortative) meaning "let us break [them = the peoples' ports]." This form is unattested in the Bible. Therefore I consider it unlikely.

[3] As in the case of נשברה, נסבה is a *niph'al* perfect 3rd person feminine plural with an old ending in ā (ה‚). The subject is דלתות העמים as well. Alternatively נסבה can be taken as an active *hiph'il* future 1st person plural with paragogic ה (cohortative) from the root (סבב) meaning "let us bring [it]." This form is attested in 1 Chr. 13:3 only. If this were the case, נסבה would imply a more active Tyrian participation in bringing trade to her ports.

[4] The subject of this verb is once again "the peoples' ports" (דלתות העמים).

actions against Judah. The Hebrew word translated as "ports" (דלתות) is used here in an unconventional, technical way to designate the ports of the Mediterranean area.[5]

Now the economic tenor and interpretation of Ez. 26:2 becomes clear. Ez. 26:2 is a response to the historical situation characteristic of the final years of the 7th century BCE when the Philistine ports, "the peoples' ports" (דלתות העמים in Hebrew), suffered a major destruction at the hands of Nebuchadnezzar.[6] During most of her history, Judah lacked an exit to the sea. The Philistine cities were the natural outlet to import and export products and commodities.[7] Tyre counted on benefiting from the shift of the southern trade, to control all the ports, to be the only place to ship goods.[8] In this situation, the expressions "they have come round to me" (נסבה אלי) and "I will be filled" (אמלאה) are fully justified. Tyre knew of the Neo-Babylonian policy of not resettling destroyed areas and expected to capitalize on the trade vacuum resulting from the destruction of the Philistine ports.[9] The importance of ports

---

[5] In singular דלת usually means "door, leaf of a door" (*HALOT*, 223b). The plural and dual forms sometimes mean "gates" of a city (Deut. 3:5; Jos. 6:26; Jug. 16:3; 1 Sam. 23:7; 2 Chr. 8:5; 14:6) and sometimes are used in cosmic contexts or metaphorically. This is the case in Job 38:8-10 where the dual form refers to the possibility of shutting the "sea with doors" (דלתים) and setting a boundary to it, in Ps. 78:23 where it designates "the doors of heaven" (דלתי שמים), and here. The Akkadian cognate *daltu* (door) is used in cosmic contexts as well. The use of the parallel expression "the seaports" (מבואת ים) designating Tyre's harbors in Ez. 27:3 together with a comparison with other Hebrew expressions meaning port (מחוז, מזח, חוף אניות, and מפרץ) reinforce the idea that דלתות in 26:2 designates some kind of structure that surrounds, encircles, "girdles" the sea, i.e., a port (see Schwarzenbach, *Terminologie*, 1954, 79ff.; Stieglitz, *Maritime Activity*, 1971, 61, 66-70; Greenberg, *Ezekiel 21-37*, 1997, 548; *HALOT*, 541b).

[6] Ashkelon was destroyed in 604 BCE, Gaza in 601 BCE, and Ashdod c. 600 BCE. Ekron, not a city port but very close to the seashore, was destroyed in 603 BCE.

[7] This phenomenon is known as transshipment.

[8] Katzenstein already suggested this possibility (*History*, 1997, 311). He did not link this shift of the southern trade to Ez. 26:2 though.

[9] If נסבה is a cohortative *hiph'il* form, it would hint at a direct Tyrian involvement in bringing about this trade shift and in cutting out trade from Judah (ירושלם in the text). The same can be said of נשברה ("are destroyed") if it is a cohortative *qal* form. I find it unlikely though.

during the Iron II and earlier periods can not be overemphasized. They were vital in the economic process known as transshipment.[10]

The following verses in Ezekiel 26 announce the imminent siege and destruction of Tyre that is the direct result of Tyre's actions against Jerusalem listed in verse 2. Even though the focus of these verses is on the siege and destruction of Tyre, a number of sections hint at economic factors intimating that the ultimate reason for Tyre's destruction is economic. Following the order in which they appear in the oracle itself, such indications will be analyzed.

Verse 4 mentions the destruction of Tyre's walls and the breaking down of her towers. The result is, as verse 5 notices, that "the magnificent structures of the commercial capital of the Mediterranean will be replaced by fishermen's nets, spread out on the bare rock to dry, in the midst of the sea."[11] Verse 9 gives a similar image of desolation: Nebuchadnezzar directs the stroke of his battering ram against Tyre's walls and breaks her towers with his axes. The destruction of Tyre's walls and towers is in sharp contrast with Tyre's past economic success and splendor portrayed in 27:11 where mercenaries of Arwad and Helek were on Tyre's walls and Gammadites hang their shields on her towers.

Another reference to Tyre's past economic power is expressed in the sentence "with the hoofs of his [Nebuchadnezzar's] horses he will trample down all your bazaars/marketplaces"[12] (verse 11a). The sentence "and your mighty pillars to the ground they will fall" is also a reference to Tyre's past wealth. The expression "your mighty pillars" (מצבות עזך) alludes both to the pillars supporting Tyre's magnificent

---

[10] Stager has studied this process which he calls "port power" in the Levantine coastal areas during the Early and Middle Bronze Age. His conclusions are applicable to the Iron Age IIC (722-586 BCE) as well. For a summary of Stager's "port power" notion, see Levine, "Biblical 'Town'," in *Urbanization and Land Ownership*, eds. Hudson and Levine, 1999, 2.442.

[11] Block, *Ezekiel 25-48*, 1998, 37.

[12] I follow Mazar and Stager in understanding חוצות as "bazaar, marketplace" rather than "street." Stager translates חוצות אשקלון "bazaars of Ashkelon" in 2 Sam. 1:20 (see Stager, "Archaeology of Destruction," 1996, 65). Mazar suggested the same translation in "The Philistines," in *Early Biblical Period*, eds. Ahituv and Levine, 1986, 67 and in "The Phoenicians," in *Early Biblical Period*, eds. Ahituv and Levine, 1986, 222, note 32.

buildings and to all the bases of Tyrian security.[13] The expression may convey a reference to the temple of Heracles (=Melkart) described by Herodotus. According to the Greek historian (2.44), "In it [the temple] were two pillars, one of pure gold, the other of emerald which gleamed brightly at night."[14]

An explicit reference to Tyre's past glory and to economic factors is in verse 12 that reads as follows: "And they will steal your wealth and plunder your merchandise; they will break down your walls and destroy your desirable houses. Your stones, your timber, and rubble, they will hurl into the waters." "Wealth" (חילך) and "merchandise" (רכלתך) refer to the products listed in greater detail in chapter 27.[15] Notice that here the plundering of the city comes before the demolition of the walls showing that this was the main motivation for the siege of the city.[16] The expression "your desirable houses" (בתי חמדתך) could allude to the royal palace, "which is believed to have been a superb complex of buildings as symbol of Tyre's prosperity."[17]

---

[13] Block, *Ezekiel 25-48*, 1998, 38. Greenberg translates the expression as "mighty stelae" and says that "they may have been temple fixtures, symbols of the divine presence in which the Tyrians trusted for protection" (Greenberg, *Ezekiel 21-37*, 1997, 534).

[14] Zimmerli translates מצבות עזך as "the pillars in which you stubbornly trusted" and sees a connection between the expression and the temple of Heracles in Tyre (see Zimmerli, *Ezekiel 2*, 1983, 36-37). The close relation between Melkart, the city god, and Tyre's trading enterprises comes to mind in this context. The mention of the fall of the mighty pillars is a symbol intended to express the end of all resistance. The sentence "YHWH has commanded against Canaan to destroy its strongholds" (מעזניה) in Is. 23:11b can be related to מצבות עזך here.

[15] עץך can also refer to the precious woods used in the construction of the ship Tyre (27:5-6).

[16] Compare to Zimmerli, *Ezekiel 2*, 1983, 36. Nebuchadnezzar's looting of the city Ezekiel had expected did not finally take place. In the oracles against Egypt, Ezekiel recognizes this fact: "And neither he [Nebuchadnezzar] nor his forces received any compensation from Tyre for the great effort that they performed against her." In compensation, the prophet announces, Nebuchadnezzar will receive the land of Egypt to plunder and loot it (Ez. 29:18-19).

[17] Thus Van Dijk, *Prophecy*, 1968, 22-23. According to him, "The plural *bāttîm* for 'palace' accords with the Ugaritic use of employing the plural to indicate the various buildings of which a temple or palace consists" (p. 23). Notice that Joel 4:5 states that "Tyre and Sidon have taken my [Judah's] silver and gold, and have carried my most valuable things into your palaces" (היכליכם) (cf. sections 3.5 and 3.8.f).

Verses 15-16 describe the international dimension of Tyre's sudden fall and the neighboring princes' and commercial allies' lament at the news of her fall: "Will not […] the coastland regions shake at the slaughter by the sword in your midst? (16) Then all the princes of the sea will descend from their thrones, remove their robes[18] and take off their embroidered garments." The reference in verse 15 to "the coastland regions" (האיים) is important. As D. I. Block has noticed,[19] this term designates the maritime lands, islands, and coastal cities included, that were the primary benefactors of Tyre's mercantile ventures. Ez. 26:18 (twice), 27:3, 15, and 35 contain other references to these "coastal regions" as major trading partners of Tyre. A similar reaction to Tyre's downfall is presented in Isaiah's oracle against Tyre in Is. 23:2. The text reads: "Be still, O inhabitants of the coast (ישבי אי), O merchants of Sidon."[20] Is. 23:5-6 depicts the international reaction to Sidon's ruin which is patterned on the reaction to Tyre's fall:

> When the report reaches Egypt, they will be in anguish just as at the time of[21] the news about Tyre.[22]
> Cross over to Tarshish, howl,
> O inhabitants of the coast (ישבי אי).

The lamentation (קינה) used in verses 17-18 is similar to the one in 27:33-36 where the fact that these coastland regions were among the main trading partners of Tyre is even more evident. Verse 17 says:

> How you have vanished, the one inhabited from the seas (מימים),[23]

---

[18] מעיליהם denotes robes worn by men of rank. See 1 Sam. 15:27; 18:4; 24:5, 12; 28:14; Job 1:20; 2:12; Ezra 9:3, 5.

[19] Block, *Ezekiel 25-48*, 1998, 44.

[20] Ez. 27:35 refers also to the impact of Tyre's fall on "the inhabitants of the coastal regions" (ישבי האיים).

[21] See *BDB* (454b [כ3b]) on the use of כ with a temporal value.

[22] *The New Oxford Annotated Bible* (ed. Metzger and Murphy, 1994, 894) renders כשמע צר as "over the report about Tyre" as if the news were on Tyre's fall not on Sidon's.

the famous city
that was powerful on the sea,[24]
both her and her inhabitants;
that imposed (or inspired) terror of them,[25]
all her inhabitants (לכל־יושביה).[26]

As M. Greenberg has pointed out, the lament in 26:17-18 highlights: "The benefit and enrichment Tyre bestowed on all who dealt with her." W. Zimmerli acknowledged the overall economic content of this oracle. In his assessment, Tyre, as a calculating merchant, rejoiced at Jerusalem's destruction expecting to profit from it.[27]

Economic considerations are present in chapter 26 in both the indictment (verse 2) and in the description of Tyre's siege, destruction, and looting that follows. As we have seen, the economic nature of the

---

[23] The preposition "from" (מן) here indicates "the remoter cause, the ultimate ground *on account of* which something happens or is done" (*BDB*, 580 [מן2f]; see also *HALOT*, 598 [מן4]). It stresses the idea that the ultimate cause for Tyre's prosperity was sea trade (compare to Greenberg, *Ezekiel 21-37*, 1997, 536). Many commentators (Elliger in *BHS*, Block, Zimmerli) follow here the Greek reading נשבת ("you have perished, ceased").

[24] For Van Dijk, the ־ב in חזקה בים is a case of comparative *beth*. According to him, Tyre's fame was the result of her being the Queen of the sea reigning over the see through her traffic and imposing her will on the waves (Van Dijk, *Prophecy*, 1968, 37). If this were the case, it would reinforce the economic character of the whole passage. For his part, Greenberg (*Ezekiel 21-37*, 1997, 537) takes חזקה בים as a superlative and translates it "that was strongest in the sea." Block (*Ezekiel 25-48*, 1998, 46) translates חזקה "ruler" and compares Tyre with the modern day superpowers. He comments that both Tyre and her merchants controlled the shipping lanes and imposed their own conditions on their trading partners. Notice the importance of the sea in the Tyrian oracles. The word (in singular or plural) appears twenty times. The presence of words such as מלח (27:9, 27, 29) and חובל (27:8, 27, 28) reinforces this impression as well. Outside Ezekiel 27 מלח is attested only once in Jon. 1:5 and חובל appears again only in Jon. 1:6. The sea (ים) is the source of Tyre's strength (Ez. 26:17); wealth and prosperity (27:3, 9, 25); splendor and beauty (27:4); and of other peoples' prosperity as well (27:33).

[25] On the political dimensions of this statement, see section 4.2.

[26] I follow Greenberg in taking לכל־יושביה "as introducing an explication of the preceding subject: namely, 'each and everyone of her (i.e., Tyre's) inhabitants' inspired fear of themselves" (*Ezekiel 21-37*, 1997, 538; see also Zimmerli, *Ezekiel 2*, 1983, 31).

[27] Zimmerli, *Ezekiel 2*, 1983, 40.

indictment against Tyre in Ez. 26:2 is unquestionable. The verse sets the tone for the entire series of Tyrian oracles. Tyre estimated that the trade vacuum resulting from the destruction of the Philistine ports represented a golden opportunity for her. She anticipated a major trade shift and rejoiced at the prospect of having trade shifted to the North, to the Tyrian ports. Potentially, this situation would result in the economic ruin of Jerusalem and Judah. These economic calculations on Tyre's part, together with her oppressive trading policies, were the ultimate motivation for Ezekiel's condemnation of the city.

In the economic factors present in the rest of chapter 26, a *crescendo* can be distinguished: first Tyre's siege and desolation is depicted. The destruction of her walls and towers (vv. 4-5, and 9) is in sharp contrast with the glorious past of the city. At a second stage, the account focuses on the economic consequences of the destruction: Tyre's economic "pillars," her bazaars, and temple, have ceased to exist (v. 11). Then the economic motivations for the siege, looting her wealth and plundering her merchandise, are introduced (v. 12). Finally, the oracle presents the international reaction to Tyre's fall and the lament of her trading partners in full detail (vv. 15-18).

b. The Second Oracle (Ezekiel 27)

The second oracle in chapter 27 has an unmistaken economic character. Written in the form of a lament (קינה), it presents an impressive picture of the worldwide scope of Tyre's economic and trading ventures. The oracle first portrays Tyre as a superb ship (3-11), a list of Tyre's trading partners and their goods follows (12-24), and the description of the sudden sinking of the ship and of the mourners and morning signs closes the oracle (25-36). Each of these three parts contributes to create an impressive image of economic might.

First of all we learn about Tyre's strategic position and key role in trade. Verse 3 reads:

And say to Tyre, the one dwelling on the seaports,[28] merchant of the nations to many coastal lands. Thus said the Lord YHWH:

---

[28] מבואת ים here and דלתות העמים in 26:2 are parallel expressions (see note 5).

> 'O Tyre you have said:
> "I am perfect in beauty."
> Your boundaries are in the heart of the seas,
> your builders perfected your beauty.'

The hyperbole "merchant of the nations" (רכלת העמים) illustrates very well Tyre's economic importance. As one author has commentated, "Tyre serves as middleman for the world, transferring products to and from the most distant ports."[29] The fact that Tyre boasts of "dwelling on the seaports" (מבואת ים) and of having her boundaries "in the heart of the seas" (בלב ימים) intimates that Tyre's prosperity was the result of her strategic position, on the one hand, and of her sea trade, on the other.

The sentence "your builders perfected your beauty" (בניך כללו יפיך) at the end of verse 3 introduces us to Tyre's prosperity as manifested in the luxury materials employed in building her. Verses 5-8 present such description.[30] It has been rightly noticed that[31] "beauty and splendor are synonyms in this oracle and refer to the imposing magnificence and opulence that Tyre manifested to the beholder."

The luxury items used in the construction of Tyre that convey this impressive image of splendor are presented in the following chart.

VERSE	PRODUCT	PROVENANCE	USAGE
5	junipers	Senir	all your planks
	cedar	Lebanon	mast
6	oaks	Bashan	your oars
	ivory-inlaid cypresses	the coasts of Cyprus[32]	your deck[33]

---

[29] Greenberg, *Ezekiel 21-37*, 1997, 548. Notice the similarity between "merchant of the nations" (רכלת העמים) and "you were the profit (traffic, gain) of peoples" (ותהי סחר גוים) in Is. 23:3b.

[30] The expression כללו יפיך appears again in verse 11 where it is Tyre's mercenaries (Arwadites, Helekites, and Gammadites) that "perfected her beauty."

[31] Greenberg, *Ezekiel 21-37*, 1997, 548.

[32] The oracle against Tyre in Isaiah 23 confirms the close economic links between Tyre and Cyprus. Is. 23:1 says: "When they [= the ships of Tarshish] came in from Cyprus, it was revealed to them [Tyre's destruction]." Verse 12 conveys a similar idea even though the subject there is Sidon not Tyre.

[33] The term probably refers to a framing structure for some covering similar to a tabernacle. Van Dijk (*Prophecy*, 1968, 63) renders this word as "pavilion" noticing that

| 7 | fine embroidered linen Egypt | | your sail |
| | blue and red purple | the coasts of Elishah[34] | awning |

Verse 9[35] provides a new glimpse into Tyre's trading preeminence. It reads: "All the ships of the sea and their sailors were in you to bring your imports."

Verses 12-24 contain an impressive list of Tyre's trading partners and the commodities they traded in:

VERSE TRADE PARTNER	MERCHANDISE	TYRE'S PRODUCTS ADDITIONAL DATA
12 Tartessus, Spain	silver, iron, tin, lead[36]	your exports[37]
13 Javan, Tubal, Meshech[38]	slaves and copper implements	your imports[39]

W. F. Albright took קרש as "a trellised throne-room, as a pavilion, and this is the most common interpretation." Zimmerli (*Ezekiel 2*, 1983, 43) translates it "deck" with a question mark and observes that קרש in Ex. 26:15ff. and "elsewhere in the description of the Tent of Meeting means 'a plank.'" Diakonoff ("Naval Power," 1992, 172) prefers the meaning "benches." Block (*Ezekiel 25-48*, 1998, 57) comments that his "rendering of *qereš* as 'hull' is tentative. Appealing to Ugar. *qereš*, which is used of some sort of dwelling place or pavilion for El, some have seen here a reference to a fancy cabin decorated with ivory carvings."

[34] Or Carthage according to Diakonoff's interpretation ("Naval Power," 1992, 176).

[35] Section 4.2 on the political status of Tyre deals in detail with verses 8-11.

[36] The Septuagint includes gold among the commodities imported from Tartessus.

[37] עזבונים is a Phoenician technical term that appears seven times in Ezekiel 27 and comes from a root עזב of which there are several homonyms. Most scholars derive עזבונים from עזב.I meaning "to leave, forsake, loose" (*BDB*, 736b; *HALOT*, 806b). To my knowledge, only Van Dijk (*Prophecy*, 1968, 75-76) has put forward an alternative etymology. In his opinion, עזבונים is related to the term *'dbt* (עזב III) meaning "convoy." (The term in context would still mean "wares, merchandise.") While scholars agree on the etymology of the word, they disagree on its meaning in context. They render the term as "stored goods" (Rüger, *Tyrusorakel*, 1961, 53); "wares, merchandise" (Zimmerli, *Ezekiel 2*, 1983, 64; Block, *Ezekiel 25-48*, 1998, 70); "a space for storing (leaving) goods" (Diakonoff, "Naval Power," 1992, 184); and "exports" (Greenberg, *Ezekiel 21-37*, 1997, 553). The expression בצאת עזבוניך in Ez. 27:33 shows that עזבון is something that "goes forth" implying that it designates goods the trader leaves (*'azab*) in a given place, i.e. exports (Greenberg, *Ezekiel 21-37*, 1997, 556). For this reason, I join Greenberg in translating עזבונים as exports.

[38] "Ionia, Cilicia, Phrygia" according to Diakonoff ("Naval Power," 1992, 185).

[39] מערב is the counterpart of עזבונים. This collective noun masculine singular is a Phoenician technical term that appears nine times in Ezekiel 27 and is one of the most

| 14 | Beth-Togarma[40] | chariot horses, steeds,[41] and mules | your exports |
| 15 | Rhodians[42] / | ivory tusks and ebony | finished products[43] |

difficult in the Tyrian oracles. מערב derives from a root ערב, but several homonyms with this combination of consonants exist. The interpretations of its etymology are as follows: 1) מערב is a noun from a root ערב meaning "to take one pledge, give in pledge, exchange" (DDD, 786b [II. ערב]); "to stand surety for" (HALOT, 876b [II ערב]); "to answer or vouch for" (Rüger, Tyrusorakel, 1961, 54); "to pledge, bind oneself, bind oneself with a pledge, barter" (Zimmerli, Ezekiel 2, 1983, 64). In context מערב means "articles of exchange, merchandise" (BDB, 786b); "trade, barter" (HALOT, 615b [מערב]) and 876 [I ערב 4]); "merchandise, goods for barter(ing)" (Zimmerli, Ezekiel 2, 1983, 64). 2) מערב is a noun from a root ערב (originally ġrb) meaning "to enter." This interpretation was first suggested by Müller ("Sarkophag," Wiener Zeitschrift für die Kunde des Morgenlandes 8 [1894]: 4) and is supported by Lipiński ("Products," 1985, 216); Liverani ("Trade Network," 1991, 77); Diakonoff ("Naval Power," 1992, 183-84); Block (Ezekiel 25-48, 1998, 63). Supporters of this etymology often translate מערב as "merchandise" or "goods" but also as "shipment" (Lipiński, "Products," 1985, 216) or "incoming goods, exports" (Diakonoff, "Naval Power," 1992, 184). 3) מערב derives from a root 'rb meaning "to give" (Driver, "Difficult Words," in Old Testament Prophecy, ed. Rowley, 1950, 64-66). This suggestion has not found much support among scholars. 4) מערב is related to 'arab "to offer, bring in." Greenberg has suggested this proposal on the basis of a Phoenician inscription in which the root 'rb seems to mean "to bring, offer." For him the meaning of מערב in Ezekiel 27 is "import(s)" (Greenberg, Ezekiel 21-37, 1997, 551). I agree with Greenberg's analysis and rendering of the term.

[40] Cappadocia according to Diakonoff, "Naval Power," 1992, 187 (see page 187, note 285).

[41] The usual meaning of פרשים "horsemen" does not seem to feet the context. The term is variously translated as "saddle-horses" (Zimmerli, Ezekiel 2, 1983, 47); "geldings" (Diakonoff, "Naval Power," 1992, 187); "chariot teams" (Block, Ezekiel 25-48, 1998, 72).

[42] With BHS and most scholars I prefer here the reading רדן that makes better sense in this context. דדן appears again in verse 20 of the list.

[43] אשכרך appears only here and in Ps. 72:10 where it is in parallelism with מנחה (gift). It is a loanword from Akkadian iškaru that in turn comes from Sumerian eš-gar. Akkadian iškaru means, among other things: 1) "work assigned to be performed;" 2) "materials or supplies for workmen to process or with which to manufacture objects;" 3) "finished products, staples or materials, etc., to be delivered" (CAD, I/J, 245 [1-2], 246 [3]). The term is variously rendered as "tribute" (HALOT, 95); "due" (Zimmerli, Ezekiel 2, 1983, 64); "gift" (BDB, 1016b); "repayment" (Lipiński, "Products," 1985, 218); "products to be delivered" (Greenberg, Ezekiel 21-37, 1997, 555); "in payment" (Van Dijk, Prophecy, 1968, 78); "payment" (Block, Ezekiel 25-48, 1998, 70); "allotted task in labor or delivered produce" (Diakonoff, "Naval Power," 1992, 184). Following

	many coastlands		
16	Edom[44]	turquoise, purple, embroidery, byssus, coral, and agate[45]	your exports
17	Judah and the Land of Israel	wheat from Minnith, *pannag*,[46] honey, balsam, and oil	your imports
18-19	Damascus	wine of Helbon, reddish-gray[47] wool, wine from Uzal,[49] wrought iron, cassia, and calamus	your manufactures[48]
20	Dedan	saddlecloths for riding	
21	Arabia and all the chieftains of Qedar	lambs, rams, and goats	
22	The traders of Sheba and the land Raamah	the choicest of all perfumes, all [kinds of] precious stones, gold	all your exports
23-24	Haran, Canneh, Eden, Sheba's traders,	perfect garments, clothes of blue and embroidered work,	in your market-place

---

Rüger, I prefer to render אשכר as "finished products." In my opinion, the verb השיב used in connection with אשכר here, determines the meaning of אשכר by linking meaning 2 and 3 of Akkadian *iškaru*. In other words, אשכר here designates finished products such as ivory tusks and ebony made of raw materials previously delivered from a third party and once again "brought back" or "returned" into the market (interpretation first suggested by Rüger, *Tyrusorakel*, 1961, 57).

[44] With most commentators I follow *BHS*' emendation from ארם to אדם that suits better the products listed in the verse.

[45] See Diakonoff, "Naval Power," 1992, 187, for a different interpretation of the meaning of some of these luxury commodities.

[46] פנג is a *hapax legomenon* of uncertain meaning. Diakonoff renders it "olives" ("Naval Power," 1992, 185); Block "resin" (*Ezekiel 25-48*, 1998, 72); Greenberg "meal" (*Ezekiel 21-37*, 1997, 556); Zimmerli does not translate it (*Ezekiel 2*, 1983, 48). It designs some kind of food.

[47] Diakonoff, "Naval Power," 1992, 188, suggests an emendation of the Massoretic text from ṣaḥar to ṣoḥar, "white." Some commentators identify צחר with a place name. The Septuagint renders it Miletus.

[48] מעשיך is a key word in understanding Tyrian trade: Tyre's trading partners, for the most part, supplied her with raw materials and exotic products receiving manufactured products in exchange (see Block, *Ezekiel 25-48*, 1998, 71; Liverani, "Trade Network," 1991, 76-77). The translation "your manufactures" (*BDB*, 797a [מעשה2a]) encapsulates this idea that is absent in a number of translations such as "your products" (Zimmerli, *Ezekiel 2*, 1983, 47); "your production" (Van Dijk, *Prophecy*, 1968, 69); "your enterprises" (Greenberg, *Ezekiel 21-37*, 1997, 555).

[49] The Massoretic text here (ודן ויין מאוזל) is difficult. I follow the minor emendations suggested by Millard ("Wine Trade," *Journal of Semitic Studies* 7 [1962]: 201-03): ודני יין מאזל "and casks of wine from Uzal." So does Block (*Ezekiel 25-48*, 1998, 67).

Ashur, and Chilmad   colorful chests[50] bound with solid cords

Tartessos / Spain (תרשיש) opens and closes the list. V. 25 reads:
"The ships of Tarshish[51] transported [52] your imports for you.
As a result you were filled (ותמלאי)[53] and heavily laden in the midst of
the seas."

Verses 26-32a depict the wreck of the Tyrian ship. An east wind
wrecks the ship in the heart of the seas (v. 26). The description in verse
27 says: "Your wealth and your exports, your imports, your sailors and
mariners, the repairers of your fissures, those bringing you imports, all
your warriors in your midst along with all your company within you will
fall into the heart of the seas on the day of your fall."

By referring back to verses 8-11, repeating three special terms for
her cargo "your wealth" (הוניך), "your exports" (מערבך), and "your
imports" (עזבוניך), and listing the role of the different seamen on board,

---

[50] גנזי ("chests") is a word of doubtful meaning. Zimmerli (*Ezekiel 2*, 1983, 51) renders
it "fabric of two colors;" Block (*Ezekiel 25-48*, 1998, 72) translates it "carpets;" *BDB*
(170b) suggests "*chests* of variegated cloth;" Diakonoff ("Naval Power," 1992, 188)
offers the translation "crates (or chests)."

[51] תרשיש here may not be a geographical reference but just an allusion to a type of
large seagoing merchant ship (see comment in next note).

[52] *BDB* (1003b, I. [שור]) translates שרותיך "[the ships of Tarshish] were *thy travellers*
(i.e. traders)" but considers the participle improbable and presents several emendations
to the text such as שרות לך ב "[they] *journey for thee* with thy wares" (Kraetzschmar)
and שרתוך "[they] *served thy*" (Cornill). Greenberg (*Ezekiel 21-37*, 1997, 561) renders
the participle as "they traveled for you." Once again we see here a reference to Tyre's
trading empire. Isaiah, in his oracle against Tyre in Is. 23:1 underscores also the close
economic ties that existed between Tyre and "the ships of Tarshish:" "Howl, O ships of
Tarshish, for it is destroyed, without a house (port?)." Verse 10 insists on the same idea:
"Cross over to your own land, like the Nile, O ships of Tarshish; this is no harbor (or
dock, shipyard) anymore." Verse 14 repeats almost word by word verse 1.

[53] Notice the use of the verb מלא in the Tyrian oracles. It appears only three times in
26:2; 27:26; and 28:16. In the first two verses it is in the *niph'al* stem and in the third
one in the *qal* stem but in every single instance it has clear economic overtones.
Economic and political implications go hand in hand in 28:16. The same root in the
Pi'el stem (מלאוך) with similar economic connotations recurs in the oracle against
Tyre in Is. 23:2 where messengers crossing over the sea are said to have "replenished
you."

the text "heightens the scope and economic significance of the disaster, [...] all of Tyre's wealth and all her noble sailors will sink with her."[54]

Verses 32b-36 contain a lament over the wreck of the Tyrian ship. Verse 33 states Tyre's past glory showing clearly the motive of the nations' lament: they have enriched and profited themselves from Tyre's commercial successes what explains the intensity of their reaction at her fall. The verse reads as follows: "When your exports went forth[55] by[56] sea, you enriched many nations, by your abundant wealth[57] and imports, you made the kings of the earth rich."

Verse 34 expands on the same reaction:

Now you have been wrecked by the seas
in the deep waters,
your imports and all your company (or crew) (קהלך)
within you have sunk.

Verses 35 and 36a continue the portrayal of the observers' surprise over Tyre's sudden fall. They expand on 26:18 with a more vivid description.

All the inhabitants of the coastlands
are appalled over you,
their kings' hair bristles with horror
and their faces tremble.[58]
The merchants among the peoples

---

[54] Block, *Ezekiel 25-48*, 1998, 84.

[55] As commented earlier (note 37), this is a key verse for the understanding of the technical term עזבונים "exports." In his translation of this verse, Greenberg (*Ezekiel 21-37*, 1997, 547) interpolates here the word "collected" between brackets.

[56] Together with Cooke (*Ezekiel*, 1936, 307) and Van Dijk (*Prophecy*, 1968, 86-87), I consider the significance of מימים to be not "from the sea" but "by sea." Van Dijk refers to the frequent interchange of ־ב and מן, ־ב having the ablative sense "from, by" and מן shearing the meaning "in, over" (p. 87).

[57] הון is a noun meaning "wealth, prosperity [that] speaks of the wealth one's work and business ventures produce" (*HALOT*, 242b [והון]). The term alludes to the financial basis for trade (Liverani, "Trade Network," 1991, 76-77).

[58] Or "are convulsed." Isaiah 23:10b-11 contains a similar reaction to Tyre's destruction. Tyre has ceased to be a harbor (אין מזח עוד) and YHWH "has stretch out his hand over the sea and has shaken the kingdoms."

whistle over you.

As D. I. Block has pointed out, chapter 27 stands out for its apparent disinterest in human affairs. The oracle depicts Tyre's splendor as the legitimate reward for her business acumen, diligence, and skill.[59]

The economic character of the second Tyrian oracle in chapter 27 is overwhelming. The chapter starts out by stating Tyre's economic importance as "the merchant of the nations" "dwelling on the seaports" and showing that her prosperity is due to the fact that "her boundaries are in the heart of the seas" (v. 3). A full description of Tyre's splendor and glory manifested in the materials employed in building her follows (vv. 5-8). Tyre's preeminence in trade is then expressed (v. 9) and her worldwide net of trading partners and luxury products listed (vv. 12-25). The sudden and unexpected wreck of the Tyrian ship shows the scope and economic significance of the disaster (26-32a). The subsequent lamentation over Tyre's past glory underscores the motivation for the nations' lament and is the clue to determine the economic character of the unit: all nations have enriched and profited themselves from Tyre's commercial success (26-36). Chapter 27 serves as the backdrop for the two oracles in chapter 28. The latter judge Tyre's commercial success as driven by arrogance and haughtiness.

c. The Third and Fourth Oracles (Ez. 28:1-19)

The two oracles in chapter 28 are directed against the prince of Tyre (1-10) and the king of Tyre (11-19). They confirm the fact that economic motivations were the predominant reasons for the entire series of oracles.[60]

---

[59] Block, *Ezekiel 25-48*, 1998, 87.

[60] These two oracles are among the most intriguing and difficult of the entire book. Block (*Ezekiel 25-48*, 1998, 87) has enumerated the problems, many of which still defy satisfactory solution. Some of them are as follows: the determination of the limits of the unit, the relationship between the two parts that integrate it, the relationship of these two oracles with those in the previous two chapters, textual difficulties, hapax legomena, the origin of Ezekiel's ideological notions, the relationship of this text to the narratives of Genesis 1-3 and to the Priestly material in Exodus 28, and the message the prophet wants to convey to his own people.

Verses 4-5, placed between two indictments against Tyre in verses 2 and 6, show that Tyre's prosperity "that had been such a prominent motif in the foregoing oracles was the result of deliberate and official royal policy."[61] The verses read:

(4) By your wisdom[62] and understanding you have amassed[63] wealth for yourself and have accumulated gold and silver in your treasuries. (5) In the greatness of your wisdom you have increased your wealth by your trade and your heart has become haughty[64] on account of your wealth.

רכלה ("trade") (v. 5) is the key word in these two verses. As commented earlier, most scholars translate it "trade,"[65] "traffic,"[66] or "dealing."[67] The meaning of רכלה becomes clearer in verses 16 and 18 where it appears again and I fully discuss it.

---

[61] Block, *Ezekiel 25-48*, 1998, 97.

[62] Meyers and Meyers (*Zechariah 9-14*, 1993, 98) notice that the term חכמה "encompasses a broad range of meanings, including technical skill, as that of an artisan, political or economic diplomacy or shrewdness, and even everyday pragmatism or cleverness." In this text, חכמה is used in the technical sense of wisdom "in the administration of affairs" (*BDB*, 314b [חכם2]). Van Dijk (*Prophecy*, 1968, 103) renders the term as "skill" and תבונה as "shrewdness."

[63] עשה in the sense of "to acquire" recurs rather often in biblical usage (see *BDB*, 795b [עשהII.7]). *BDB* compares it to English "make money."

[64] The same root (גבה) appears twice in 28:2 and 17. Among the nations Ezekiel mentions in the oracles against foreign nations, only Egypt in Ez. 31:10 is blamed for having a similar haughty attitude. For Ezekiel, Egypt and Tyre belonged to an entirely different category than the rest of Judah's neighbors and he treated them accordingly. He saw them under a different light: they were the two major regional powers. The reasons for their arrogance, nevertheless, were different. Egypt's haughtiness derived from her political and military power. Tyre's arrogance on the other hand, resulted from her economic prosperity and splendor. On top of that, it is evident that both Egypt and Tyre shared a policy of active resistance to the Neo-Babylonian empire. Ultimately Ezekiel might have considered them responsible for the destruction of Jerusalem and the rest of the small states of the area. At every opportunity they had sparked the anti-Babylonian sentiments of these small petty states of Palestine and incited them to rebel.

[65] *HALOT*, 1237b (רכלה*a); Van Dijk (*Prophecy*, 1968, 105); Zimmerli (*Ezekiel 2*, 1983, 75); Block (*Ezekiel 25-48*, 1998, 91).

[66] *BDB*, 940a (ורכלה1).

[67] Greenberg, *Ezekiel 21-37*, 1997, 574.

A second oracle against the king of Tyre that starts in verse 12 contains the statement "you [...] are perfect in beauty" (אתה כליל יפי).[68] In the similar sentence in 27:3 "O Tyre you have said: "I am perfect in beauty" (צור את אמרת אני כלילת יפי), it was noticed that beauty in the context of the oracles refers to the magnificence and opulence that Tyre (the king of Tyre in this instance) manifested to the beholder. So, again an economic factor appears here. As in 27:3, where the sentence "your builders perfected your beauty" introduces us to Tyre's prosperity as manifested in the luxury materials employed in her construction, here the reference to the "perfect beauty" of Tyre's king serves as a preamble to the list of precious stones that were his "covering."[69]

Ezekiel now adds a new dimension to the proverbial richness of the king of Tyre. The prophet places him in Eden, the garden of God and the representation of a utopian realm of prosperity, luxury, splendor, and joy. Verse 13a reads as follows:

> In Eden, the garden of God, were you. All precious stones were your covering:[70] Ruby, topaz, and diamond; chrysolite, onyx, and

---

[68] This second oracle presents serious difficulties of interpretation that start already in the translation. These difficulties extend to the determination of its formal structure and are related to the fact that the oracle has been edited extensively (see Zimmerli, *Ezekiel 2*, 1983, 87).

[69] The obscure expression at the beginning of the verse חותם תכנית "*thou* wast one *sealing proportion,* i.e. *perfection,*" "complete perfection," "*a sealer of symmetry*" (*BDB*, 368a [חתם2]); "you were the sealer of proportion" (Greenberg, *Ezekiel 21-37*, 1997, 580) can have the same effect and serve a similar purpose. In this sense, Block (*Ezekiel 25-48*, 1998, 105) suggests that the expression "highlights the status, magnificence, and beauty of the king of Tyre."

[70] מסכה (covering) is a feminine noun of the root סכך. *BDB* (697a) translates it "*thy covering* (= *thou wast covered* with them)" (thus also Gesenius and Koehler-Baumgartner). Alternative etymologies and renderings have been offered. Zimmerli (*Ezekiel 2*, 1983, 82) prefers the translation "your garment;" Greenberg (*Ezekiel 21-37*, 1997, 581) suggests "your hedge;" Block (*Ezekiel 25-48*, 1998, 99) renders it "adorned you;" and Van Dijk chooses "was your defence" (*Prophecy*, 1968, 92, 116-17). In view of the degree of uncertainty about the meaning of most of these precious stones listed, some of whom are *hapax legomena*, I recommend Zimmerli's survey of the various interpretations of these terms (*Ezekiel 2*, 1983, 82-84). Block (*Ezekiel 25-48*, 1998, 108) has a useful comparative chart with "Modern Versional Renderings of Ezekiel's Jewels" and discusses them in page 109. The purpose of the present study is not so

jasper; sapphire, turquoise, and emerald; and worked in gold were your sockets[71] and settings in you in the day that you were created they were established.

Many commentators see here a reference to a garment similar to that of the high priest. The nine names of the precious stones, arranged in three sets of three, correspond with minor rearrangements in sequence to the stones of the first two and fourth rows of jewels on the high priest's breastplate in Ex. 28:17-20.[72] What matters to this study is the way in which the king of Tyre is portrayed in all his glory. He is a paradigm of prosperity, opulence, and wealth.

Verses 15-18a depict a change in the Tyrian king's behavior and are key in understanding the economic motivation of the oracles. Verses 15-18a read:

(15) You were blameless in your behavior from the day that you were created, until wickedness[73] was found in you. (16a) By the abundance[74] of your trade[75] you filled your heart[76] with

---

much to determine the exact precious stone these technical terms refer to but to highlight the economic underpinnings of each of the four Tyrian oracles.

[71] The meaning of תפיך remains obscure. Gesenius identifies it with "the bezel or hollow in which a gem is set" (*Hebrew-Chaldee Lexicon*, 1984, 871a, root # 8596, s.v. תף2). A derivation from תף "tambourine, hand-drum" (thus *BDB* [1074a]; Greenberg [*Ezekiel 21-37*, 1997, 579]) does not seem likely. Zimmerli (*Ezekiel 2*, 1983, 84) considers other suggestions such as Driver's "earrings, pendant jewel" and Jahnow's "your engravings." Block (*Ezekiel 25-48*, 1998, 100) and Van Dijk (*Prophecy*, 1968, 118) derive it from יפי and render it "your beauty."

[72] See Greenberg (*Ezekiel 21-37*, 1997, 582); Block (*Ezekiel 25-48*, 1998, 106-12).

[73] Other translations of עולתה are "iniquity" (Van Dijk, *Prophecy*, 1968, 93); "wrongdoing" (Greenberg, *Ezekiel 21-37*, 1997, 585); "misconduct" (Block, *Ezekiel 25-48*, 1998, 101). *BDB* (732b) renders it "injustice, unrighteousness, wrong." The word often conveys the idea of "*violent deeds of injustice*" (*BDB*, 732b [עולה1]).

[74] Or "by the magnitude," "by the scope" following Greenberg (*Ezekiel 21-37*, 1997, 579-80) who renders ברב here by the expression "because of your many (dealings)" and מרב in verse 18 by "by your many (iniquities)." Block (*Ezekiel 25-48*, 1998, 101) uses the expression "by the magnitude (of your iniquities)" to translate מרב in verse 18.

[75] Even though I translated רכלתך as "trade," the account refers to national trade, driven by palace and royal policy. The underlying concept is thus plural and refers to

violence[77] and sinned. [...] (17a) Your heart became haughty on account of[78] your beauty;[79] you corrupted your wisdom[80] for the

---

"your trading policies" or "your commercial policies" here and in Ez. 28:5 and 18. In my assessment, *רכלה is one of a number of feminine singular words, generally feminine participles used substantivally in a collective sense "as the comprehensive designation of a number of *persons*, [...] living beings, [...] dead bodies" (GKC, # 122s [p. 394]). Some of them are: ארחה, travelling company, i.e. travelling person (a caravan); גולה, the company of exiles; דלה, the unimportant, the poor population; חיה, cattle, beasts; דגה, fish (almost always collective); and נבלה, corpses in Is. 5:25; 26:19. Another example not listed by Gesenius is כבודה "valuable things" according to *HALOT* (458a) or "abundance, riches" in *BDB* (459b). Even the *hapax legomena* *סחרה "commercial activity" (Ez. 27:15) and מרכלת "brokerage, class of merchants" (Ez. 27:24) can have a collective meaning. Chapter 3 presents a full discussion of the "trading policies" referred to by the word רכלתך.

[76] Zimmerli (*Ezekiel 2*, 1983, 86) understands תוכך in a plural sense as "all who are in you."

[77] חמס is a general term for violent actions. *TLOT* suggests that the root חמס can be associated with the root חמץ "to oppress" (1.437). Prophetic diction often uses שוד "misdeed, destruction" as a synonym for חמץ. The difference, according to *TLOT*, "may lie in the fact that *šōd* emphasizes the active doing, *ḥāmās* the nature or consequence of the deed" (1.437). Haag (*TDOT*, 4.478-87) shows that חמס implies "cold-blooded and unscrupulous infringement of the personal rights of others, motivated by greed [...] and often making use of physical violence and brutality. [...] The primary context of *chāmās* is society" (482-83). Block (*Ezekiel 1-24*, 1997, 267) has pointed out that the use of חמס in Ez. 7:23 and here suggests that "these crimes were characteristic especially of the community leaders, who hold the lives of ordinary folk in their hands. These are the very crimes against humanity for which Habakkuk had condemned Babylon (Hab. 2:8, 11, 17)." Zimmerli (*Ezekiel 2*, 1983, 93) comments on מלו חמס that it refers "to the violence which has arisen as a result of Tyre's trading." Greenberg (*Ezekiel 21-37*, 1997, 585) uses the expression "lawless gain" to translate חמס and adds that this is a meaning "found first in Amos 3:10: 'They treasure up lawless gain and rapine in their palaces.'"

[78] The preposition ב can have a causal force meaning "through, on account of, because of" in some instances (see *BDB*, 90a [בIII.5]).

[79] As in 27:3, 11; and 28:12 "beauty" (יפיך) has to do with the luxury, magnificence, and opulence of Tyre and her rulers. The same applies to "your beaming splendor" (יפעתך) in this same verse (17).

[80] The Hebrew noun חכם has a broad range of meanings (see note 62 above), in general it means "someone who has a masterful understanding of something" (*TLOT*, 1.420). Here, as Greenberg (*Ezekiel 21-37*, 1997, 576) has noticed, חכמה can refer to "commercial genius."

sake of your beaming splendor.[81] [...] (18a) By[82] all[83] your iniquities, in the wickedness[84] of your trade, you profaned your sanctuary.[85]

This final section of the Tyrian oracles is an apt culmination to the entire series of oracles. It reveals that Tyre's prosperity was the result of deliberate and official royal policy. The wisdom of the prince of Tyre had enabled him to amass wealth, gold, and silver (vv. 4-5). The account places the prince/king of Tyre in Eden, a utopian realm of prosperity, luxury, splendor, and joy. There all kinds of precious stones were his "covering" (v. 13a). He is a paradigm of prosperity, opulence, and wealth. Nevertheless, a careful reading of the two oracles in chapter 28 makes the economic grounds for Tyre's condemnation come to the fore. They indicate that Tyre's prosperity[86] was the result of "wickedness" and "violent acts of injustice" (עולתה). Tyre's "trade" and trading policies

---

[81] I follow here HALOT's translation of יפעתך (424b).

[82] The preposition מן can be used to express the ultimate or remote cause of something as is the case here (see BDB, 580a [מן 2f]). This use is frequent in מרב. BDB translates this מן as "on account of, by reason of, from, because of." The preposition can be also rendered as "through" as does Zimmerli (Ezekiel 2, 1983, 86).

[83] Or "multiple" (רב). HALOT (1174b) translates רב עצמותי in Job 4:14 as "all my bones." Greenberg (Ezekiel 21-37, 1997, 580) renders רב by "many."

[84] Or "dishonesty" (see HALOT, 798a [עול2]). Block (Ezekiel 25-48, 1998, 101) renders עול as "unscrupulous."

[85] Cooke (Ezekiel, 1936, 324) was the first to suggest that מקדשיך stands for a single temple and denotes a single sanctuary with its precincts. The plural here can denote the different elements or various structures that make up the sacred precinct "which normally included the temple itself, the walls, and the gardens" (Block, Ezekiel 25-48, 1998, 101, note 70; see also HALOT, 626a). מקדשיך here is ambiguous. Many commentators interpret it as an allusion to "the holy garden/mountain of God" (Greenberg, Ezekiel 21-37, 1997, 586) or to "the sacred precinct on God's holy mountain" (Block, Ezekiel 25-48, 1998, 101). Zimmerli (Ezekiel 2, 1983, 94) explains this unique accusation according to which Tyre had desecrated her sanctuaries as "the result of commodities forcibly seized from the people that had found their way into the temple treasury." I agree with Zimmerli's interpretation. Notice the use of the word "your palaces/temples" (היכליכם) in Joel 4:5 which I translate "for you have taken my silver and gold and have carried my most valuable things into your palaces." מקדשיך here and היכליכם in Joel 4:5 can be related (cf. sections 3.5 and 3.8.f).

[86] The king of Tyre is just the representative of the city.

(ויכולינך) had enabled her to partake in the Assyrian oppression, to establish alliances with Egypt and Babylon, to enter into trade partnerships with the Philistines, to entertain economic relations with Edom, to have a share in the lucrative Arabian trade, and to extend her commercial influence. In fact, through her trading and commercial policies, Tyre had managed to control the trade routes and the metal and horse trade, two vital sectors for the Judean economy (cf. sections 3.8 and 3.10). But this economic success came with a price. Tyre had filled herself with "violence" and "lawless gain" (חמס).[87] In pursuing economic success and beaming splendor (יפעתך),[88] she corrupted (שחת) her business acumen (חכמתך) and even profaned (חללת) in this way her own temple (מקדשיך). As we have seen (cf. section 3.14), Phoenician trade in the West began under the aegis of Melkart, the Tyrian city god, and most Tyrian foundations in the Mediterranean were linked to a temple, which, in most cases was dedicated to Melkart. The temple had a share, a tenth part of the products of trade, in the benefits of Tyrian maritime trade as well. It is in light of these facts that the sentence in verse 18a, "by all your iniquities, in the wickedness of your trade, you profaned your sanctuary" (מרב עוניך בעול רכלתך חללת

---

[87] As we have seen in section 3.11, Homer describes the Phoenicians as "greedy merchant men" and pirates (*The Odyssey*, 15.415). For Hosea 12:8 the typical trader is a cheat. The word he uses for trader is "Canaan" whose first born was Phoenician Sidon. According to Hosea, he has "false scales in his hands, to oppress he loves." Is. 23:15-18 presents the wide network of Tyrian trading partners as the clientele of a prostitute that would do anything for gain (see Chiera, "Is. 23," *RSF* 14 [1986]: 18). Amos 8:4-6 condemns the merchants who are impatient for the holy days to pass so that they can resume their fraudulent business. Commerce by Jew and Tyrian alike overrode the Sabbath rest in post-exilic Jerusalem according to Neh. 13:15-16.

[88] The ך suffix in יפעתך and in the following words is 2nd masculine singular. It refers to the king of Tyre not to the city. Ez. 28:7b announces also the end of Tyre's beaming splendor. It predicts the arrival of the Neo-Babylonian army that "will draw their swords against the beauty of your wisdom and profane your beaming splendor" (וחללו יפעתך). In his oracle against Tyre in Is. 23:8, Isaiah confirms the importance of the city, whom he called "Tyre the crown-bestower" (צר המעטירה), and acknowledges the high social status of her merchants ("whose merchants were princes and whose traders were the honored of the earth"). At the same time he announces that YHWH has planned "to defile the pride of all glory" (לחלל גאון כל־צבי). The word Isaiah uses, צבי, "beauty, decoration, ornament, splendor" has a meaning similar to יפעתך in Ez. 28:16.

מקדשיך) is to be understood.

2. Political Status of Tyre as Reflected in Ezekiel 26:1-28:19

There are only a few references hinting at the political status of Tyre as a regional power and at her relation to other Phoenician cities. Nevertheless some key terms and passages give us a glimpse into Tyre's political influence in the area. It is also possible to correlate the insights from the text with some historical events. In what follows I will discuss Tyre's political status as reflected in Ez. 26:17 and 28:8-11.

a. The Expression "and her Inhabitants, Who Imposed their Terror, All her Inhabitants" in Ez. 26:17

The key word in the sentence "and her inhabitants, who imposed (or spread) their terror, all her inhabitants" in Ez. 26:17 is חתיתם ("terror"). The word is often emended to חתיתה[89] even though the sentence makes perfect sense as it is and no emendation is necessary. The passage has been traditionally understood in economic terms. M. Greenberg, for example, after stating that Tyre did not wield political or military control over her trading partners at any time, comments that it was Tyre's primacy in trade "that 'inspired terror'-which is a hyperbole for acknowledgment of Tyre's primacy in trade."[90]

While I agree with Greenberg's assessment of Tyre's economic role, I think that one should not rule out a political dimension to this "terror" inspired by Tyre among her trading partners. While it is impossible to determine the exact forms of the colonies' dependence upon Tyre due to the insufficiency of our data, it is a recognized fact that the colonies had to pay a tribute to the Tyrian ruler consisting on the tenth part of the profits of trade (cf. section 3.14). Utica's refusal to pay such tribute prompted the king's punitive expedition (Josephus, *Ant.*, 8.5.3 [146]). Tyre's political-military control over her colonies is evident also in that, at the close of the 8th century, a revolt in Kition (Cyprus)

---

[89] Thus *BHS*, *BDB* (369b [חתית), the Greek version, Ewald, and Cornill.
[90] Greenberg, *Ezekiel 21-37*, 1997, 538.

was suppressed by king Elulaos (Josephus, *Ant.*, 9.14.2 [284]). Other revolt attempts, even though not documented, are not at all unlikely.[91]

Furthermore, it is known that there was a *sukin* in Cyprus who called himself king Hiram's slave (*'bd hrm mlk sdnm*)[92] and who seems to have carried out the administration and judicature in this city. This shows a "rather rigid control of the king over the Cyprian colony." Later on, Carthage governed her colonies by a representative, "one who is above the community."[93] Carthage may have borrowed this practice from Tyre. The Melkart cult, pre-eminent in Spain, Cyprus, Sicily, Sardinia, and Malta was another factor in this economic, political, and religious dependency of the colonies from the metropolis. To some degree, the above facts show that Tyre's "terror" had both economic and political dimensions.

a. The Description of the Crew of the Ship Tyre in Ez. 27:8-11

Ez. 27:8-11 depicts the crew of the ship Tyre with words as follows:

The inhabitants of Sidon and Arwad
were your oarsmen;
your wise men, O Tyre, were in you
as your sailors;
the elders of Byblos and her wise men were in you
as repairers of your fissures;
all the ships of the sea and their sailors were in you
to bring your imports;
[Men of] Paras, Lud, and Put were in your army,
as your warriors;
shield and helmet they hung on you;
they constituted your splendor;
Men of Arwad and Helek[94] were on your walls all around;

---

[91] Tsirkin, "Tyrian Power," 1998, 185-87.
[92] *KAI* 31, 1. The term appears also in the Aḥiram sarcophagus of Byblos (*KAI* 1, 2).
[93] Tsirkin, "Tyrian Power," 1998, 185.
[94] The term חיל here is identical with the one in verse 10 which I translated "your army." A geographical reference no longer recognizable could lie behind this וחיל. Commentators have connected it to Akkadian *ḫilakku* and Aramaic and Phoenician *ḫlk*

and Gammadites on your towers;
Their shields (?) they hang on your walls all around;
they perfected your beauty.

The passage shows that economic supremacy and political dominion went hand in hand. Tyre's political supremacy is conveyed here by the fact that the nobles of Tyre's neighbor cities perform different, sometimes menial duties on the ship.[95] Verses 8 and 9 show men of Sidon, Byblos, and Arwad employed in the Tyrian navy and army "partly as citizens of dependent *poleis*, tributary to Tyre(?), partly perhaps as mercenaries. Tyrians themselves seem to have occupied senior positions."[96] The very fact that Tyre was strong enough to withstand the Babylonians for thirteen years demonstrates the strength of her army, navy, and fortifications.[97] It seems that Tyre's navy was the strongest in the Mediterranean at the time and was capable of supplying the besieged city.[98]

A number of historical data confirm Tyrian political superiority over the other Phoenician cities:[99]

1) Nebuchadnezzar II's ration tablets listing deliveries of oil for the subsistence of prisoners of war identified by name, profession, and/or nationality. They date from the 10th to the 35th year of Nebuchadnezzar II (595/4-570/69 BCE). One text mentions 126 men from Tyre and in another at least 190 mariners from Tyre are listed.

---

meaning Cilicia. The parallelism with Arward favors this possibility (see Greenberg, *Ezekiel 21-37*, 1997, 552).

[95] Zimmerli, *Ezekiel 2*, 1983, 58. See also Block's commentary on these verses (*Ezekiel 25-48*, 1998, 62-66).

[96] Diakonoff, "Naval Power," 1992, 181.

[97] The population of Tyre in ancient times is estimated in 25,000 people. A significant number of people from the mainland could have used the island as a refuge during wartime (see Wildberger, *Isaiah 13-27*, 1997, 420). Today about 12,000 inhabitants live there.

[98] Diakonoff, "Naval Power," 1992, 181.

[99] Ez. 27:8-11 contains a list of nations supplying Tyre with mercenaries. A number of commentators (Zimmerli, Block) see in the first group of nations (Paras, Lud, Put) a traditional list of Egyptian allies. In their opinion, this attests to the close relationship between Tyre and Egypt in the early 6th century BCE (see Block, *Ezekiel 25-48*, 1998, 64-65; Zimmerli, *Ezekiel 2*, 1983, 59-60).

The number of mariners from other Phoenician cities is much smaller (eight for Byblos and three for Arwad).[100]

2) The fact that Nebuchadnezzar's "court calendar" mentions a "king of Tyre"[101] suggests that Nebuchadnezzar did not achieve an actual military conquest of Tyre and that Tyre had once again become subject to Babylon.

3) The presence of a *šandabakku* or Babylonian chief commissioner as a witness is attested in a document from Nebuchadnezzar's forty-first year (564/3). The text was written in Tyre itself and suggests the presence of a Babylonian chief commissioner alongside king Baal who replaced the rebel Ithobal.[102]

The description of Tyre in Ez. 27:5-11 concentrates on Tyre's naval power but it contains observations about her military might as well.[103] Verses 10-11 show that Tyre employed mercenary troops from Persia (פרס),[104] Lydia (לוד) and Libya (פוט),[105] Arwadites (בני ארוד)[106] and Gammadites (גמדים).[107] Ez. 27:27 contains another reference to Tyre's אנשי מלחמתך, "your fighting men," "men of war," or "warriors."

---

[100] See *ANET* 308 and references in sections 2.6 and 2.10.

[101] See Unger, *Babylon*, 1970, 293; *ANET* 308.

[102] See Unger, "Nebukadnezar II," 1926, 314-17 and section 2.10.

[103] Diakonoff, "Naval Power," 1992, 171.

[104] Many scholars find out of context a mention of Persia at a date as early as 586 BCE. Diakonoff, for example ("Naval Power," 1992, 174), emends *prs* (Persia) to *trs* (Asian Thrace).

[105] In his lengthy discussion of the texts and contexts where the term פוט appears, Diakonoff ("Naval Power," 1992, 177-81) concludes that "*Puṭ* should be read *Pōṭ* and should be regarded as a Phoenician rendering of Greek *Pontos*, 'sea,' meaning of course, the 'Peoples of the Sea'" (p. 181).

[106] As mentioned above חילך in verse 11 can be a geographical term referring to Cilicia (see note 94 in this chapter).

[107] Diakonoff ("Naval Power," 1992, 181) emends *gmdym* to *gmrym* and concludes that Cimmerians were manning Tyre's towers. Cimmerians and Scythians excelled as archers. Block (*Ezekiel 25-48*, 1998, 65) suggests an equation of *gmdym* with the *Qumidi* mentioned in the Amarna Tablets.

3. New Interpretation and Dating of the Oracles Based on Historical and Literary Grounds

In this context the way in which Tyre threatened Jerusalem makes sense. Ezekiel 26:2 refers to the destruction of the Philistine ports ("the peoples' ports" or דלתות העמים in Hebrew) in the late 7th century. As commented earlier (cf. sections 3.3, 3.5, and 4.1.a), Ashkelon was destroyed in 604 BCE, Gaza in 601 BCE, and Ashdod c. 600 BCE.[108] The prophet was describing the situation of desolation and ruin that followed the destruction of the Philistine ports (and specially Ashkelon) in the early years of the 6th century BCE. Throughout most of its history Israel and Judah lacked an exit to the sea. The Philistine cities were their natural outlet to import and export products and commodities.

If this historic and literary reconstruction is correct, Tyre's malicious joy is understandable. Tyre anticipated a major trade shift. She rejoiced at the prospect of having trade shifted to the North to Tyre itself. The expressions "they have come round to me" (נסבה אלי) and "I will be filled, satisfied" (אמלאה) make perfect sense in this context. This trade vacuum in the Philistine coast represented a real opportunity for Tyre. It meant also the economic ruin for Jerusalem and Judah (on this matter, see discussion in 4.1.a).

The historical analysis of Ezekiel's oracles against Tyre in the previous chapter has demonstrated that economic and political factors were the main reasons for Ezekiel's condemnation of Tyre. Social and religious reasons were also present but of minor importance.

As we saw (cf. section 3.2), a major Tyrian expansion took place under the protection of the Neo-Assyrian Empire during the 8th century. This expansion was motivated by the search for new metal sources and raw materials and was geared to the West Mediterranean. The study has shown that the period between 720 and 700 BCE was characterized by a spectacular growth in the number of settlements and that maximum economic growth took place during the 7th century BCE in the Phoenician settlements in the West Mediterranean and elsewhere. The archaeological data gathered together shows that this expansion continued until the beginning of the 6th century BCE when most

---

[108] Ekron was destroyed around this time too (c. 603).

Phoenician settlements experienced a deep economic crisis. In the Iberian Peninsula, silver extraction and trade were abandoned in Riotinto and Gadir respectively. Phoenician activities came to a halt in the years 600-580 BCE. The process culminated with the abandonment of the Phoenician settlements around 580-550 BCE and with the transition from the Phoenician to the Punic phases that took place in 550 BCE. At about the same time (c. 580 BCE), the import of Phoenician luxury products such as stone, alabaster, shell, and metal vases stopped suddenly in the Italian Peninsula. The number of amulets peculiar to Egypt's 26th dynasty found at Carthage sharply decreased in the second half of the 6th century BCE as well.

Nebuchadnezzar's siege of Tyre (c. 588/7-573 BCE) marked the end of Tyre's economic success (cf. section 2.9). Both textual sources and the archaeological record point to the decade between 580 and 570 BCE as the *terminus ad quem* for the major shift of trade from Tyre itself to Carthage. After the siege, Tyre's power was exhausted. Tyre lost her overseas territories with the exception of her colonies in Cyprus. This is the main historical argument in support of dating the oracles to Ezekiel's time. A more precise dating of the oracles on historical grounds is not possible.

5
Summary and Conclusions

The present study seeks to answer a number of puzzling questions about the Tyrian oracles in Ezekiel 26:1-28:19. Chapter 1 shows how textual and archaeological sources indicate that Judah's neighbors were taking advantage of Judah's situation in the period immediately before and after the destruction of Jerusalem. Arad ostracon # 24, line 20 mentions an Edomite advance in the Eastern Negev (c. 598 BCE). Edom was guilty of violence against Judah (Ez. 35:5, Joel. 4:19) and may even have assisted the Babylonians in the sack of Jerusalem (Obad. 11, 13-14; Ps. 137:7; Lam. 4:21-22).

2 Kgs. 24:2 indicates that, after Jehoiakim's rebellion against Nebuchadnezzar, Arameans,[1] Ammonites, and Moabites, participated in a Babylonian attack against Judah c. 598 BCE. Ammon rejoiced at the destruction of the Temple, the desolation of the land of Israel, and the exile of the Judeans (Ez. 25:3, 6) and Moab showed a disdainful attitude toward Judah (Ez. 25:8). All Transjordanian states (Edom included) enjoyed a relative prosperity in the period around the destruction of Jerusalem. No destruction layer has been found in Ammonite territory. On the contrary, Ammon experienced a period of prosperity between the end of the 7th century and the beginning of the 6th century. Jer. 49:1 condemns Ammon for having seized one-time Israelite territory. In the wake of Jerusalem's destruction, Jer. 40:13 states that Baalis, king of Ammon, instigated the assassination of Gedaliah, the Judean governor appointed by Nebuchadnezzar.

After Hezekiah's rebellion against Sennacherib, the Philistines had received several Judean cities in the Shephelah. This event had severely weakened Judah economically and politically. They enjoyed great prosperity during the 7th century until Nebuchadnezzar's

---

[1] Many scholars emend the text to "Edom" and connect this campaign to the aforementioned Arad ostracon # 24, line 20 mentioning an Edomite encroachment in the Eastern Negev c. 598 BCE. Due to the similarity of the Hebrew consonants ר and ד that distinguish Aram (ארם) and Edom (אדם), the confusion between the two is very frequent (on this matter, see discussions in sections 2.6 and 2.9).

destruction of Ashkelon in 604 BCE. Similarities of vocabulary link the oracle against Philistia in Ez. 25:15 to the Edomite oracles in 25:12 and 35:5 where the Edomites are accused of having participated in acts of vengeance against Israel.

Egypt, finally, is condemned for being an unreliable political ally (Ez. 29:6). The historical evidence presented in chapter 2 shows the persistent role Egypt played in instigating Judean uprisings, only to fail to support the Judeans adequately for a successful outcome.

In this context, Tyre is the only exception among the seven nations mentioned in Ezekiel's oracles against foreign nations[2] in that the stated reasons for her condemnation do not explain the nature of Tyre's negative actions against Judah. Tyre and Judah had no common boundaries and entertained good relations during most of their history. Nonetheless Tyre appears in a series of oracles against foreign nations that includes Judah's worst enemies Ammon, Moab, Edom, and the Philistine cities and the three chapters dedicated to her are longer than the oracles against these other four nations combined. Only the oracles against Egypt in chapters 29-32 are longer than the Tyrian oracles and they state clearly the motive for Egypt's condemnation: Egypt was an unreliable political ally.

Scholars have not provided a convincing explanation for Tyre's condemnation or taken into account historical circumstances and the oracles themselves do not seem to provide a clue for it. This surprising situation raises important questions: what was Tyre doing to Judah and in what way(s) was harming her? What were the reasons for the condemnation? What core of historical events does the prophet refer to and what set of historical circumstances does the prophecy echo? What is the *historical reality* of the prophecy? Why did Ezekiel consider Tyre a threat and in which way was Tyre a threat to Judah? Finally, why would Tyre turn against Judah? No previous study of Ezekiel has fully explored these questions or given a satisfactory answer to them. They are the focus of the present study that takes into account economic and political factors never before applied fully to this subject.

---

[2] No reason is given for the inclusion of Sidon in the oracles. It may be due to a quota of seven nations in the present collection or to the fact that the prophet had in mind the coast and its seaports and Sidon was one of them. Tyre and Sidon are regularly paired in the oracles against foreign nations, as, e.g., Jer. 27:3 and Joel 4:4.

Chapter 2 provides the historical framework for the Tyrian oracles. It is a historical survey of the main events between 626 and 573 BCE. The year 626 marked the beginning of the rapid decline of the Assyrian empire with the death of the Assyrian king Assurbanipal and 573 is the generally accepted date for the end of Nebuchadnezzar's siege of Tyre. The chapter shows the insufficiency of historical sources for the period. This is the main obstacle to an accurate reconstruction of the events that took place between 626 and 573 BCE.

The Neo-Babylonian Chronicles show that the Assyrian king Sin-šar(ra)-iškun was beaten in Babylon in August, 626 BCE. The Neo-Babylonian king Nabopolassar gained control of Nippur (622), Suḫu and Ḫindanu (616) and defeated the Assyrians in Qablinu (616). An Assyro-Egyptian alliance was concluded on that year. Then Assur (615), Nineveh (614), and Harran (610) were conquered.

In 609 pharaoh Necho II (609-595/4 BCE) killed King Josiah (640-609 BCE) in Meggido (2 Chr. 35:20; 2 Kgs. 23:29). What happened at Megiddo and the circumstances surrounding Josiah's death are an enigma to this very day. Afterwards, "the people of the land" made his youngest son Jehoahaz king in his place (2 Kgs. 23:29-30). He reigned for three months. Necho established his headquarters at Carchemish to protect his interests in Syria and support the Assyrians. The Euphrates became the border between Egypt and Babylon for the next few years. Subsequently, Necho made Eliakim, Jehoahaz' half-brother, king with the name of Jehoiakim (609-597 BCE).

The Babylonian advance continued with the capture of Kimuḫu (607) a strategic site which the Egyptians recaptured in 606. The following year, Nebuchadnezzar (605-562 BCE), beat the Egyptians in a decisive battle at Carchemish. The battle of Carchemish meant the end of the Egyptian domination of the Levant (2 Kgs. 24:7). Soon afterwards, Nebuchadnezzar marched against the city of Ashkelon, captured, and destroyed it (November/December 604). In the next three years (603-601) he marched yearly to the Ḫatti-land to collect his annual tribute. In 601 Nebuchadnezzar attacked Egypt, Necho II mustered his army, and both met in open battle. Both sides suffered heavy losses.

Around 600, King Jehoiakim refused to pay tribute to the Babylonians (2 Kgs. 24:1). Nebuchadnezzar, according to the

Babylonian Chronicle, "seized the city and captured the king" in the year 597. 2 Kgs. 24:10-17 shows that Jehoiachin (December 598-March 597), not Jehoiakim, was the king of Judah who surrendered to Nebuchadnezzar. Nebuchadnezzar took the treasures of the Temple and Palace and exiled the elite. He appointed Mattaniah, Jehoiachin's uncle, as king and changed his name to Zedekiah (597-586 BCE) who was the last king of Judah. Cuneiform documents shed some light on Jehoiachin's fate in exile. He was held as a royal hostage together with Aga, the king of Ashkelon, and many mariners from Tyre and some from other Phoenician cities.

The fall of Jerusalem in 597 was the decisive event in the progressive disintegration of the land of Judah. The looting of the Royal and Temple treasuries decimated the economic resources of the tiny state and the deportation to Babylon of the Judean elite (including Ezekiel) destroyed the social fabric of the Judean community. The year 597 started a period of unprecedented political instability in Judah. Zedekiah, the last Judean king, lacked experienced advisers. Jer. 27:3 mentions a meeting of envoys from Edom, Moab, Ammon, Tyre, and Sidon at Jerusalem (594).[3] The meeting is traditionally interpreted as a conspiracy against the king of Babylon. In 593 Psammetichus II (595-589 BCE) engaged in a successful campaign in Nubia. Graffiti at Abu-Simbel show Phoenician, Greek, and Judean participation in this campaign. Then he set out for Palestine and the Phoenician coast.

The exact date for the outbreak of Zedekiah's rebellion is not known but must have taken place in the late 590's or early in the 580's. Nebuchadnezzar's retaliation took place soon afterwards. Jerusalem withstood the Babylonians for eighteen months (Jan. 587-July/August 586) (2 Kgs 25:1-3; Jer. 39:1-2; 52:4-11). As a result of the intervention of an Egyptian army in Palestine (Jer. 37:5-11), the siege was temporarily relaxed. Egyptian involvement in the revolt is certain (Ez. 17:15 and Lachish ostracon # 3). The Egyptian attack, commanded by pharaoh Apries (588-570 BCE), must have taken place around the time of Ezekiel's prophecy against Egypt dated in January, 587 (Ez. 29:1). Herodotus (2.161) indicates that Apries fought a sea-battle against the king of Tyre. It is not clear whether he was attacking the Phoenician

---

[3] The account does not mention the Philistine cities. This may indicate that they had ceased to exist by this time.

states or the Babylonians, or whether his campaign in Phoenicia was connected with the Egyptian march to liberate Jerusalem.

The capture of Jerusalem was followed by the slaughter of the Judean nobles, the blinding of Zedekiah who was taken to Babylon, the destruction of the Temple, the removal of the cultic objects to Babylon, and the deportation of her population (2 Kgs. 25:13-17; Jer. 39:1-10). Evidence of Babylonian destruction in Judea at this time is extensive. Only some cities in the land of Benjamin (Tell el-Ful, Mizpah, Gibeon) escaped the Babylonian destruction. Nebuchadnezzar appointed Gedaliah over the people left in the land of Judah. A certain Ishmael assassinated him and decided to flee to Ammon first, and then to Tahpanhes in Egypt, taking Jeremiah along with him (Jer. 42:1-43:7). Babylonian reprisals took place in 582/1 with a new deportation (Jer. 52:30). Early during his Egyptian exile, Jeremiah prophesied an imminent invasion of Egypt by the Babylonians (43:8-13). There is no evidence for this invasion in Babylonian, Egyptian, or Greek histories.

Ezekiel 26-28 refers to a siege of Tyre in Nebuchadnezzar's time. Ez. 26:1 dates it to "the eleventh year, on the first day of the month" which corresponds to March-March 587-586. Ez. 29:17, which is part of the oracles against Egypt, contains the latest date in the book: "In the twenty-seventh year, on the first day of the month" or March-April 571 and implies that the siege had by then already ended but there was no capitulation of Tyre. Josephus (*Ag. Ap.*, 1.21 [156-59]) indicates that the siege lasted thirteen years. Although the dating of the siege of Tyre is not fully settled, most scholars would accept the year 588/7 for the beginning of the siege and the year 573 for the end of it. The siege may have consisted of a long blockade of the mainland opposite Tyre and have required the annual replacement of the attacking troops. It seems to have ended with a treaty by which the royal Tyrian house had to reside in Babylon. Together with the Babylonian king, a commissioner had to reside in Ušu. A part of the population was deported. A tablet with an official receipt mentioning provisions "for the king and the soldiers who went with him against the land of Tyre" published in 1926 is the only archeological evidence for the siege.

Eleven archival documents from the city of Ṣurru, that seems to have been a city of Tyrian deportees, dated between the years 573-563 give further insights into the later history of Tyre. Ṣurru disappeared with the beginning of Evil-Merodach's reign in 562. Around that time a change in the political system of Tyre took place with the beginning of the government of the judges. Nebuchadnezzar's death may have marked the return of the Tyrian exiles and a change in government.

The reasons for the siege of Tyre had to do with Egypt, with whom Tyre had good relations. Nebuchadnezzar needed to establish a safe base for his ultimate goal: the conquest of Egypt. This is the motivation for the conquest of the small states in Western Asia and of the Phoenician cities of Arwad, Sidon, and Tyre. It is also probable that the new Egyptian navy could have represented a threat to Babylon as long as the Phoenician states were independent. The thirteen-year siege may have been the occasion for Apries' naval campaign in which he fought "a battle with the king of Tyre by sea" (Herodotus, 2.161).

After the siege, Tyre's power was exhausted. Tyre lost her overseas territories with the exception of the colonies in Cyprus. Carthage became an independent state and took over Tyre's overseas territories.

Chapter 3 deals with the motivations for the Tyrian oracles and shows that answers to the questions in chapter 1 are complex. They involve economic, political, social, and religious factors. In the end, Judah's restraint of trade and economic stagnation were the direct result of Tyre's economic policies and trade practices. Metals and horses were the commodities Judah needed most, and Tyre exerted a practical monopoly over their trade and distribution. Tyre could have curbed easily Judah's access to such commodities or imposed tariffs on their distribution. Tyre collaborated with Assyria, Egypt, and Babylon, the empires that ruled Palestine from the mid-7th century to the first half of the 6th century. She entered into trade partnerships with the Philistines, entertained economic relations with Edom, and had a share in the lucrative Arabian trade. Judah's lack of both strategic metals (iron, copper, tin) and tribute metals (silver, gold), along with Tyre's control of overland and sea routes and her monopoly of important raw materials and outlets enabled her to curb effectively Judah's access to the metal resources the Judean economy desperately needed. Horses, necessary for military purposes, were subject to similar trade restrictions. A Tyrian economic and territorial penetration process in the territory of the old kingdom of Judah, observable in the Persian and Hellenistic Periods and probably going back to the Neo-Babylonian Period, completed these trading policies.

Slave trade was another factor in Tyre's dealings with Judah. Sources unequivocally document Phoenician slave trade in the 1st millennium BCE. Joel 4:6 and Am. 1:9 accuse Tyre of selling Judean slaves in the period following the destruction of Jerusalem in 586 BCE.

Social factors and social criticism are observable in the oracles as well. Tyrian products were status symbols. They represented the oppression of a dishonest Tyrian merchant elite that sold itself to the highest bidder.

Finally, a clear link between Tyre's religion and her economic activities is observable. Tyrian economic and colonizing activities were a continuation of her Canaanite religion under the patronage of Melkart, the city god. This constituted another reason for rejecting altogether Tyrian political and economic influence and activities.

Chapter 4 concentrates on the core economic focus of each of the oracles and on their individual contribution to the overall economic content and nature of the Tyrian oracles.

The chapter starts out by correlating Ez. 26:2 with known historical events. In 26:2, Ezekiel describes the situation of desolation and ruin that resulted from Nebuchadnezzar's destruction of the Philistine ports (Ashkelon in 604 BCE, Gaza in 601, and Ashdod c. 600). Throughout most of its history, Israel lacked an exit to the sea. The Philistine cities were the natural outlet for import and export of products and commodities. Tyre anticipated a major trade shift to the North, to Tyre itself. This is the meaning conveyed by the verb אמלאה ("I will be filled"). The fact that נסבה ("they have come round to me") is a perfect niph'al form may indicate that the trade shift had already taken place. In this case, a date after 600 and closer to the destruction of Jerusalem would be very likely.

The oracle in chapter 26 continues depicting Tyre's siege and desolation. The destruction of her walls and towers (vv. 4-5, 9) is in sharp contrast with the glorious past of the city. At a second stage, the account focuses on the economic consequences of the destruction: Tyre's economic "pillars," her bazaars and temple, have ceased to exist (v. 11). Then the economic motivations for the siege become clear, the looting of her wealth and plundering of her merchandise are introduced (v. 12).

Finally, the international reaction to Tyre's fall and the lament of her trading partners are presented in full detail (vv. 15-18).

The economic character of the second oracle against Tyre in Ezekiel 27 is self-evident. Most *hapax legomena* and Phoenician technical terms are concentrated in it. The chapter starts out by stating Tyre's economic importance as "the merchant of the nations" (רכלת העמים), "dwelling on the seaports (ישבתי על־מבואת ים)," and attributing her prosperity to the fact that "her boundaries are in the heart of the seas" (בלב ימים גבוליך) (v. 3). A full description of Tyre's splendor and glory manifested in the materials employed in building her follows (vv. 5-7). Tyre's preeminence in trade is then stated (v. 9) and her worldwide net of trading partners and luxury products listed (vv. 12-25). The sudden, unexpected wreck of the Tyrian ship shows the scope and economic significance of the disaster (26-32a). The subsequent lamentation over Tyre's past glory underscores the motivation for the nations' lament and is an indication of the economic character of the unit: all the nations have enriched and profited from Tyre's commercial success (vv. 26-36).

The final section of the Tyrian oracles in chapter 28 is an apt culmination to the entire series of oracles. It reveals that Tyre's prosperity was the result of deliberate and official royal policy (vv. 4-5). The account places the prince/king of Tyre in Eden, a utopian realm of prosperity, luxury, splendor, and joy. There, all kinds of precious stones were his "covering" (מסכתך) (v. 13a). He is depicted as a paradigm of prosperity, opulence, and wealth. Nevertheless, a careful reading of the two oracles in chapter 28 makes the economic grounds for Tyre's condemnation come to the fore. They indicate that Tyre's prosperity (the king of Tyre represents the city) was the result of "wickedness" and "violent deeds of injustice" (עולתה) (v. 15). Tyre's "trade" or "trading policies" (רכלתך) (vv. 16a, 18a) had enabled her to partake in the Assyrian oppression, to establish alliances with Egypt and Babylon, to enter into trade partnerships with the Philistines, to entertain economic relations with Edom, to have a share in the lucrative Arabian trade, and to extend her commercial influence. In fact, through her trading and commercial policies, Tyre had managed to control the trade routes and the metal and horse trade, two vital sectors for the Judean economy, and to curb Judah's access to them. But this economic success came with a price. Tyre had filled herself with "violence" and "lawless gain" (חמס) (v. 16a). In pursuing economic success and "beaming splendor" (יפעתך), she corrupted (שחת) her business acumen (חכמתך) (v. 17a) and even profaned (חללת) her own temple (מקדשיך) (v. 18a). As we have seen, Phoenician trade in the west began under the aegis of Melkart, the Tyrian city god, and most Tyrian foundations in the Mediterranean were linked to a temple, which, in most cases was dedicated to Melkart. The temple had a share, a tenth part of the profits of trade, in the benefits of Tyrian maritime trade as well. It is in light of these facts that the sentence in 18a "by all your iniquities, in the wickedness of your trade, you profaned your sanctuary" (מרב עוניך בעול רכלתך חללת מקדשיך) is to be understood.

The Tyrian oracles reveal a political dimension to Tyre's "terror" (חתיתם) (Ez. 26:17). Tyrian colonies paid a tribute to the Tyrian ruler, Tyre organized military campaigns against rebellious colonies, and a *sukin*, carried out the administration and judicature of the Cyprian colony. The description of the ship Tyre in Ez. 27:8-11 proves that economic supremacy and political dominion went hand in hand and demonstrates Tyre's political superiority over the other Phoenician cities. Historical data, to a certain extent, confirms this situation. The very fact that Tyre was strong enough to withstand the Babylonians for thirteen years shows the strength of her army, navy, and fortifications.

The conclusion of chapter 4 dates the Tyrian oracles to the period between 600 and 586 BCE on both literary and historical grounds. Ez. 26:2 refers to the desolation and ruin that followed the destruction of the main Philistine ports in the early years of the 6th century. Tyre considered that this trade vacuum in the Philistine coast represented a golden opportunity for her. Trade, she thought, would be shifted to the north, to her own ports. This trade shift would ruin the economy of the tiny Judean state.

On historical grounds, the archaeological data shows that the Tyrian expansion in the West Mediterranean continued until the beginning of the 6th century BCE when most Phoenician settlements in the Iberian Peninsula and elsewhere suffered a deep economic crisis. All Phoenician activities in Riotinto and Gadir came to a halt in the years 600-580 BCE. The process culminated with the abandonment of the Phoenician settlements around 580-550 BCE and with the transition

from the Phoenician to the Punic phases that took place in 550 BCE. At
about the same time (c. 580 BCE), the import of Phoenician luxury
products stopped suddenly in the Italian Peninsula, a similar process was
observable in Carthage.

The archaeological record thus points to the decade 580 and 570
BCE as the *terminus ad quem* for the major shift of trade from Tyre to
Carthage. This is the main historical argument in support of dating the
oracles to Ezekiel's time. A more precise dating of the oracles on
historical grounds is not possible. However textual and historical
evidence shows that Nebuchadnezzar's siege of Tyre took place between
c. 588/7 and c. 573 and the literary analysis of Ez. 26:2 in correlation
with the Neo-Babylonian Chronicles and the archaeological record
points to a dating to the period immediately after 600. Both on literary
and historical grounds, we can allocate the oracles to Ezekiel's time in
the period between 599 and 573.

Bibliography

Aberbach, D.
   1993   *Imperialism and Biblical Prophecy.* New York: Rouledge.

Ackroyd, P. R.
   1968   *Exile and Restoration: A Study of Hebrew Thought of the Sixth Century B.C.* OTL. Philadelphia: Westminster.

Aharoni, Y.
   1979   "The Negeb and the Southern Borders." In *World History of the Jewish People.* Vol. 4/2. *The Age of the Monarchies: Culture and Society,* ed. A. Malamat, 290-307. Jerusalem: Massada.
   1981   *Arad Inscriptions.* Jerusalem: Israel Exploration Society.

Ahituv, S. and B. A. Levine, eds.
   1986   *The Early Biblical Period.* Jerusalem: Israel Exploration Society.

Ahlström, G. W.
   1971   *Joel and the Temple Cult of Jerusalem.* Leiden: Brill.
   1993   *The History of Ancient Palestine,* ed. D. Edelman. Minneapolis: Fortress.

Albright, W. F.
   1932   "Seal of Eliakim and the Latest Preexilic History of Judah." *JBL* 51: 77-106.
   1941   "New Light on the Early History of Phoenician Colonization." *BASOR* 83: 14-22.

Allen, M. J.
   1997   *Contested Peripheries: Philistia in the Neo-Assyrian World-System.* University of California at Los Angeles, Ph.D. dissertation, unpublished.

Althann, R.
   1992a   "Gedaliah." *ABD,* ed. D. N. Freedman, 2:925-26. New York: Doubleday.
   1992b   "Josiah." *ABD,* ed. D. N. Freedman, 3:1015-18. New York: Doubleday.

Alvar, J.
 1982 "Aportaciones al estudio del Tarshish bíblico." *RSF* 10:
  211-30.
Alvar, J. C. Martínez Maza, and M. Romero.
 1995 "Cartago versus Tartesos. Un problema histórico y un
  debate historiográfico." In *Atti del III Congresso
  internazionale di studi fenici e punici*, 3.I.60-70. Tunis:
  Institut National du Patrimoine.
Amadasi Guzzo, M. G.
 1993 "Osservazioni sulle stele iscritte di Tiro." *RSF* 21: 157-63.
Amadasi Guzzo, M. G. et al., eds.
 1992 *Dizionario della civiltà fenicia*. Rome: Gremese.
Andersen, F. I. and D. N. Freedman.
 1989 Amos: A New Translation with Introduction and
  Commentary. AB 24A. New York: Doubleday.
Anderson, B. W.
 1984 *Creation in the Old Testament*. IRT 6, ed. B. W.
  Anderson. Philadelphia/London: Fortress/SPCK.
Arcari, E.
 1990 "La politica estera di Nabucodonosor in Siria-Palestina."
  RSF 17: 159-72.
Aristotle.
 1936 *Minor Works*. Trans W. S. Hett. Loeb Classical Library
  Cambridge: Harvard University Press.
Arrian.
 1949-54 *Anabasis*. Trans. E. I. Robson. Loeb Classical Library.
  Cambridge: Harvard University Press.
Asher, A. H. E.
 1996 *Judah and her Neighbours in the Seventh Century BCE*.
  Ph.D. dissertation, University of South Africa,
  unpublished.
Aubet, M. E.
 1988 "Spain." In *TP*, ed. S. Moscati, 226-42. New York:
  Abbeville.
 1993 *Phoenicians and the West: Politics, Colonies and Trade*.
  Trans. M. Turton. Cambridge: Cambridge University
  Press.

1996   "Notas sobre arqueología funeraria fenicia en Andalucía."
            In *Alle soglie della classicità il Mediterraneo tra
            tradizione e innovazione*, ed. E. Acquaro, 2.497-508. Pisa
            – Rome: Istituti editoriali e poligrafici internazionali.

Avienus, Rufus Fustus.
1977   *Ora Maritima*. Trans. J. P. Murphy. Chicago: Ares.

Avigad, N.
1975   "Jerusalem, the Jewish Quarter of the Old City, 1975."
            IEJ 25: 260-61.

1978   "חותמו של שריהו בן נריהו." *EI* 14 (1978): 86-87

1983   *Discovering Jerusalem*. Nashville: Thomas Nelson.

Avigad, N. and J. C. Greenfield.
1982   "A Bronze *phiale* with a Phoenician Dedicatory
            Inscription." *IEJ* 32: 118-28.

Avigad, N. and B. Sass.
1997   *Corpus of West Semitic Stamp Seals*. Jerusalem: The
            Israel Academy of Sciences and Humanities – The Israel
            Exploration Society – The Institute of Archaeology - The
            Hebrew University Press.

Bachmann, H. G.
1993   "The Archaeometallurgy of Silver." In *Archeologia delle
            attività estrattive e metallurgiche. V ciclo di lezioni sulla
            ricerca applicata in archeologiacertosa di pontignano
            (SI) – Campiglia Marittima (LI), 9-21 settembre 1991*, ed.
            R. Francovich, 487-95. Siena: Quaderni del Dipartimento
            di Archeologia e Storia delle Arti Sezione Archeologia,
            Università di Siena.

Baker, D. W.
1992   "Ophir." *ABD*, ed. D. N. Freedman, 5:26-27. New York:
            Doubleday.

Balmuth, M. S., ed.
2001   *Hacksilver to Coinage: New Insights into the Monetary
            History of the Near East and Greece*. Numismatic Studies
            24. New York: The American Numismatic Society.

Barag, D.
1963   "A Survey of Pottery Recovered from the Sea off the
            Coast of Israel." *IEJ* 13: 13-19.

1982-83   "Tyrian Currency in Galilee." *INJ* 6-7: 7-13.
1985   "Phoenician Stone Vessels from the Eighth-Seventh Centuries BCE." *EI* 18 (Avigad Volume): 215-32.

Barnett, R. D.
1982   *Ancient Ivories in the Middle East.* Qedem 14. Jerusalem: The Hebrew University Press.
1978   "Phoenicia and the Ivory Trade." *BASOR* 229: 87-97.
1980   "Phrygia and the Peoples of Anatolia in the Iron Age." In *CAH*, 2nd ed. Vol. 2, part 2. *History of the Middle East and the Aegean Region c. 1380-1000 B.C.*, eds. I. E. S. Edwards et al., 417-27. Cambridge: Cambridge University Press.

Bartlett, J. R.
1982   "Edom and the Fall of Jerusalem, 587 B.C." *PEQ* 114: 13-23.
1992   "Edom." *ABD*, ed. D. N. Freedman, 2:292-93. New York: Doubleday.

Bartoloni, P.
1988a   "Ships and Navigation." In *TP*, ed. S. Moscati, 72-77. New York: Abbeville.
1988b   "Commerce and Industry." In *TP*, ed. S. Moscati, 78-86. New York: Abbeville.
1993   "Considerazioni sul 'tofet' di Tiro." *RSF* 21: 153-56.
1995a   "Navires et navigation." In *CPP*, ed. V. Krings, 282-89. Leiden: Brill.
1995b   "Techniques et sciences." In *CPP*, ed. V. Krings, 354-61. Leiden: Brill.
1996   "Appunti sulla ceramica fenicia tra Oriente e Occidente dall'VIII al VI sec. A.C." *Transeuphratène* 12: 85-95.

Barton, J.
1980   *Amos's Oracles against the Nations. A Study of Amos 1.3-2.5.* Cambridge: Cambridge University Press.

Baslez, M. F.
1987   "Le rôle et la place des Phéniciens dans la vie économique des ports de l'Égée." In *Phoenicia and the East Mediterranean in the First Millennium B.C.* SP 5, ed. E. Lipiński, 267-85. Leuven: Uitgeverij Peeters.

1992 "Ivoires." In *DCPP*, ed. E. Lipiński, 233-37. Paris: Brepols.

Baurain, C. I. and A. Destrooper-Georgiades.
 1995 "Chypre." In *CPP*, ed. V. Krings, 597-631. Leiden: Brill.

Beit-Arieh, I.
 1996 "Edomites Advance into Judah." *BAR* 22 (1996): 28-36.

Ben Abed, F.
 1995 "Les Phéniciens dans la peninsule iberique." In *Atti del III Congresso internazionale di studi fenici e punici*, 3.I.109-22. Tunis: Institut National du Patrimoine.

Bentzen, A.
 1950 "The Ritual Background of Amos 1:2-2:16." *OTS* 8: 85-99.

Benz, F. L.
 1972 *Personal Names in the Phoenician and Punic Inscriptions*. Studia Pohl 8. Rome: Pontifical Biblical Institute.

Berridge, J. M.
 1992a "Jehoiachin." *ABD*, ed. D. N. Freedman, 3:661-63. New York: Doubleday.
 1992b "Jehoiakim." *ABD*, ed. D. N. Freedman, 3:664-65. New York: Doubleday.

Bickerman, E. J.
 1979-80 "Nebuchadnezzar and Jerusalem." *PAAJR* 46-47: 69-85.

Bierling, M. R., ed.
 2002 *The Phoenicians in Spain: An Archaeological Review of the Eighth-Sixth Centuries B.C.E. - A Collection of Articles Translated from Spanish*. Winoma Lake: Eisenbrauns.

Bikai, P. M.
 1978 *The Pottery of Tyre*. Warminster: Aris and Phillips.

Bikai, P. M.
 1991 *The Cedar of Lebanon: Archaeological and Dendrochronological Perspectives*. Ph.D. dissertation, University of California, Berkeley, unpublished.

Blanco, A. and J. M. Luzón.
  1969   "Pre-Roman Silver Miners at Riotinto." *Antiquity* 43: 124-31.
Blázquez, J. M.
  1975   *Tartessos y los orígenes de la colonización fenicia en Occidente*, 2nd ed. Salamanca: Universidad [Secretariado de Publicaciones e Intercambio Científico].
  1983   "Panorama general de la presencia fenicia y púnica en España." *Atti del I Congresso internazionale di studi fenici e punici*, 1.313-33. Rome: Consiglio nazionale delle ricerche.
Bloch-Smith, E.
  1992   *Judahite Burial Practices and Beliefs about the Dead.* JSOTSup 123. Sheffield: Sheffield Academic Press.
Block, D. I.
  1984   "'Israel' – 'Sons of Israel:' A Study in Hebrew Eponymic Usage." *SR* 13: 301-26.
  1997   *The Book of Ezekiel – Chapters 1-24*. Grand Rapids: William B. Eerdmans.
  1998   *The Book of Ezekiel – Chapters 25-48*. Grand Rapids: William B. Eerdmans.
Bloom, J. B.
  1988   *Material Remains of the Neo-Assyrian Presence in Palestine and Transjordan.* Ph.D. dissertation, Bry Mawr College, unpublished.
Boadt, L.
  1980   *Ezekiel's Oracles against Egypt: A Literary and Philological Study of Ezekiel 29-32.* BibOr 37. Rome: Pontifical Biblical Institute.
  1986   "Rhetorical Strategies in Ezekiel's Oracles of Judgment." In *Ezekiel and His Book: Textual and Literary Criticism and their Interrelation.* BETL 74, ed. J. Lust, 182-200. Leuven: Leuven University Press and Uitgeverij Peeters Leuven.
  1992   "Ezekiel, Book of." *ABD*, ed. D. N. Freedman, 2:711-22. New York: Doubleday.

Boardman, J. et al., eds.
  1982   *CAH*, 2nd ed. Vol. 3, part 3, *The Expansion of the Greek World, Eighth to Sixth Centuries B.C.* Cambridge: Cambridge University Press.
  1991   *CAH*, 2nd ed. Vol. 3, part 2, *The Assyrian and Babylonian Empires and Other States of the Near East, from the Eighth to the Sixth Centuries B.C.* Cambridge: Cambridge University Press.

Bondi, S. F.
  1990   "I Fenici in Erodoto." *Hérodote et les peuples non Grecs*, EAC 35. 250-300. Vandoeuvres – Genève: Fondation Hardt.
  1995   "Le commerce, les échanges, l'économie." In *CPP*, ed. V. Krings, 268-81. Leiden: Brill.

Bongenaar, A. C. V. M.
  1999   "Money in the Neo-Babylonian Institutions." In *Trade and Finance in Ancient Mesopotamia*, ed. J. G. Dercksen, 159-74. Leiden – Istanbul: Nederlands Historisch-Archaeologisch Instituut and te Istanbul.

Bonnet, C.
  1988   *Melqart. Cultes et mythes de l'Héraclès Tyrien en Méditerranée.* SP 8. Leuven: Uitgeverij Peeters – Presses Universitaires de Namur.

Bordreuil, P.
  1992   "Phoceens." In *DCPP*, ed. E. Lipiński, 353. Paris: Brepols.

Bosch Gimper, P.
  1952   "Problemas de la historia fenicia en el extremo Occidente." *Zephyrus* 3: 15-30.

Botterweck, G. and H. Ringgren, eds.,
  1974-   *Theological Dictionary of the Old Testament.* 10 vols. Trans. D. E. Green. Grand Rapids: William B. Eerdmans.

Braun, T. F. R. G.
  1982a   "The Greeks in the Near East." In *CAH*, 2nd ed. Vol. 3, part 3, *The Expansion of the Greek World, Eighth to Sixth Centuries B.C.*, eds. J. A. Boardman et al., 1-31. Cambridge: Cambridge University Press.

1982b   "The Greeks in Egypt." In *CAH*, 2nd ed. Vol. 3, part 3, *The Expansion of the Greek World, Eighth to Sixth Centuries B.C.*, eds. J. A. Boardman et al., 32-56, Cambridge: Cambridge University Press.

Breasted, J. H.
1962   *Ancient Records of Egypt; Historical Documents from the Earliest Times to the Persian Conquest.* 5 vols. Reprint. New York: Russell and Russell.

Briant, P.
1998   *A History of the Persian Empire.* Winoma Lake: Eisenbrauns.

Bright, J.
1965   *Jeremiah.* AB 21. Garden City: Doubleday.

Briquel-Chatonnet, F.
1992   *Les relations entre les cités de la côte phénicienne et les royaumes d'Israël et de Juda.* SP 12. Leuven: Uitgeverij Peeters and Departement Oriëntalistiek.

1995   "Syro-Palestine et Jordanie." In *CPP*, ed. V. Krings, 583-96. Leiden: Brill.

Broshi, M.
1974   "The Expansion of Jerusalem in the Reigns of Hezekiah and Manasseh." *IEJ* 24: 21-26.

Brown, F., S. R. Driver, and C. A. Briggs.
1979   *The New Brown – Driver – Briggs – Gesenius Hebrew and English Lexicon.* Peabody: Hendrickson.

Buhl, F.
1890   *Die sozialen Vehältnisse der Israeliten.* Berlin: Reuter.

Bunnens, G.
1978   "La mission d'Ounamon en Phénicie. Point de vue d'un non-égyptologue." *RSF* 6: 1-16.

1979   *L'expansion phénicienne en Méditerranée. Essai d'interprétation fondé sur une analyse des traditions littéraires.* Brussels – Rome: Institut Historique Belge de Rome.

1983   "Tyre et la mer." In *Redt Tyrus / Sauvons Tyr.* SP 1, eds. E. Gubel et al., 7-21. Leuven: Uitgeverij Peeters.

1985   "Le luxe phénicien d'après les inscriptions royales assyriennes." In *Phoenicia and its Neighbours*. SP 3, eds. E. Gubel and E. Lipiński, 121-33. Leuven: Uitgeverij Peeters.

1986   "Aspects religieux de l'expansion phénicienne." In *Religio Phoenicia.* SP 4, eds. C. Bonnet et al., 205-30. Namur.

1995   "L'histoire événementielle *partim* Orient." In *CPP*, ed. V. Krings, 222-36. Leiden: Brill.

Buttrick, G. A., ed.
1962   *The Interpreter's Dictionary of the Bible.* 4 vols. Nashville: Abingdon.

Cahill, J. M. and D. Tarler.
1994   "Excavations Directed by Yigal Shiloh at the City of David, 1978-1985." In *Ancient Jerusalem Revealed*, ed. H. Geva, 31-45. Jerusalem: Israel Exploration Society.

Callender, D. E.
1995   *The Significance and Use of Primal Man Traditions in Ancient Israel.* Ph.D. dissertation, Harvard University.

2000   *Adam in Myth and History: Ancient Israelite Perspectives on the Primal Human.* Winoma Lake: Eisenbrauns.

Carrol-Spillecke, M., ed.
1992   *Der Garten von der Antike bis zum Mittelalter.* Kulturgeschichte der antiken Welt 57. Mainz am Rhein: Philipp von Zabern.

Carter, C.
1999   *The Emergence of Yehud in the Persian Period: A Social and Demographic Study.* JSOTSup 294. Sheffield: Sheffield Academic Press.

Carter, J. B.
1984   *Greek Ivory-Carving in the Orientalizing and Archaic Periods.* Ph.D. dissertation, Harvard University, unpublished.

Cary, M.
1932   "Les Sources of Silver for the Greek World." In *Mélanges Gustave Glotz*, 133-42. Paris: Les Presses Universitaires de France.

Casson, L.
>   1959   *The Ancient Mariners, Seafarers and Sea Fighters of the Mediterranean in Ancient Times*. New York: The Macmillan Company.

Cazelles, H.
>   1977   "L'arrière-plan historique d'Amos 1.9-10." In *VIth Congress of Jewish Studies*, 1.71-76. Jerusalem: The World Union of Jewish Studies.
>   1981   "La vie de Jérémie dans son contexte national et international." In *Le Livre de Jérémie*. BETL 54, ed. P. M. Bogaert, 21-39. Leuven: Uitgeverij Peeters.

Cecchini, S. M.
>   1995   "L'art. Ivoirerie." In *CPP*, ed. V. Krings, 516-26. Leiden: Brill.

Chamorro, J. G.
>   1987   "Survey of Archaeological Research on Tartessos." *AJA* 91: 197-232.

Chazan, R., W. W. Hallo, and L. H. Schiffman, eds.
>   1999   *Ki Baruch Hu: Ancient Near Eastern, Biblical, and Judaic Studies in Honor of Baruch A. Levine*. Winoma Lake: Eisenbrauns.

Chiera, G.
>   1986   "Is. 23: L'elegia su Tiro." *RSF* 14: 3-19.

Ciasca, A.
>   1988   "Phoenicia." In *TP*, ed. S. Moscati, 140-51. New York: Abbeville.
>   1995   "La ceramologie." In *CPP*, ed. V. Krings, 137-47. Leiden: Brill.

Clifford, R. J.
>   1971   *The Cosmic Mountain in Canaan and the Old Testament*. HSM 4. Cambridge: Harvard University Press.

Clifford, R. J. and J. J. Collins, eds.
>   1992   *Creation in the Biblical Traditions*. CBQMS 24. Washington: Catholic Biblical Association of America.

Cogan, M.
   1974   *Imperialism and Religion: Assyria, Judah, and Israel in the Eighth and Seventh centuries B.C.E.* SBLMS 19. Missoula: Scholars.

Cogan, M. and H. Tadmor.
   1988   *II Kings*. AB 11. New York. Doubleday.

Cohen, H. R.
   1978   *Biblical Hapax Legomena in the Light of Akkadian and Ugaritic.* SBLDS 37. Missoula: Scholars.

Cole, S. W.
   1996   *Nippur in Late Assyrian Times, c. 755-612 B.C.* SAAS 5, Helsinki: Neo-Assyrian Text Corpus Project.

Colombier, A. M.
   1987   "Céramique grecque et échanges en Méditerranée orientale: Chypre et la côte syro-palestinienne (fin VIIIe-fin IVe siècles av. J.-C.)." In *Phoenicia and the East Mediterranean in the First Millenium.* SP 5, ed. E. Lipiński, 239-48. Leuven: Uitgeverij Peeters.

Cook, S. L.
   1999   "Creation Archetypes and Mythogems in Ezekiel: Significance and Theological Ramifications." In SBLSPS 38: 123-46.

Cooke, G. A.
   1936   *A Critical and Exegetical Commentary on the Book of Ezekiel.* Edinburg: T. and T. Clark.

Cowley, A.
   1992   *Aramaic Papyri of the Fifth Century B.C.* Oxford: Oxford University Press.

Cross, F. M. and D. N. Freedman.
   1953   "Josiah's Revolt against Assyria." *JNES* 12: 56-58.

Crowfoot, J. W. and J. M. Crowfoot.
   1938   *Early Ivories from Samaria.* London: Palestine Exploration Fund.

Culican, W.
   1966   *The First Merchant Venturers: The Ancient Levant in History and Commerce.* London: McGraw-Hill.

1970   "Phoenician Oil Bottles and Tripod Bowls." *Berytus* 19: 5-16.

1991   "Phoenicia and Phoenician Colonization." In *CAH*, 2nd ed. Vol. 3, part 2, *The Assyrian and Babylonian Empires and Other States of the Near East, from the Eighth to the Sixth Centuries B.C.*, eds. J. A. Boardman et al., 461-546. Cambridge: Cambridge University Press.

Curtis, J., ed.
1988   *Bronzeworking Centers of Western Asia c. 1000-539 BC.* London: Kegan Paul International.

D'Agostino, F.
1996   "Da Neriglissar a Nabonedo e oltre (considerazioni sulla storia economica neo-babilonese)." In *Alle soglie della classicità il Mediterraneo tra tradizione e innovazione,* ed. E. Acquaro, 1.117-27. Pisa – Rome: Istituti editoriali e poligrafici internazionali.

Danker, F. W.
1992   "Purple." *ABD*, ed. D. N. Freedman, 5:557-60. New York: Doubleday.

Darnell, J. C.
1992   "The *Knb.wt* Vessels of the Late Period." In *Life in a Multi-Cultural Society: Egypt from Cambises to Constantine and beyond.* SAOC 51, ed. J. H. Johnson, 67-89. Chicago: Oriental Institute of the University of Chicago.

Davis, E. F.
1989   *Swallowing the Scroll: Textuality and the Dynamics of Discourse in Ezekiel's Prophecy.* JSOTSup 78. Sheffield: Sheffield Academic Press and Almond.

Debergh, J.
1988   "Index des Studia Phoenicia I-VI." In *Carthage.* SP 6, ed. E. Lipiński, 259-80. Leuven: Uitgeverij Peeters.

Delavault, B. and A. Lemaire.
1979   "Les Inscriptions Phéniciennes de Palestine." *RSF* 7: 1-39.

Demsky, A.
1997 "The Name of the Goddess of Ekron: A New Reading."
   JANES 25: 1-5.
1998 "Discovering a Goddess: A New Look at the Ekron
   Inscription Identifies Mysterious Deity." *BAR* 24: 53-58.

Dercksen, J. G., ed.
1999 *Trade and Finance in Ancient Mesopotamia. Proceedings*
   of the First MOS Symposium. Nederlands – Istanbul:
   Nederlands Historisch-Archaeologisch Instituut and te
   Istanbul.

De Spens, R.
1998 "Droit internationale et commerce au début de la XXIe
   dynastie. Analyse juridique du rapport d'Ounamon." In
   Le commerce en Égypte ancienne. BdÉ 121, eds. N.
   Grimal and B. Menu, 105-26. Cairo: Institut Français
   d'Archéologie Orientale.

Deutsch, R.
1999 "Seal of Ba'alis Surfaces." *BAR* 25 (1999): 46-49.

Dever, W. G.
1984 "Asherah, Consort of Yahweh? New Evidence from
   Kuntillet 'Ajrud. *BASOR* 255: 21-37.
1995 "Social Structure in Palestine in the Iron II Period on the
   Eve of Destruction." In *The Archaeology of Society in the*
   Holy Land, ed. T. E. Levy, 416-31. New York: Acts on
   File.

Diakonoff, I. M.
1969 "Main Features of the Economy in the Monarchies of
   Ancient Western Asia." In *Third International*
   Conference of Economic History Munich 1965, 13-32.
   Paris: Mouton.
1992 "The Naval Power and Trade of Tyre." *IEJ* 42: 168-93.

Dicou, B.
1994 *Edom, Israel's Brother and Antagonist: The Role of Edom*
   in Biblical Prophecy and Story. JSOTSup 169. Sheffield:
   Sheffield Academic Press.

Dícs Cusi, E.
    1994   *Phoenician Architecture in the Iberian Peninsula and its Influence on Indigenous Cultures.* Ph.D. dissertation, Universitat de Valencia (Spain), unpublished.

Diodorus of Sicily.
    1933 67 *Bibliothooa Historioa.* Trano. C. H. Oldfather. Loeb Classical Library. Cambridge: Harvard University Press.

Dornemann, R. H.
    1983   *The Archaeology of the Transjordan in the Bronze and Iron Ages.* Milwaukee: Milwaukee Public Museum.
    1997   "Amman." In *Oxford Encyclopedia of Archaeology in the Near East,* ed. E. Meyers, 1.98-102. Oxford: Oxford University Press.

Dothan, M.
    1992   "Ashdod." *ABD,* ed. D. N. Freedman, 1:477-82. New York: Doubleday.

Dothan, T. and S. Gitin.
    1992   "Ekron." *ABD,* ed. D. N. Freedman, 2:415-22. New York: Doubleday.

Dougherty, R. P.
    1923   *Archives from Erech, Time of Nebuchadnezzar and Nabonidus.* New Haven: Yale University Press.

Drioton, E. and J. Vandrier.
    1938   *L'Égypte.* Paris: Les Presses Universitaires de France.

Driver, G. R.
    1950   "Difficult Words in the Hebrew Prophets." In *Studies in Old Testament Prophecy,* ed. H. H. Rowley, 52-72. Edinburgh: Clark.

Dussaud, R.
    1946-48 "Melqart." *Syria* 25: 205-30.

Edens, C. and G. Bawden.
    1989   "History of Tayma' and Hejazi Trade during the first millenium BC." *JESHO* 32: 48-103.

Egberts, A.
    1991   "The Chronology of *The Report of Wenamun.*" *JEA* 77: 57-67.

BIBLIOGRAPHY 193

1998 "Hard Times: The Chronology of 'The Report of Wenamun' Revised." *ZÄS* 125: 93-108.

Eichrodt, W.
1979 *Ezekiel, A Commentary.* Trans. C. Quin. OTL. Philadelphia: Westminster.

Eissfeldt, O.
1933 "Das Datum der Belagerung von Tyrus durch Nebukadnezzar." *Forschungen und Fortschritte (= Kleine Schrift* II, 1-3) 9: 421-22.

Eitan, A.
1994 "Rare Sword of the Israelite Period Found at Vered Jericho." *Israel Museum Journal* 12: 61-62.

Eitam D. and A. Shomroni.
1987 "Research of the Oil-Industry During the Iron Age at Tel Miqne." In *Olive Oil in Antiquity*, eds. M. Heltzer and D. Eitam, 37-56. Haifa: University of Haifa Press.

Elat, M.
1971 *Tribute and Booty in the Economies of the Countries of the Near East in the Time of the Kingdom of Israel.* Ph.D. dissertation, Hebrew University, unpublished (Hebrew).
1977 *Economic Relations in the Lands of the Bible c. 1000-539 B.C.E.* Jerusalem: Bialik (Hebrew).
1978 "The Economic Relations of the Neo-Assyrian Empire with Egypt." *JAOS* 98: 20-34.
1979a "Trade and Commerce." In *World History of the Jewish People.* Vol. 4/2, *The Age of the Monarchies: Culture and Society*, ed. A. Malamat, 173-86. Jerusalem: Jewish History Publications – Massada.
1979b "The Monarchy and the Development of Trade in Ancient Israel." In *State and Temple Economy in the Ancient Near East.* OLA 5, ed. E. Lipiński, 2.527-46. Leuven: Departement Oriëntalistiek.
1982 "The Impact of Tribute and Booty on Countries and People within the Assyrian Empire." *Archiv für Orientforschung* 18: 244-51.
1983 "The Iron Export from Uzal (Ezekiel XXVII 19)." *VT* 33: 323-30.

1991   "Phoenician Overland Trade within the Mesopotamian
            Empires." In *Ah Assyria...Studies in Assyrian History and
            Ancient Near Eastern Historiography Presented to Hayim
            Tadmor*. SH 33, eds. M. Cogan and I. Eph'al, 21-35.
            Jerusalem: Magnes and The Hebrew University Press.

Elayi, J.
1978   "L'essor de la Phénicie et le passage de la domination
            assyro-babylonienne à la domination perse." *Baghdader
            Mitteilungen* 9: 25-38.

1987   *Recherches sur les cités phéniciennes à l'époque Perse*.
            Supplemento n. 51 agli Annali, vol. 47.2. Naples: Istituto
            Universitario Orientale.

1988   "L'exploitation des cèdres du Mont Liban par les rois
            assyriens et néo-babyloniens." *JESHO* 31: 14-41.

Elayi, J. and G. Bunnens.
1992   "Bois." In *DCPP*, ed. E. Lipiński, 76. Paris: Brepols.

Elayi, J. and J. Sapin.
1998   *Beyond the River: New Perspectives on Transeuphratene*.
            Trans. J. Edward Crowley. Sheffield: Sheffield Academic
            Press.

Elliger, K. and W. Rudolph, eds.
1984   *Biblia Hebraica Stuttgartensia*. Stuttgart: Deutsche
            Bibelgessellschaft.

Emery, A. C.
1998   *Weapons of the Israelite Monarchy: A Catalogue with Its
            Linguistic and Cross-Cultural Implications*. Ph.D.
            dissertation, Harvard University, unpublished.

Emerton, J. A.
1982   "New Light on Israelite Religion: The Implications of the
            Inscription from Kuntillet 'Ajrud." *ZAS* 94: 2-20.

Eph'al, I.
1979a   "Assyrian Dominion in Palestine." In *World History of
            the Jewish People*. Vol. 4/1, *The Age of the Monarchies:
            Political History*, ed. A. Malamat, 276-89, Jerusalem:
            Massada.

1979b   "The Western Minorities in Babylonia in the 6th-5th
          Centuries B.C.: Maintenance and Cohesion." *Or* 47: 74-
          90.
1982   *The Ancient Arabs. Nomads on the Borders of the Fertile
          Crescent 9th-5th Centuries B.C.* Leiden: Brill.
Even-Shoshan, A.
1989   *A New Concordance of the Bible.* Jerusalem: "Kyriat
          Sefer" (Hebrew).
Fantar, M.
1988   "L'impact de la présence phénicienne et de la fondation
          de Carthage en Méditerranée occidentale." In *Carthago*.
          SP 6, ed. E. Lipiński, 3-14. Leuven: Uitgeverij Peeters.
Fechter, F.
1992   *Bewältigung der Katastrophe: Untersuchungen zu
          ausgewählten Fremdvölkersprüchen im Ezechielbuch.*
          BZAW 208. Berlin: de Gruyter.
Ferjaoui, A.
1993   *Recherches sur les relations entre l'Orient phénicien et
          Carthage.* OBO 124. Fribourg – Göttingen – Carthage:
          Vandenhoeck and Ruprecht.
Fernández-Miranda, M.
1991   "Tartessos: indígenas, fenicios y griegos en Huelva." In
          *Atti del II Congresso internazionale di studi fenici e
          punici*, 2.87-96. Rome: Consiglio nazionale delle ricerche.
Fernández Uriel, P.
1995   "Algunas consideraciones sobre la púrpura: su expansión
          por el lejano occidente." In *Atti del III Congresso
          internazionale di studi fenici e punici*, 3.II.39-53. Tunis:
          Institut National du Patrimoine.
Finegan, J.
1950   "The Chronology of Ezekiel." *JBL* 64: 61-66.
1998   *Handbook of Biblical Chronology.* Peabody:
          Hendrickson.
Finkelstein, I.
1988   *The Archaeology of the Israelite Settlement.* Jerusalem:
          Israel Exploration Society.

1992   "Ḥorvat Qitmit and the Southern Trade in the Late Iron Age II." *ZDPV* 108: 156-70.

1995   *Living on the Fringe: The Archaeology and History of the Negev, Sinai, and Neighbouring Regions in the Bronze and Iron Ages*. MMA 6. Sheffield: Sheffield Academic Press.

Finkelstein, I., ed.

1993   *Shiloh: The Archaeology of a Biblical Site*. MSIATAU 10. Jerusalem: The Institute of Archaeology of Tel Aviv University.

Finkelstein, I. and Z. Lederman, eds.

1997   *Highlands of Many Cultures: The Southern Samaria Survey: The Sites*. Tel Aviv: The Institute of Archaeology of Tel Aviv University.

Fisher, J. R.

1998   *Ammon (עמוני / עמון) in the Hebrew Bible: A Textual Analysis and Archaeological Context of Selected References to the Ammonites of Transjordan*. Ph.D. dissertation, Andrews University, unpublished.

Fleming, W.

1915   *Tyre: The History of Tyre*. New York: Columbia University Press.

Forbes, R. J.

1971-72 *Studies in Ancient Technology*. Vols. 8-9. Leiden: Brill.

Frankenstein, S.

1979   "The Phoenicians in the Far West: A Function of Neo-Assyrian Imperialism." In *Power and Propaganda: A Symposium on Ancient Empires*, ed. M. T. Larsen. 263-94. Copenhagen: Akademisk Forlag.

Freedman, D. N., ed.

1992   *The Anchor Bible Dictionary*. 6 vols. New York: Doubleday.

Freedy, K. S. and D. B. Redford.

1970   "The Dates in Ezekiel in Relation to Biblical Babylonian, and Egyptian Sources." *JAOS* 90: 462-85.

Fretz, M. J.
  1992   "Weapons and Implements of Warfare." *ABD*, ed. D. N.
            Freedman, 6:893-95. New York: Doubleday.
Friedrich, J., W. Röllig, M. G. Amadasi Guzzo, and W. R. Mayer.
  1999   *Phönizisch-punische Grammatik*, 3rd ed. Rome: Pontifical
            Biblical Institute.
Gale N. H.
  1989   "Lead Isotope Analyses Applied to Provenance Studies –
            A Brief Review." In *Archaeometry. Proceedings of the
            25th International Symposium*, ed. Y. Maniatis, 469-503.
            Amsterdam: Elsevier.
Gallagher, W. R.
  1999   *Sennacherib's Campaign to Judah: New Studies*. Leiden:
            Brill.
Garbini, G.
  1980   *I Fenici. Storia e religione*. Naples: Istituto Universitario
            Orientale.
  1993   "Iscrizioni funerarie da Tiro." *RSF* 21: 3-6.
Gardiner, A. H.
  1961   *Egypt of the Pharaohs, an introduction*. Oxford:
            Clarendon.
Gesenius, H. W. F.
  1984   *Gesenius' Hebrew and Chaldee Lexicon to the Old
            Testament*. Reprint. Grand Rapids: Baker.
Geva, S.
  1982   "Archaeological Evidence for the Trade Between Israel
            and Tyre?" *BASOR* 248: 70-72.
Gibson, J. C. L.
  1971-82   *Textbook of Syrian Semitic Inscriptions*. 3 vols. Oxford:
            Oxford University Press.
Gill, D. W. J.
  1988   "Silver Anchors and Cargoes of Oil." *PBSR* 56: 1-12.
Ginsberg, H. L.
  1950   "Judah and the Transjordan States from 734 to 582
            B.C.E." In *A. Marx Jubilee Volume*, ed. S. Liberman,
            117-58. New York: Theology Seminary of America.

1987   "Urban and Growth Decline at Ekron in the Iron II
             Period." *BA* 50: 206-22.

Gitin, S.
   1989   "Tel Miqne-Ekron in the 7th c. BCE. City Plan
             Development." In *Olive Oil in Antiquity*, eds. M. Helzer
             and D. Eitam, 81-97. Haifa: University of Haifa Press.
   1990a   "Ekron of the Philistines. Part II: Olive-Oil Suppliers to
             the World." *BAR* 16: 33-42, 59.
   1990b   "The Effects of Urbanization on a Philistine City-State:
             Tel Miqne-Ekron in the Iron Age II Period." In
             *Proceedings of the Tenth World Congress of Jewish
             Studies*, 277-84. Jerusalem: The World Union of Jewish
             Studies.
   1996   "Royal Philistine Temple Inscription Found at Ekron." *BA*
             59: 101-02.

Gitin, S. and W. G. Dever.
   1989   *Recent Excavations in Israel: Studies in Iron Age
             Archaeology.* Winona Lake: Eisenbrauns.

Gitin, S., T. Dothan, and J. Naveh.
   1997   "A Royal Dedicatory Inscription from Ekron." *IEJ* 48: 1-
             18.

Glueck, N.
   1935   *Exploration in Eastern Palestine, II.* AASOR 15. New
             Haven: American Schools of Oriental Research.
   1959   *Rivers in the Desert a History of the Negev.* New York:
             Straus and Cudahy.
   1970   *The Other Side of Jordan.* Cambridge: American Schools
             of Oriental Research.

Goedicke, H.
   1975   *The Report of Wenamun.* Baltimore: Johns Hopkins
             University Press.

Gómez Bellard, C.
   1996   "Quelques réflexions sur les premiers établissements
             phéniciens à Ibiza." In *Alle soglie della classicità il
             Mediterraneo tra tradizione e innovazione*, ed. E.
             Acquaro, 2.763-79. Pisa – Rome: Istituti editoriali e
             poligrafici internazionali.

González-Wagner, C.
    1986   "Tartessos y las tradiciones literarias." *RSF* 14: 201-28.
Gosse, B.
    1986   "Le recueil d'oracles contre les nations d'Ézéchiel XXV-
                XXXII dans la rédaction du livre d'Ézéchiel." *RB*: 535-
                62.
    1993   "Le Psaume 83, Isaïe 62, 6-7 et la tradition des oracles
                contre les nations des livres d'Isaïe et d'Ézéchiel." *BN* 70:
                9-12.
Gowan, D. E.
    1964   *The Significance of the Oracles against the Nations in the
                Message of Ezekiel*. Ph.D. dissertation, the University of
                Chicago, unpublished.
    1971   "The Use of *ya'an* in Biblical Hebrew." *VT* 21: 168-85.
Gowen, H. H.
    1922   "Hebrew Trade and Trade Terms in Old Testament
                Times." *Journal of the American Oriental Research*, 6: 1-
                16.
Graham, A. J.
    1982a   "The colonial expansion of Greece." In *CAH*, 2nd ed. Vol.
                3, part 3, *The Expansion of the Greek World, Eighth to
                Sixth Centuries B.C.*, eds. A. Boardman et al., 83-162.
                Cambridge: Cambridge University Press.
    1982b   "The Western Greeks." In *CAH*, 2nd ed. Vol. 3, part 3, *The
                Expansion of the Greek World, Eighth to Sixth Centuries
                B.C.*, eds. A. Boardman et al., 163-95. Cambridge:
                Cambridge University Press.
Gran Aymerich, J. M. J.
    1983   "Malaga, ville phénicienne d'Espagne." *Archeologia,
                prehistoire et archeologie* 179: 39-40.
Gras, M., P. Rouillard, and J. Teixidor.
    1989   *L'Univers Phénicien*. Paris: Arthaud.
Grayson, A. K.
    1975   *Assyrian and Babylonian Chronicles*. Locust Valley: J. J.
                Augustin.
    1980   "Assyria and Babylonia." *Or.* 49: 140-94.

1991   "Assyria 668 635 B.C.: The Reign of Assurbanipal." In *CAH*, 2nd ed. Vol. 3, part 2, *The Assyrian and Babylonian Empires and Other States of the Near East, from the Eighth to the Sixth Centuries B.C.*, eds. J. A. Boardman et al., 144-61. Cambridge: Cambridge University Press.

Green, M.
1986a   "Wenamun's Demand for Compensation." *ZÄS* 113: 115-19.

1986b   "*m-k-m-r* und *w-r-k-t-r* in der Wenamun-Geschichte." *ZÄS* 113: 115-19.

Greenberg, M.
1957   "Ezekiel 17 and the Policy of Psammetichus II." *JBL* 76: 304-09.

1980   "The Vision of Jerusalem in Ezekiel 8-11: A Holistic Interpretation." In *The Divine Helmsman*, eds. J. Crenshaw and S. Sandmel, 143-63. New York: Ktav.

1983   *Ezekiel 1-20*. AB 22. New York: Doubleday.

1986   "What Are Valid Criteria for Determining Inauthentic Matter in Ezekiel?" In *Ezekiel and His Book: Textual and Literary Criticism and their Interrelation*. BETL 74, ed. J. Lust, 123-35. Leuven: Leuven University Press and Uitgeverij Peeters Leuven.

1997   *Ezekiel 21-37*. AB 22A. New York: Doubleday.

Griffith, F. L.
1909   *Catalogue of the Demotic Papyri in the John Rylands Library, Manchester, with facsimiles and complete translations*. 3 vols. Manchester – London: Manchester University Press and B. Quaritch.

Gubel, E.
1987   *Phoenician Furniture*. SP 7. Leuven: Uitgeverij Peeters.

1992   "Huile." In *DCPP*, ed. E. Lipiński, 221. Paris: Brepols.

Haag, H.
1980   "חמס." In *Theological Dictionary of the Old Testament*, eds. G. Botterweck and H. Ringgren, 4.478-87. Grand Rapids: William B. Eerdmans.

Hackett, J., ed.
   1989   *Warfare in the Ancient World.* New York: Sidgwick and
               Jackson.
Hallo, W. W.
   1980   "Biblical History in its Near Eastern Setting. The
               Contextual Approach." In *Scripture in Context: Essays on
               the Comparative Method.* Pittsburgh Theological
               Monograph Series 34, eds. C. D. Evans, W. W. Hallo, and
               J. B. White, 1-26. Pittsburgh: Pickwick.
   1982   "Nebuchadnezzar Comes to Jerusalem." In *Through the
               Sound of Many Voices. Writings Contributed on the
               Occasion of the 70th Anniversary of W. Gunther Plaut,* ed.
               J. W. Plaut, 40-57. Lester and Orpen Dennys.
   1990   "Compare and Contrast: The Contextual Approach to
               Biblical Literature." In *The Bible in Light of Cuneiform
               Literature; Scripture in Context III.* Ancient Near Eastern
               Texts and Studies 8, eds. W. W. Hallo, B. W. Jones, and
               G. L. Mattingly, 1-30. Lewiston: E. Mellen.
Hals, R. M.
   1989   *Ezekiel.* FOTL XIX. Grand Rapids: William B.
               Eerdmans.
Hamdeh, A.
   1985   *Die sozialen Strukturen im Phönizien des ersten
               Jahrtausends v. Chr.* Ph.D. dissertation, Würzburg
               University, unpublished.
Hanson, R. S.
   1980   *Tyrian Influence in the Upper Galilee.* Meiron excavation
               project 2. Cambridge: Cambridge University Press.
Haran, M.
   1968   "Observations On the Historic Background of Amos 1:2-
               2:6." *IEJ* 18: 201-13.
Harden, D.
   1962   *The Phoenicians.* New York: Frederick A. Praeger.
Har-El, M.
   1976   "The Valley of the Craftsmen (Ge' Haharašim)." *PEQ*
               109: 75-86.

Harper, R. P., ed.
    1892-1914 *Assyrian and Babylonian Letters Belonging to the Kouyounjik Collection of the British Museum.* 14 vols. London: British Museum.

Harris, Z. S.
    1936   *A Grammar of the Phoenician Language.* AOS 8. New Haven: American Oriental Society.

Hayes, J. H.
    1968   "The Usage of Oracles against Foreign Nations in Ancient Israel." *JBL* 87: 81-92.

Hayes, J. H. and J. M. Miller.
    1986   A History of Ancient Israel and Judah. Philadelphia: Westminster.

Heltzer, M. and D. Eitan, eds.
    1987   *Olive Oil in Antiquity.* Haifa: University of Haifa Press.

Herr, L. G.
    1999   "The Ammonites and Moabites in the Late Iron Age and Persian Period." In *Ancient Ammon.* Studies in the History and Culture of the Ancient Near East 17, eds. B. Macdonald and R. W. Younker, 219-37. Leiden: Brill.

Herrera, M. D.
    1992   "Galilée." In *DCPP*, ed. E. Lipiński, 184. Paris: Brepols.

Herzog, C. and M. Gichon.
    1997   *Battles of the Bible.* Mechanicsburg: Stackpole Books.

Hestrin, R. and M. Dayagi.
    1979   *Ancient Seals: First Temple Period. From the Collection of the Israel Museum.* Jerusalem: The Israel Museum.

Hiebert, T.
    1992   "Joel, book of." *ABD*, ed. D. N. Freedman, 3:873-80. New York: Doubleday.

Hobbs, T. R.
    1989   *A Time for War: A Study of Warfare in the Old Testament.* Wilmington: Michael Glazier.

Hoch, J. E.
    1994   *Semitic Words in Egyptian Texts of the New Kingdom and Third Intermediate Period.* Princeton: Princeton University Press.

Hoftijzer J. and K. Jongeling.
    1995   *Dictionary of the North-West Semitic Inscriptions*. 2 vols.
            HOS 2. Leiden: Brill.
Holladay, J. S.
    1986   *Jeremiah I.* Philadelphia: Fortress.
    1990   *Jeremiah II.* Minneapolis: Fortress.
    1992   "Maskhuta, Tell el-." *ABD*, ed. D. N. Freedman, 4:588-
            92. New York: Doubleday.
Homer.
    1992   *The Odyssey*. Trans. A. T. Murray. Loeb Classical
            Library. Cambridge: Harvard University Press.
    1999   *The Iliad*. Trans. A. T. Murray. Loeb Classical Library.
            Cambridge: Harvard University Press.
Homsky, M. and S. Moshkovitz.
    1976   "The Distribution of Different Wood Species of the Iron
            Age II at Tel Beer-Sheba." *TA* 3: 42-48.
Howie, C. G.
    1950   *The Date and Composition of Ezekiel*. JBLMS 4.
            Philadelphia: Society of Biblical Literature.
Hudson, M. and B. Levine, eds.
    1999   *Urbanization and Land Ownership in the Ancient Near
            East*. Vol. 2. Cambridge: Harvard University Press.
Huebner, U.
    1992   "Idumea." *ABD*, ed. D. N. Freedman, 3:382-83. New
            York: Doubleday.
Huss, W.
    1985   *Geschichte der Karthager*. Munich: Beck.
    1990   *Die Karthager*. Frankfurt am Main: Buchergilde
            Gutenberg.
Hutchens, K. D.
    1998   *Although Yahweh Was There: The Land in the Book of
            Ezekiel*. Ph.D. dissertation, Emory University,
            unpublished.
Isserlin, B. S. J.
    1998   *The Israelites*. London: Thames and Hudson.

Ishida, T.

    1992   "Solomon." *ABD*, ed. D. N. Freedman, 6:105-13. New York: Doubleday.

James, T. G. H.

    1991   "Egypt: the Twenty-fifth and Twenty-sixth Dynasties." In *CAH*, 2nd ed. Vol. 3, part 2, *The Assyrian and Babylonian Empires and Other States of the Near East, from the Eighth to the Sixth Centuries B.C.*, eds. J. A. Boardman et al., 677-747. Cambridge: Cambridge University Press.

Jankowska, N. B.

    1969   "Some Problems of the Economy of the Assyrian Empire." In *Ancient Mesopotamia*, ed. I. M. Diakonoff, 253-95. Moscow: "Nauca."

Jenni, E. and C. Westerman, eds.

    1971-76   *Theologisches Handwörterbuch zum Alten Testament.* 2 vols. Munich: Kaiser.

Jensen, L. B.

    1963   "Royal Purple of Tyre." *JNES* 22: 104-18.

Joannès, F.

    1982   "La localization de Ṣurru a l'époque néo-babylonienne." *Semitica* 32: 35-42.

    1987   "Trois textes de Ṣurru a l'époque néo-babylonienne." *RA* 81: 147-58.

    1999   "Structures et opérations commerciales en Babylonie a l'époque néo-babylonienne." In *Trade and Finance in Ancient Mesopotamia*, ed. J. G. Dercksen, 175-94. Leiden – Istanbul: Nederlands Historisch-Archaeologisch Instituut and te Istanbul.

Justinus, Marcus Junianus.

    1994-97   *Epitome of the Philippic History of Pompeius Trogus / Justin.* Trans. J. C. Yardley. Clarendon Ancient History. New York: Clarendon Press.

Kaplony, P.

    1992   "Papyrus Bologna 1086 und der 'Stab des Thoth.'" In *The Intellectual Heritage of Egypt* (Kákosy Festschrift). Studia aegyptiaca 14, ed. U. Luft, 309-22. Budapest: [s.n].

Karageorghis, V.
 1976   *Kition. Mycenean and Phoenician Discoveries in Cyprus.*
         New York: Thames and Hudson.
 1982   *Cyprus from the Stone Age to the Romans.* New York:
         Thames and Hudson.
 1982   "Cyprus." In *CAH*, 2nd ed. Vol. 3, part 3, *The Expansion
         of the Greek World, Eighth to Sixth Centuries B. C.*, eds.
         J. A. Boardman et al., 57-70. Cambridge: Cambridge
         University Press.
 1988   "Cyprus." In *TP*, ed. S. Moscati, 152-65. New York:
         Abbeville.

Karageorghis, V., ed.
 1985   *Archaeology in Cyprus, 1960-1985.* Nicosia: A. G.
         Leventis Foundation.

Kassianidou, V., B. Rothenberg, and P. Andrews.
 1993   "Silver Production in the Tartessian Period. The Evidence
         from Monte Romero." *Arx* 1: 17-34.

Katzenstein, H. J.
 1983   "Before Pharaoh conquered Gaza (Jeremiah xlvii 1)." *VT*
         33: 249-51.
 1991   "Phoenician Deities Worshipped in Israel and Judah
         During the Time of the First Temple." In *Phoenicia and
         the Bible*. SP 11, ed. E. Lipiński, 187-91. Leuven:
         Uitgeverij Peeters.
 1992a   "Gaza (Prehellenistic)." *ABD*, ed. D. N. Freedman, 2:912-
         15. New York: Doubleday.
 1992b   "Tyre." *ABD*, ed. D. N. Freedman, 6:686-90. New York:
         Doubleday.
 1993   "Nebuchadnezzar's Wars with Egypt." *EI* (Avraham
         Malamat Volume) 24: 184-86 (Hebrew).
 1996   "Some Reflections on the "Tarshish Ship."" In *Alle soglie
         della classicità il Mediterraneo tra tradizione e
         innovazione*, ed. E. Acquaro, 1.237-48. Pisa – Rome:
         Istituti editoriali e poligrafici internazionali.
 1997   *The History of Tyre. From the Beginning of the Second
         Millenium B.C.E. until the Fall of the Neo-Babylonian*

Empire in 539 B.C.E., 2nd ed. Beer Sheva: Ben Gurion University of the Negev.

Katzenstein, H. J. and D. Edwards.

1992 "Tyre." *ABD*, ed. D. N. Freedman, 6:686-92. New York: Doubleday.

Kempinski, A. and R. Reich, eds.

1992 *The Architecture of Ancient Israel from the Prehistoric to the Persian Periods.* Jerusalem: Israel Exploration Society.

Kestemont, G.

1983 "Tyr et les Assyriens." In *I. Redt Tyrus / Sauvons Tyr.* SP 1, eds. E. Gubel et al., 53-78. Leuven: Uitgeverij Peeters.

1985 "Les Phéniciens en Syrie du Nord." In *Phoenicia and its Neighbours in the First Millenium B.C.* SP 3, eds. E. Gubel and E. Lipiński, 135-61. Leuven: Uitgeverij Peeters.

Kindler, A.

1967 "The Mint of Tyre: The Major Source of Silver Coins in Ancient Palestine." *EI* 8: 318-24.

Kitchen, K. A.

1973 *The Third Intermediate Period in Egypt.* Westminster. Aris and Phillips.

Knauf, E. A.

1992a "The Ishmaelites." *ABD*, ed. D. N. Freedman, 3:513-20. New York: Doubleday.

1992b "Seir." *ABD*, ed. D. N. Freedman, 4:1072-73. New York: Doubleday.

Koch, M.

1984 *Tarschisch und Hispanien. Historisch-geographische und namenkundliche Untersuchungen zur Phönikischen Kolonisation der Iberischen Halbinsel.* Berlin: Walter de Gruyter.

Koehler, L. and W. Baumgartner, eds.

1967-90 *Hebräisches und aramäisches Lexikon zum Alten Testament.* 4 vols. Leiden: Brill.

Koehler, L. and W. Baumgartner, eds.
1994-00   *The Hebrew and Aramaic Lexicon of the Old Testament.* 5
           vols. Trans. M. E. J. Richardson. Leiden: Brill.
Kohler, J. and A. Ungnad.
1913   *Assyrische Rechtsurkunden.* Leipzig: E. Pfeiffer.
Koopmans, W. T.
1993   "Poetic Reciprocation: The Oracles against Edom and
           Philistia in Ezek. 25:12-17." In *Verse in Ancient Near
           Eastern Prose.* AOAT 42, ed. W. G. E. Watson, 113-22.
           Neukirchen-Vluyn: Neukirchener.
Kopcke, G. and I. Tokumaru, eds.
1992   *Greece between East and West: 10th-8th Centuries BC.*
           Mainz: Philipp von Zabern.
Krahmalkov, C. R.
2000   *Phoenician-Punic Dictionary.* SP 15. Leuven: Uitgeverij
           Peeters and Departement Oosterse Studies.
2000   *A Phoenician-Punic Grammar.* Leiden: Brill.
Krings, V., ed.
1995   *La civilisation phénicienne et punique – manuel de
           recherche.* Leiden: Brill.
Kroeze, J. H.
1961   "The Tyre-Passages in the Book of Ezekiel." In *Studies
           on the Book of Ezekiel. Papers read at the 4th Meeting of
           Die O.T. Werkgemeenskap in Suid-Africa,* 10-23. Pretoria:
           University of South Africa.
Kuan, K.
1994   *Assyrian Historical Inscriptions and Israelite/Judean–
           Tyrian–Damascene Political and Commercial Relations
           in the Ninth-Eighth Centuries BCE (Eighth Century BC,
           Ninth Century BC, Israel, Judah, Tyre, Sidon, Damascus).*
           Ph.D. dissertation, Emory University, unpublished.
Kuhrt, A.
1995   *The Ancient Near East.* New York: Rouledge.
Laato, A.
1992   *Josiah and David Redivivus: The Historical Josiah and
           the Messianic Expectations of Exilic and Postexilic Times.*

ConBOT 33. Stockholm: Almqvist and Wiksell International.

LaBianca, O. S. and R. W. Younker.
1995   "The Kingdoms of Ammon, Moab and Edom: The Archaeology of Society in Late Bronze/Iron Age Transjordan (ca. 1400-500 BCE)." In *The Archaeology of Society in the Holy Land*, ed. T. Levy, 399-415. New York: Acts on File.

Lackenbacher, S.
1982   *Roi batisseur: les récits de construction Assyriens des origines à Teglatphalasar III.* Paris: Éditions recherche sur les civilizations.

Lambdin, T. O.
1953   "Egyptian Loan Words in the Old Testament." *JAOS* 73: 145-55.

Lancel, S.
1995   "Les prospections et "surveys" *partim* Orient." In *CPP*, ed. V. Krings, 106-18. Leiden: Brill.
1997   *Carthage, A History.* Trans. A. Nevill. Malden: Blackwell.

Lebrun, R.
1987   "L'Anatolie et le monde phénicien du Xe au IVe siècle av. J.-C." In *Phoenicia and the East Mediterranean in the First Millennium B. C.* SP 5, ed. E. Lipiński, 23-35. Leuven: Uitgerij Peeters.

Leclant, J.
1968   "Les relations entre l'Égypte et la Phénicie du voyage d'Ounamon a l'expédition d'Alexandre." In *The Role of the Phoenicians in the Interaction of Mediterranean Civilizations*, ed. W. A. Ward, 9-31. Beirut: American University of Beirut.
1995   "Carthage et l'Égypte." In *Atti del III Congresso internazionale di studi fenici e punici*, 3.I.41-50, Tunis: Institut National du Patrimoine.

Leemans, W. F.
1977   "The Importance of Trade." *Iraq* 39: 1-2.

Lemaire, A.
    1982   "Une inscription phénicienne de Tell es-Sai'diyeh." *RSF*
               10:11-12.
    1984   "Date et origine des inscriptions hébraïques et
               phéniciennes de Kuntillet 'Ajrud." *SEL* 1: 131-43.
    1987   "Les Phéniciens et le commerce entre la mer Rouge et la
               mer Méditerranée." In *Phoenicia and the East
               Mediterranean in the First Millenium B. C.* SP 5, ed. E.
               Lipiński, 49-60. Leuven: Uitgeverij Peeters.
    1992a   "Édom." In *DCPP*, ed. E. Lipiński, 143-44. Paris:
               Brepols.
    1992b   "Samarie." In *DCPP*, ed. E. Lipiński, 386. Paris: Brepols.
    1995   "La circulation monétaire phénicienne en Palestine a
               l'époque perse." In *Atti del III Congresso di studi fenici e
               punici*, 3.II.192-202. Tunis: Institut National du
               Patrimoine.
Levine, B. A.
    1999   "The Biblical 'Town' as Reality and Typology:
               Evaluating Biblical Reference to Towns and their
               Functions." In *Urbanization and Land Ownership in the
               Ancient Near East*, eds. M. Hudson and B. A. Levine,
               2.421-53. Cambridge. Harvard University Press.
Levy, T. E., ed.
    1995   *The Archaeology of Society in the Holy Land.* New York:
               Facts on File.
Lindsay, J.
    1976   "The Babylonian Kings and Edom, 605-550 B.C." *PEQ*
               108: 23-39.
Liphschitz, N. and Y. Waisel.
    1973   "Dendroarchaeological Investigations in Israel. (Tell
               Beersheba and Arad in the Northern and Eastern Negev)."
               IEJ 23: 30-36.
Lipiński, E.
    1972   "The Egypto-Babylonian War of the Winter of 601-600
               B.C." *Annali dell'Istituto Orientale di Napoli* 32: 235-41.

1973   "Garden of Abundance, Image of Lebanon." *ZAW* 85: 359-60.

1975   "Deux marchands de blé phéniciens à Ninive." *RSF* 3: 65-76.

1979   "Les temples néo-assyriens et les origines du monnayage." In *State and Temple Economy in the Ancient Near East*. OLA 6, ed. E. Lipiński, 2.565-88. Leuven: Departement Oriëntalistiek.

1985a   "Products and Brokers of Tyre according to Ezekiel 27." In *Phoenicia and its Neighbors*. SP 3, eds. E. Gubel and E. Lipiński, 213-20. Leuven: Uitgeverij Peeters.

1985b   "Phoenicians in Anatolia and Assyria, 9th-6th Centuries B.C." *OLP* 16: 81-90.

1986   "Les formules de datation dans Ézéchiel a la lumière des données épigraphiques récentes." In *Ezekiel and His Book: Textual and Literary Criticism and their Interrelation*. BETL 74, ed. J. Lust, 359-66. Leuven: Leuven University Press and Uitgeverij Peeters.

1992a   "Israël et Juda." In *DCPP*, ed. E. Lipiński, 231-32. Paris: Brepols.

1992b   "Jérusalem." In *DCPP*, ed. E. Lipiński, 238-39. Paris: Brepols.

1995   *Dieux et déesses de l'univers phénicien et punique*. Leuven: Uitgeverij Peeters.

Lipiński, E., ed.

1992   *Dictionnaire de la civilization phénicienne et punique*. Paris: Brepols.

Littauer, M. A. and J. H. Crowel.

1979   *Wheeled Vehicles and Ridden Animals in the Ancient Near East*. Leiden: Brill.

1992   "Chariots." *ABD*, ed. D. N. Freedman, 1:888-92. New York: Doubleday.

Liverani, M.

1990   "Wen-Amun and Zakar-Ba'al: Gift or Trade?" In *Prestige and Interest: International Relations in the Near East ca.*

1600-1100 B.C. HANES 1, ed. M. Liverani, 247-54.
Padova: Sargon.

1991   "The Trade Network of Tyre according to Ezek. 27." In
*Ah Assyria...Studies in Assyrian History and Ancient
Near Eastern Historiography Presented to Hayim
Tadmor.* SH 33, eds. M. Cogan and I. Eph'al, 65-80.
Jerusalem: Magnes and Hebrew University Press.

Luckenbill, D. D.
1926-27   *Ancient Records of Assyria and Babylonia.* 2 vols.
Chicago: The University of Chicago Press.

Lundbom, J. R.
1999   *Jeremiah 1-20: A New Translation with Introduction and
Commentary.* AB 21A. New York: Doubleday.

Lust, J.
1986   *Ezekiel and His Book: Textual and Literary Criticism and
their Interrelation.* BETL 74. Leuven: Leuven University
Press and Uitgeverij Peeters Leuven.

Macdonald, B. and R. W. Younker, eds
1999   *Ancient Ammon.* Studies in the History and Culture of the
Ancient Near East 17. Leiden: Brill.

Machinist, P.
1992   "Palestine, Administration of (Assyro-Babylonian)."
ABD, ed. D. N. Freedman, 5:69-81. New York:
Doubleday.

Mackay, C.
1934   "The King of Tyre." *CQR* 117: 239-58.

Maddin, R., T. S. Wheeler, and J. D. Muhly.
1977   "Tin in the Ancient Near East: Old Questions and New
Finds." *Expedition* 19: 35-47.

Madroñero, A.
1992   "The Ancient Tin Trade in Galicia and its Interpretation
through Petroglyphs." In *Bulletin of the Metals Museum*
18: 44-88.

Maisler, B.
1951   "Two Hebrew Ostraca from Tell Qasile." *JNES* 10: 265-
67.

Malamat, A.

1950a   "The Historical Setting of Two Biblical Prophecies on the Nations." *IEJ* 1: 149-59.

1950b   "The Last Wars of the Kingdom of Judah." *JNES* 9: 218-27.

1956   "A New Record of Nebuchadrezzar's Palestinian Campaigns." *IEJ* 6: 246-55.

1968   "The Last Kings of Judah and the Fall of Jerusalem: an Historical-chronological study." *IEJ* 18: 137-56.

1973   "Josiah's Bid for Armageddon: The Background of the Judean-Egyptian Encounter in 609 B.C." *JANES* 5 [Gaster Festschrift]: 267-79.

1979   "The Last Years of the Kingdom of Judah." In *World History of the Jewish People*. Vol. 4/1 *The Age of the Monarchies: Political History*, ed. A. Malamat, 205-21. Jerusalem: Masada.

1988   "The Kingdom of Judah Between Egypt and Babylon: A Small State Within a Great Power Confrontation." In *Text and Context. Old Testament and Semitic Studies for F.C. Fensham*. JSOTSup 48. ed. W. Classen, 117-29. Sheffield: Sheffield Academic Press.

1990   "The Kingdom of Judah between Egypt and Babylon." *ST* 44: 65-77.

1999   "Caught Between the Great Powers." *BAR* 25: 34-41, 64.

Malbran-Labat, F.

1982   *L'armée et l'organisation militaire de L'Assyrie*. Paris: Librairie Droz.

Malkin, I.

1999   *Myth and Territory in the Spartan Mediterranean*. Paris: Belles Lettres.

Manor, D. W. and G. A. Herion.

1992   "Arad." *ABD*, ed. D. N. Freedman, 1:331-36. New York: Doubleday.

Marcotte, D.

1992   "Pseudo-Skylax." In *DCPP*, ed. E. Lipiński, 418-19. Paris: Brepols.

Markoe, G. E.
  2000   *Phoenicians.* Berkeley – Los Angeles: University of
            California Press.
Massinger, M. O.
  1967   *Babylon in Biblical Prophecy.* Ph.D. dissertation, Dallas
            Theological Seminary, unpublished.
Masson, O. and M. Sznycer.
  1972   *Recherches sur les Phéniciens à Chypre.* Genève-Paris:
            Droz.
May, H. G.
  1984   *Oxford Bible Atlas,* 3rd ed. Oxford: Oxford University
            Press.
Mayerson, P.
  1992   "The Gaza 'Wine' Jar (*Gazition*) and the 'Lost' Ashkelon
            Jar (*Askalonion*)." *IEJ* 42: 76-80.
Mazar, A.
  1990   *Archaeology of the Land of the Bible, 10,000-586 B.C.E.*
            Garden City: Doubleday.
  1997   *David King of Israel Alive and Enduring?* Jerusalem:
            Simor (Hebrew).
Mazar, B.
  1986a   "The Philistines and the Rise of Israel and Tyre." In *The
            Early Biblical Period*, eds. S. Ahituv and B. Levine, 63-
            82. Jerusalem: Israel Exploration Society.
  1986b   "The Phoenicians in the Levant." In *The Early Biblical
            Period*, eds. S. Ahituv and B. Levine, 218-30. Jerusalem:
            Israel Exploration Society.
Mazza, F.
  1988   "The Phoenicians as Seen by the Ancient World." In *TP*,
            ed. S. Moscati, 548-67. New York: Abbeville.
Mazza, F., S. Ribichini, and P. Xella.
  1988   *Fonti classiche per la civiltà fenicia e punica I, Fonti
            letterarie greche dalle origini alla fine dell'età classica.*
            Rome: Consiglio Nazionale delle Ricerche.
McEwan, G. J.
  1982   *The Late Babylonian Tablets in the Royal Ontario
            Museum.* Toronto: Royal Ontario Museum.

McNutt, P. M.
  1990   *The Forging of Israel: Iron Technology, Symbolism and Tradition.* JSOTSup 108. SWBAS 8. Sheffield: Sheffield Academic Press and Almond.

Mendelsohn, I.
  1949   *Slavery in the Ancient Near East.* Oxford: Oxford University Press.

Meshel, Z.
  1978   *Kuntillet 'Ajrud. A Religious Center from the Time of the Judean Monarchy on the Border of Sinai.* Jerusalem: The Israel Museum.

Metzger, B. M. and R. E. Murphy, eds.
  1994   *The New Oxford Annotated Bible.* Revised ed. Oxford: Oxford University Press.

Metzger, M.
  1991   "Zeder, Weinstock und Weltenbaum." In *Ernten, was man saet*, eds. D. W. Daniels et al., 197-229. Neukirchen-Vluyn: Neukirchener.

Meyers, C. L.
  1992   "Cherubim." *ABD*, ed. D. N. Freedman, 1:899-900. New York: Doubleday.

Meyers, C. L. and E. M. Meyers.
  1993   *Zechariah 9-14.* AB 25C. New York: Doubleday.

Meyers, E. M., ed.
  1997   *The Oxford Encyclopedia of Archaeology in the Near East.* 5 vols. Oxford: Oxford University Press.

Michaelidou-Nicolaou, I.
  1987   "Repercussions of the Phoenician Presence in Cyprus." In *Phoenicia and the East Mediterranean in the First Millennium B.C.* SP 5, ed. E. Lipiński, 331-38. Leuven: Uitgeverij Peeters.

Millard, A. R.
  1962   "The Wine Trade of Damascus." *JSS* 7: 201-203.

Miller, J. E.
  1993   "The Maelaek of Tyre (Ezekiel 28:11-19)." *ZAW* 105: 497-501.

Miosi, F. T.
    1992   "Re." *ABD*, ed. D. N. Freedman, 5:624-25. New York:
                Doubleday.
Mitchell, T. C.
    1991a   "Judah until the fall of Jerusalem (c. 700-586 B.C.)." In
                CAH, 2nd ed. Vol. 3, part 2, *The Assyrian and Babylonian
                Empires and Other States of the Near East from the
                Eighth to the Sixth Centuries B.C.*, eds. J. A. Boardman et
                al., 391-409. Cambridge: Cambridge University Press.
    1991b   "The Babylonian Exile and the Restoration of the Jews in
                Palestine (586-c. 500 B.C.)." In *CAH*, 2nd ed. Vol. 3, part
                2, *The Assyrian and Babylonian Empires and Other
                States of the Near East from the Eighth to the Sixth
                Centuries B.C.*, eds. A. Boardman et al., 410-60.
                Cambridge: Cambridge University Press.
Moorey, P. R. S.
    1994   *Ancient Mesopotamian Materials and Industries.* Oxford:
                Oxford University Press and Clarendon.
Mosca, G. and J. Russell.
    1987   "A Phoenician Inscription from Cebel Ires Daķi in Rough
                Cilicia." *EpAn* 9: 1-28.
Moscati, S.
    1972   *I Fenici e Cartagine.* Torino: Unione tipografico-editrice
                torinese.
    1979   *Il mondo dei Fenici.* Milan: A. Mondadori.
    1982   "L'espansione fenicia nel Mediterraneo occidentale." In
                Phönizier im Westen. Madrider Beiträge 8, ed. H. G.
                Niemeyer, 5-12. Mainz: Phillip von Zabern.
    1988a   "Territory and Settlements." In *TP*, ed. S. Moscati, 26-27.
                New York: Abbeville.
    1988b   "Colonization of the Mediterranean." In *TP*, ed. S.
                Moscati, 46-53. New York: Abbeville.
    1988c   "Substrata and Adstrata." In *TP*, ed. S. Moscati, 512-21.
                New York: Abbeville.
    1989a   *Tra Tiro e Cadice. Temi e problemi degli studi fenici.*
                Studia Punica 5. Rome: Università degli studi di Roma -
                Dipartimento di storia.

1989b   *L'ancora d'argento. Colonie e commerci fenici tra Oriente e Occidente*. Milan: Jaca Book.

1993   "Non e un tofet a Tiro." *RSF* 21: 147-51.

Moscati, S., ed.

1988   *The Phoenicians*. New York: Abbeville.

Muhly, J. D.

1970   "Homer and the Phoenicians. The Relations between Greece and the Near East in the Late Bronze and Early Iron Ages." *Berytus* 19: 19-64.

1973   *Copper and Tin*. New Haven: The Connecticut Academy of Arts and Sciences.

1982   "How Iron Technology Changed the Ancient World." *BAR* 8: 42-54.

1998   "Copper, Tin, Silver and Iron. The Search for Metallic Ores as an Incentive for Foreign Expansion." In *Mediterranean Peoples in Transition, Thirteenth to Early Tenth Centuries BCE*, eds. S. Gitin et al., 314-29. Jerusalem: Israel Exploration Society.

Müller, D. H.

1894   "Ägyptisch-minäischer Sarkophag in Museum von Gizeh." *WZKM* 8: 4.

Müller, H.P.

1971   "Phönizien in Juda in exilisch-nachexilischer Zeit." *WO* 6: 189-204.

Myers, J. M.

1962   "Some Considerations bearing on the Date of Joel." *ZAW* 74: 177-95.

1971   "Edom and Judah in the Sixth-Fifth Centuries B.C." In *Near Eastern Studies in Honor of W. F. Albright*, ed. H. Goedicke, 377-92. Baltimore: Johns Hopkins University Press.

Na'aman, N.

1991   "The Kingdom of Judah under Josiah." *TA* 18: 3-66.

1992   "Nebuchadrezzar's Campaign in Year 603 BCE." *BN* 62: 41-44.

1997   "Cow Town or Royal Capital? Evidence for Iron Age Jerusalem." *BAR* 23: 43-47, 67.

Naveh, J.
1960   "A Hebrew Letter from the Seventh Century B.C." *IEJ*
        10: 129-39.
1962   "The Excavations at Meṣad Ḥashavyaḥu-Preliminary
        Report." *IEJ* 12: 89-113.
1985   "Writing and Scripts in Seventh-Century B.C.E. Philistia.
        The New Evidence from Tell Jemmeh." *IEJ* 35: 8-21.
1987   "Unpublished Phoenician Inscriptions from Palestine."
        IEJ 37: 25-35.

Nelson, R. D.
1983   "*Realpolitik* in Judah (687-609 B.C.E.)." In *Scripture in
        Context II: More Essays on the Comparative Method*, eds.
        W. W. Hallo, J. C. Moyer, and L. G. Perdue, 177-89.
        Winona Lake: Eisenbrauns.

Neufeld, E.
1960   "The Emergence of Royal-Urban Society in Ancient
        Israel." *HUCA* 31: 31-53.

Newsome, J. D.
1979   *By the Waters of Babylon: An Introduction to the History
        and Theology of the Exile.* Atlanta: John Fox.

Niditch, S.
1993   *War in the Hebrew Bible.* Oxford: Oxford University
        Press.

Niemeyer, H. G., ed.
1982   *Phönizier im Westen.* Madrider Beiträge 8. Mainz: Philipp
        von Zabern.
1989   *Das frühe Karthago und die phönizische Expansion im
        Mittelmeerraum.* Veröffentlichungen der Joachim
        Jungius-Gesellschaft der Wissenschaften Hamburg 60.
        Göttingen: Vandenhoeck and Ruprecht.
1990   *Die Phönizier im Zeitalter Homers.* Mainz: Philipp von
        Zabern.
1993   "Trade Before the Flag? On the Principles of Phoenician
        Expansion in the Mediterranean." In *Biblical Archaeology
        Today*, eds. A. Biran and J. Aviram, 335-44. Jerusalem:
        Israel Exploration Society.

1995   "Expansion et colonisation." In *CPP*, ed. V. Krings, 247-67. Leiden: Brill.

Noth, M.
1953   "La catastrophe de Jérusalem en l'an 587 avant Jésus-Christ et sa signification pour Israël." *RHPR* 33: 81-102.
1958   "Die Einnahme von Jerusalem im Jahre 597 v. Chr." *ZDPV* 74: 133-57.

Oates, J.
1991   "The Fall of Assyria (635-609 B.C.)" In *CAH*, 2nd ed. Vol. 3, part 2, *The Assyrian and Babylonian Empires and Other States of the Near East from the Eighth to the Sixth Centuries B.C.*, eds. J. Boardman et al., 162-93. Cambridge: Cambridge University Press.

O'Connor, D. and D. P. Silverman, eds.
1995   *Ancient Egyptian Kingship*. Probleme der Ägyptologie 9. Leiden: Brill.

Oded, B.
1979a   "Judah and the Exile." In *Israelite and Judaean History*, eds. M. Hayes and J. M. Miller, 435-88. Philadelphia: Westminster.
1979b   *Mass Deportations and Deportees in the Neo-Assyrian Empire*. Wiesbaden: L. Reichert.
1979c   "Neighbors on the West." In *World History of the Jewish People*. Vol. 4/1 *The Age of the Monarchies: Political History*, ed. A. Malamat, 222-46. Jerusalem: Massada.
1979d   "Neighbors on the East." In *World History of the Jewish People*. Vol. 4/1 *The Age of the Monarchies: Political History*, ed. A. Malamat, 247-75. Jerusalem: Massada.
1995   "Observations on the Israelite/Judaean Exiles in Mesopotamia during the Eighth-Sixth Centuries BCE." In *Immigration and Emigration within the Ancient Near East*. OLA 65, eds. K. van Lerberghe and A. Schoors, 205-12. Leuven: Uitgeverij Peeters and Departement Oriëntalistiek.

Olmos Romera, R.
1990   "Tartessos y el comercio mediterráneo siglos VII al VI A. de C." In *La Magna Grecia e il lontano Occidente*, 411-

49. Naples: Istituto per la storia e l'archeologia della Magna Grecia..

Oppenheim, A. L.
1967   "Essay on Overland Trade in the First Millenium B.C." *JCS* 21: 236-54.
1969   "Comment." In *Third International Conference of Economic History. Munich 1965*, 33-44. Paris: Mouton.
1971   "Trade in the Ancient Near East." In *Fifth International Conference of Economic History Leningrad 1970*, eds. H. Van der Wee et al., 125-49. The Hague: Mouton.
1977   *Ancient Mesopotamia. Portrait of a Dead Civilization.* Chicago: Chicago University Press.

Padró, J.
1998   "Les relations commerciales entre l'Égypte et le monde phénico-punique." In *Le commerce en Égypte ancienne*. BdÉ 121, eds. N. Grimal and B. Menu, 41-58. Cairo: Institut Français d'Archéologie Orientale.

Parker, A. J.
1992   *Ancient Shipwrecks of the Mediterranean & the Roman Provinces.* BAR International Series 580. Oxford: B.A.R.

Parker, Ch. H.
1970   *"The Tyrian Oracles in Ezekiel": A Study of Ezekiel 26:1 – 28:19.* Ph.D. dissertation, Columbia University, unpublished.

Parker, R. A. and W. H. Dubberstein
1956   *Babylonian Chronology: 626 B.C.-A.D. 75.* Providence: Brown University Press.

Parpola, S.
1970   *Neo-Assyrian Toponyms.* Neukirchen-Vluyn: Butzon and Bercker Kevelaer.

Parpola, S. and K. Watanabe.
1988   *Neo-Assyrian Treaties and Loyalty Oaths.* SAA 2. Helsinki: Helsinki University.

Paul, S. M.
1991   *Amos.* Minneapolis: Fortress.

Peckham, B.
1976   "Israel and Phoenicia." In *Magnalia Dei. The Might Acts of God. In Memoriam G. E. Wright*, 224-48. Garden City: Doubleday.
1992   "Phoenicia, History of." *ABD*, ed. D. N. Freedman, 5:349-57. New York: Doubleday.

Peretti, A.
1979   *Il periplo di Scilace.* Pisa: Gardini.

Pernigotti, S.
1988   "Phoenicians and Egyptians." In *TP*, ed. S. Moscati, 522-31. New York: Abbeville.
1996   "La 'legione staniera' nell'Egitto della XXVI dinastia." In *Alle soglie della classicità il Mediterraneo tra tradizione e innovazione*, ed. E. Acquaro, 1.355-64. Pisa – Rome: Istituto editoriali e poligrafici internazionali.

Petersen, D. L.
1999   "Creation in Ezekiel: Methodological Perspectives and Theological Prospects." In SBLSPS 38: 490-500.

Pettinato, G.
1975   "I rapporti politici di Tiro con l'Assiria alla luce del 'trattato tra Asarhaddon e Baal.'" *RSF* 3: 145-60.

Picard, C.
1988   "L'essor de Carthage aux VIIe et VIe siècles." In *Carthago*. SP 6, ed. E. Lipiński, 43-50. Leuven: Uitgeverij Peeters.

Picard, G. C. and C. Picard.
1970   *Vie et mort de Carthage.* Paris: Hachette.

Pigott, V. C.
1996   "Near Eastern Archaeometallurgy: Modern Research and Future Directions." In *The Study of the Ancient Near East in the Twenty-First Century. The William Foxwell Albright Centennial Conference*, eds. J. S. Cooper and G. M. Schwartz, 139-76. Winoma Lake: Eisenbrauns.

Pleiner, R. and J. K. Bjorkman.
1974   "The Assyrian Iron Age: The History of Iron in the Assyrian Civilization." *Proceedings of the American Philosophical Society* 118: 283-313.

Pliny the Elder.
   1967-75   *Natural History*. Trans. H. Rackham. Loeb Classical
            Library. Cambridge: Harvard University Press.

Ploeger, J. G.
   1972   "אדמה." In *Theological Dictionary of the Old Testament*,
            eds. G. Botterweck and H. Ringgren, 1.88-98. Grand
            Rapids: William B. Eerdmans.

Polybius.
   1954   *The Histories*. Trans. W. R. Paton. Loeb Classical
            Library. Cambridge: Harvard University Press.

Porten, B.
   1981   "The Identity of King Adon." *BA* 44: 36-59.

Porter, B. and R. L. B. Moss.
   1951   *Topographical Bibliography of Ancient Egyptian-
            Hieroglyphic Texts, Reliefs, and Paintings*. Vol 7: *Nubia,
            the Deserts and Outside Egypt*. Oxford: Oxford
            University Press.

Postgate, J. N.
   1974   *Taxation and Conscription in the Assyrian Empire*. Studia
            Pohl: series maior 3. Rome: Pontifical Biblical Institute.

   1979   "The Economic Structure of the Assyrian Empire." In
            *Power and Propaganda: A Symposium on Ancient
            Empires*, ed. M. T. Larsen, 193-221. Copenhagen:
            Akademisk Forlag.

Pratico, G. D.
   1993   *Nelson Glueck's Excavations at Tell el-Kheleifeh: A
            Reappraisal*. American Schools of Oriental Research
            Archaeological Reports 3, ed. L. G. Herr. Atlanta:
            Scholars.

Pritchard, J. B.
   1969   *Ancient Near Eastern Texts Relating to the Old
            Testament*, 3rd ed. Princeton: Princeton University Press.

Puech, E.
   1977   "L'inscription phénicienne du trône d'Astart a Séville."
            RSF 5: 85-92.

Quaegebeur, J.
1995   "À propos de l'identification de la 'Kadytis' d'Hérodote
          avec la ville de Gaza." In *Immigration and Emigration
          within the Ancient Near East*. OLA 65, eds. K. van
          Lerberghe and A. Schoors, 245-71. Leuven: Uitgeverij
          Peeters and Departement Oriëntalistiek.

Quinn, J. D.
1961   "Alcaeus 48 (B 16) and the Fall of Ascalon (604 B.C.)."
          BASOR 164: 19-20.

Radner, K.
1999a   "Traders in the Neo-Assyrian Period." In *Trade and
          Finance in Ancient Mesopotamia*, ed. J. G. Dercksen,
          101-26. Leiden – Istanbul: Nederlands Historisch-
          Archaeologisch Instituut and te Istanbul.
1999b   "Money in the Neo-Assyrian Empire." In *Trade and
          Finance in Ancient Mesopotamia*, ed. J. G. Derscksen,
          127-57. Leiden – Istanbul: Nederlands Historisch-
          Archeologisch Instituut and te Istanbul.
1999c   *The Prosopography of the Neo-Assyrian Empire*. Vol. 1,
          part 2.B-G. Neo-Assyrian Text Corpus Project.
          Cambridge: Harvard University Press.

Rappaport, U.
1992   "Phoenicia and Galilee: Economy, Territory and Political
          Relations." In *Numismatique et histoire économique
          phéniciennes et puniques*. SP 9, eds. T. Hackens and G.
          Moucharte, 261-68. Wetteren: Cultura.

Redford, D. B.
1992   *Egypt, Canaan, and Israel in Ancient Times*. Princeton:
          Princeton University Press.

Redford, D. W.
1998   *Quest for the Crown Jewel: The Centrality of Egypt in the
          Foreign Policy of Esarhaddon*. Ph.D. dissertation,
          Hebrew Union College-Jewish Institute of Religion,
          Cincinnati, unpublished.

Reinhold, M.
1970   *History of Purple as a Status Symbol in Antiquity*.
          Brussels: Latomus.

Renan, E.
    1864   *Mission de Phénicie*. Paris: Imprimerie impériale.
Renz, T.
    1999   *The Rhetorical Function of the Book of Ezekiel*. VTSupp
              76. Leiden: Brill.
Ribichini, S.
    1995   "Les sources gréco-latines." In *CPP*, ed. V. Krings, 73-
              84. Leiden: Brill.
    1999   "Melqart." In *Dictionary of Deities and Demons in the
              Bible*, 2nd ed., eds. K. Van der Toorn et al., 1053-57.
              Leiden: Brill.
Röllig, W.
    1995   "Anatolie." In *CPP*, ed. V. Krings, 640-45. Leiden: Brill.
Röllig, W., ed.
    1974-   *Répertoire géographique des textes cuneiformes*. Beihefte
              zum Tübinger Atlas des Vorderen Orients B7.
              Wiesbaden: L. Reichert.
Rothenberg, B.
    1962   "Ancient Copper Industries in the Western Arabah." *PEQ*
              94: 5-71.
    1981   "Iron at Taanach and Early Iron Metallurgy in the Eastern
              Mediterranean." *AJA* 85: 245-68.
Rothenberg, B. and A. Blanco-Freijeiro.
    1981   *Studies in ancient Mining and Metallurgy in Southwest
              Spain: Explorations and Excavations in the Province of
              Huelva*. London: Institute for Archaeo-Metallurgical
              Studies, Institute of Archaeology, University of London.
Rouillard, P.
    1992   "Phocéens." In *DCPP*, ed. E. Lipiński, 353. Paris:
              Brepols.
Rowton, M. B.
    1951   "Jeremiah and the Death of Josiah." *JNES* 10: 128-30.
Rüger, H. P.
    1961   *Das Tyrusorakel Ezek 27*. Ph.D dissertation, Tübingen
              University, unpublished.

Sack, R. H.
1970   *An Economic, Historical Study of the Reign of Amel Marduk, King of Babylon, 562-560 BC.* Ph.D. dissertation, University of Minnesota, unpublished.
1991   *Images of Nebuchadnezzar: The Emergence of a Legend.* Selinsgrove: Susquehanna University Press.

Sader, H.
1991-92   "Phoenician Stelae from Tyre." *Berytus* 39: 101-26.
1992   "Phoenician Stelae from Tyre." *SEL* 9: 53-79.

Saggs, H. W.
1955   "The Nimrud Letters 1952: Part II." *Iraq* 17: 127-30.
1962   *The Greatness that was Babylon.* London: Sidgwick and Jackson.
1984   *The Might that was Assyria.* London: Sidgwick and Jackson.

Salles, J. -Fr.
1995   "Phénicie." In *CPP*, ed. V. Krings, 553-82. Leiden: Brill.

Salonen, A.
1956   *Hippologica accadica.* Helsinki: Suomalainen Tiedeakatemia.

Sawyer, J. F. A. and D. J. A. Clines, eds.
1983   *Midian, Moab and Edom: The History and Archaeology of Late Bronze and Iron Age Jordan and North-West Arabia.* Sheffield: Almond.

Scandone, G.
1984   "Testimonianze egiziane in Fenicia dal XII al IV sec. A.C." *RSF* 12: 133-63.
1995a   "Les sources égyptiennes." In *CPP*, V. Krings, 57-63. Leiden: Brill.
1995b   "Égypte." In *CPP*, ed. V. Krings, 632-39. Leiden: Brill.

Schmidt, W.
1965   "The deuteronomistische Redaktion des Amosbuches." *ZAW* 77: 168-93.

Schoville, K. N.
  1974   "A Note on the Oracles of Amos against Gaza, Tyre, and
          Edom." In *Studies on Prophecy*. VTSupl 26. 55-63.
          Leiden: Brill.
Schubart, H.
  1995   "Péninsule Ibérique." In *CPP*, ed. V. Krings, 743-61.
          Leiden: Brill.
Schulten, A.
  1945   *Tartessos*. Barcelona: Espasa Calpe.
Schwarzenbach, D.
  1954   *Geographische Terminologie im Hebräischen des Alten
          Testaments*. Leiden: Brill.
Seeden, H.
  1991   "A tophet in Tyre?" *Berytus* 39: 39-82.
Seevers, B.
  1998   *The Practice of Ancient Near Eastern Warfare with
          Comparison to the Biblical Accounts of Warfare from the
          Conquest to the End of the United Monarchy*. Ph.D.
          dissertation, Trinity Evangelical Divinity School,
          unpublished.
Segert, S.
  1976   *A Grammar of Phoenician and Punic*. Munich: Beck.
Seitz, C. R.
  1992   "Isaiah, book of (First Isaiah)." *ABD*, ed. D. N. Freedman,
          3:472-88. New York: Doubleday.
  1999   *Semitic Museum News, Harvard University*. Vol. 3, Nos.
          1 and 2, December 1999, pp. 1-5.
Shafer, A. T.
  1998   *The Carving of an Empire: Neo-Assyrian Monuments on
          the Periphery*. Ph.D. dissertation, Harvard University,
          unpublished.
Shanks, H.
  1995   *Jerusalem: An Archaeological Biography*. New York:
          Random House.

Shiff, L. B.

   1987   *The Nur-Sin Archive: Private Entrepreneurship in Babylon (603-507 B.C.).* Ph.D. dissertation, University of Pennsylvania, unpublished.

Shiloh, Y.

   1979   *The Proto-Aeolic Capital and Israelite Ashlar Masonry.* Qedem 11. Jerusalem: The Hebrew University Press.

   1983   "Jerusalem, City of David, 1982." *IEJ* 33: 129-31.

   1984   *Excavations at the City of David I, 1978-1982.* Qedem 19. Jerusalem.

   1985a   "The City of David: 1978-83." *Biblical Archaeology Today: Proceedings of the International Congress on Biblical Archaeology, Jerusalem, April 1984.* 451-62. Jerusalem: Israel Exploration Society - Israel Academy of Sciences and Humanities in Cooperation with the American Schools of Oriental Research.

   1985b   "The material Culture of Judah and Jerusalem in Iron Age II: Origins and Influences." In *The Land of Israel: Cross-Roads of Civilizations.* OLA 19, ed. E. Lipiński, 113-46. Leuven: Uitgeverij Peeters.

   1986   "A Group of Hebrew Bullae from the City of David." *IEJ* 36: 16-38.

   1993   "Jerusalem: The Early Periods and the First Temple Period." In *New Encyclopedia of Archaeological Excavations in the Holy Land,* ed. E. Stern, 2.698-712.

Singer, C. et al., eds.

   1954   *A History of Technology from the Earliest Times to the Fall of Ancient Empires.* Oxford: Oxford University Press.

Singer, S.

   1976   "Found in Jerusalem: Remains of the Babylonian Siege." *BAR* 2: 7-10.

   2000   "Jerusalem Update: Missing Millenium?" *BAR* 26 :34-37.

Smith, D. L.

   1989   *The Religion of the Landless: The Social Context of the Babylonian Exile.* Bloomington: Meyer Stone.

Smith, S.
    1953   "The Ship Tyre." *PEQ* 85: 97-110.
Snell, D. C.
    1992   "Trade and Commerce (ANE)." *ABD*, ed. D. N.
                Freedman, 6:625-29. New York: Doubleday.
Snodgrass, A.
    1980   "Iron and Early Metallurgy in the Mediterranean." In *The
                Coming of the Age of Iron*, eds. T. A. Wertime and J. D.
                Muhly. 335-74. New Haven: Yale University Press.
Soggin, J. A.
    1987   *The Prophet Amos.* London: SCM.
Solá Solé, J. M.
    1957   "Tarshish y los comienzos de la colonización fenicia en
                Occidente." *Sefarad* 17: 23-35.
Spalinger, A.
    1976   "Psammetichus, King of Egypt I." *JARCE* 13: 133-47.
    1977   "Egypt and Babylonia: a Survey (c. 620 B.C.-550 B.C.)."
                SAK 5: 221-44.
    1978   "Psammetichus, King of Egypt II." *JARCE* 15: 49-57.
Stager, L. E.
    1985   "The Archaeology of the Family in Ancient Israel." *ASOR*
                260: 1-35.
    1991a   "When Canaanites and Philistines Ruled Ashkelon." *BAR*
                17: 24-37, 40-43.
    1991b   "Why were Hundreds of Dogs Buried at Ashkelon." *BAR*
                17: 26-42.
    1993   "Ashkelon." In *New Encyclopedia of Archaeological
                Excavations in the Holy Land*, ed. E. Stern, 1.103-12.
    1996a   "The Fury of Babylon: Ashkelon and the Archaeology of
                Destruction." *BAR* 22: 59-69, 76-77.
    1996b   "Ashkelon and the Archaeology of Destruction: Kislev
                604 BCE." *EI* 26 (Joseph Aviram Volume): 61-74.
    1999   "Jerusalem and the Garden of Eden." *EI* 28 (Frank Moore
                Cross Volume): 183-94.
    2000   "Jerusalem as Eden." *BAR* 26: 36-47.

Stager, L. E. et al., eds.

1974   *American Expedition to Idalion, Cyprus*. Garden City: Doubleday.

2000   *The Archaeology of Jordan and Beyond: Essays in Honor of James A. Sauer*. Winoma Lake: Eisenbrauns.

Stech-Wheeler, T., J. D. Muhly, K. R. Maxwell-Hyslop, and R. Maddin.

1981   "Iron at Taanach and Early Iron Metallurgy in the Eastern Mediterranean." *AJA* 85: 245-68.

Stern, E.

1975   "Israel at the Close of the Period of the Monarchy: An Archaeological Survey." *BA* 38: 26-55.

1982   *Material Culture of the Land of the Bible in the Persian Period, 538-322*. Warminster. Aris and Phillips.

1983   "A Phoenician Art Center in Post-Exilic Samaria." *Atti del I Congresso di studi fenici e punici*, 1.211-12. Rome: Consiglio nazionale delle ricerche.

1991   "Phoenicians, Sikils, and Israelites in the Light of Recent Excavations at Tel Dor." In *Phoenicia and the Bible*. SP 11, ed. E. Lipiński, 85-95. Leuven: Uitgeverij Peeters.

1992   "Phoenician Architectural Elements During the Iron Age and the Persian Period." In *The Architecture of Ancient Israel*, eds. A. Kempinski and R. Reich, 302-04. Jerusalem: Israel Exploration Society.

1993   "The Many Masters of Dor. Part 3: The Persistence of Phoenician Culture." *BAR* 19: 38-49.

1994   *Dor Ruler of the Seas*. Jerusalem: Israel Exploration Society.

1995a   "Four Phoenician Finds from Israel." In *Immigration and Emigration within the Ancient Near East*. OLA 65, eds. K. van Lerberghe and A. Schoors, 319-34. Leuven: Uitgeverij Peeters.

1995b   "Between Persia and Greece: Trade, Administration and Warfare in the Persian and Hellenistic Periods (539-63 BCE)." In *The Archaeology of Society in the Holy Land*, ed. T. E. Levy, 432-45. New York: Facts on File.

1999   "The Archaeological Background of the History of Southern Phoenicia and the Coastal Plain in the Assyrian

Period." In *Ki Baruch Hu: Ancient Near Eastern, Biblical, and Judaic Studies in Honor of Baruch A. Levine*, eds. R. Chazan, W. W. Hallo, and L. H. Schiffman, 1-20. Winona Lake (Hebrew).

2001   *The Archaeology of the Land of the Bible*, vol. 2: *The Assyrian, Babylonian, and Persian Periods (732-332 B.C.E.)*. New York: Doubleday, 2001.

Stern, E., ed.

1993   *New Encyclopedia of Archaeological Excavations in the Holy Land.* 4 vols. Jerusalem: Israel Exploration Society.

Stern, M.

1984   *Greek and Latin Authors on Jews and Judaism.* Jerusalem: The Israel Academy of Sciences and Humanities.

Stieglitz, R. R.

1971   *Maritime Activity in Ancient Israel*. Ph.D. dissertation, Brandeis University, unpublished.

Stos-Gale, Z.

1993   "Isotopic Analyses of Ores, Slags and Artifacts: The Contribution of Archaeometallurgy." In *Archeologia delle attività estrattive e metallurgiche. V ciclo di lezioni sulla ricerca applicata in archeologiacertosa di pontignano (SI) – Campiglia Marittima (LI), 9-21 settembre 1991*, ed. R. Francovich, 593-627. Siena: Quaderni del Dipartimento di Archeologia e Storia delle Arti Sezione Archeologia – Università di Siena.

Strabo.

1960-70   *The Geography of Strabo*. Trans. Horace L. Jones. Loeb Classical Library. Cambridge: Harvard University Press.

Sudilowsky, J.

1999   "Search for Phoenician Shipwrecks. *Titanic* Explorer and Archaeologist Team Up." *BAR* 25: 16.

Sulimirski, T. and T. Taylor

1991   "The Scythians." In *CAH*. Vol 3, part 2, *The Assyrian and Babylonian Empires and Other states of the Near East, from the Eighth to the Sixth Centuries B.C.*, eds. J.

Boardman et al., 547-90. Cambridge: Cambridge University Press.

Tadmor, H.
    1956   "Chronology of the last kings of Judah." *JNES* 15: 226-30.
    1966   "Philistia under Assyrian Rule." *BA* 29: 86-102.
    1976   "The Period of the First Temple, the Babylonian Exile and the Restoration." In *A History of the Jewish People*, ed. H. H. Ben-Sasson, 91-159. Cambridge: Harvard University Press.

Taeckholm, U.
    1964   "El concepto de Tarschisch en el Antiguo Testamento y sus problemas: Tartessos y sus problemas." *V Symposio Internacional de Prehistoria Peninsular*, 79-90. Barcelona.
    1974   "Neue Studien zum Tarsis-Tartessosproblem." *Op. Rom.* 10: 41-57.

Tejera Gaspar, A.
    1979   *Las tumbas fenicias y púnicas del Mediterráneo Occidental.* PUS 44. Seville.

Te Velde, H.
    1999   "Nile." In *Dictionary of Deities and Demons in the Bible*, 2nd ed., ed. K. Van der Toorn, 626-27. Leiden: Brill.

Thiele, E. R.
    1965   *The Mysterious Numbers of the Hebrew Kings. A Reconstruction of the Chronology of the Kingdoms of Israel and Judah*, 2nd ed. Grand Rapids: Zondervan.
    1983   *The Mysterious Numbers of the Hebrew Kings. A Reconstruction of the Chronology of the Kingdoms of Israel and Judah*, 3rd ed. Grand Rapids: Zondervan.

Tomback, R. S.
    1978   *A Comparative Semitic Lexicon of the Phoenician and Punic Languages.* SBLDS 32. Missoula: Scholars.

Tsevat, M.
    1959   "The Neo-Assyrian and Neo-Babylonian Vassal Oaths and the Prophet Ezekiel." *JBL* 78: 199-204.

Tsirkin, J. B.
  1976   *The Phoenician Culture in Spain.* Moscow: Nauca
          (Russian).
  1979   "Economy of the Phoenician Settlements in Spain." In
          State and Temple Economy in the Ancient Near East.
          OLA 5, ed. E. Lipiński, 2.547-64. Leuven: Departement
          Oriëntalistiek.
  1986   "The Hebrew Bible and the Origin of Tartessian Power."
          In *Los fenicios en la Peninsula Iberica*, eds. G. del Olmo
          and M. E. Aubet, 184-85. Barcelona: AUSA.
  1988   "The Economy of Carthage." In *Carthago.* SP 6, ed. E.
          Lipiński, 125-35. Leuven: Uitgeverij Peeters.
  1990   "Socio-political Structure of Phoenicia." *Gerion* 8: 38-41.
  1998   "The Tyrian Power and her Disintegration." Trans. L.
          Chistonogova. *RSF* 26: 175-90.
Uberti, M. L.
  1988   "Ivory and Bone Carving." In *TP*, ed. S. Moscati, 404-21.
          New York: Abbeville.
Uffenheimer, B.
  1999   *Early Prophecy in Israel.* Jerusalem: Magnes.
Unger, E. A.
  1926   "Nebukadnezzar II und sein *šandabakku* (Oberkommisar)
          in Tyrus." *ZAW* 44: 314-17.
  1970   *Babylon: Die heilige Stadt nach der Beschreibung der
          Babylonier*, 2nd ed., ed. R. Borger. Berlin: de Gruyter.
Van Beek, G. W.
  1960   "Myrrh and Frankincense." *BA* 23: 70-95.
  1982   "The Drawings from Ḥorvat Teiman (Kuntillet Ajrud)."
          TA 9: 3-86.
  1993   "Jemmeh, Tell." In *New Encyclopedia of Archaeological
          Excavations in the Holy Land*, ed. E. Stern, 2.667-74.
          Jerusalem: Israel Exploration Society.
Van Berchen, D.
  1967   "Sanctuaires d'Hercule-Melqart. Contribution a l'étude de
          l'expansion phénicienne en Méditerranée." *Syria* 44: 73-
          109, 307-36.

Vanderhooft, D. S.
1999   *The Neo-Babylonian Empire and Babylon in the Latter Prophets.* HSM 59. Atlanta: Scholars.

Van der Toorn, K. et al., eds.
1999   *Dictionary of Deities and Demons in the Bible.* 2nd ed. Leiden: Brill.

Van Dijk, H. J.
1968   *Ezekiel's Prophecy on Tyre (Ez. 26,1-28,19): A New Approach.* BibOr 20. Rome: Pontifical Biblical Institute.

Van Gucht, W.
1992   "Esclaves." In *DCPP*, ed. E. Lipiński, 157. Paris: Brepols.

Vercoutter, J.
1945   *Les objects égyptians et égyptisants du mobilier funéraire carthaginois.* Paris: P. Geuthner.

Vogelstein, M.
1950-51 "Nebuchadnezzar's Reconquest of Phoenicia and Palestine and the Oracles of Ezekiel." *HUCA* 23: 197-220.

Von Voigtlander, E. N.
1964   *A Survey of Neo-Babylonian History.* Ph.D. dissertation, University of Michigan, unpublished.

Wagner, C. G.
1983   *Fenicios y cartaginenses en la Península Ibérica.* Ph.D. dissertation, Universidad Complutense, unpublished.

1996   "Elementos cronológicos y consideraciones históricas para una periodización de la presencia fenicia en la Península Ibérica." In *Alle soglie della classicità il Mediterraneo tra tradizione e innovazione*, ed. E. Acquaro, 1.423-40. Pisa – Rome: Istituti editoriali e poligrafici internazionali.

Wagner, C. G. and J. Alvar.
1989   "Fenicios en Occidente. La colonización agrícola." *RSF* 17: 61-102.

Waldbaum, J. C.
1978   *From Bronze to Iron: The Transition from the Bronze Age to the Iron Age in the Eastern Mediterranean.* Göteborg: Paul Astroems Foerlag.

1979   "The Chronology of Early Greek Pottery: New Evidence from Seventh-Century Destruction Levels in Israel." *AJA* 101: 23-40.

1980   "The First Archaeological Appearance of Iron and the Transition to the Iron Age." *The Coming of the Age of Iron*, eds. T. A. Wertime and J. D. Muhly, 69-98. New Haven: Yale University Press.

1994   "Early Greek Contacts with the Southern Levant, ca. 1000-600 B.C.: The Eastern Perspective." *BASOR* 293 (1994): 53-66.

Ward, A. W.
1968   *The Role of the Phoenicians in the Interaction of the Mediterranean Civilizations*. Beirut: American University of Beirut.

1997   "Tyre." In *Oxford Encyclopedia of Archaeology in the Near East*, ed. Eric M. Meyers, 5.247-50. Oxford: Oxford University Press.

Warning-Tuemann, B.
1978   "West-Phoenician Presence on the Iberian Peninsula." *The Ancient World* 1: 15-32.

Waterfield, R.
1998   *Herodotus: The Histories*. Oxford: Oxford University Press.

Watkins, T.
1989   "The Beginnings of Warfare." In *Warfare in the Ancient World*, ed. J. Hackett, 15-35. New York: Sidgwick and Jackson.

Weidner, E.
1939   "Jojachin, König von Juda, in babylonischen Keilschrifttexten." In *Mélanges syriens offerts à Monsieur René Dussaud*, 2.923-35. Paris: P. Geuthner.

Weinfeld, M.
1986   "The Protest against Imperialism in Ancient Israelite Prophecy." In *The Origins and Diversity of Ancient Israelite Culture*, ed. S. N. Eisenstadt, 169-82. New York: SUNY.

Wevers, J. W.
  1969   *Ezekiel.* NCBC. Grand Rapids: William B. Eerdmans.
Wheeler, T. S., J. D. Muhly, and R. Maddin.
  1979   "Neo-Assyrian Ironworking Technology." *Proceedings of the American Philosophical Society* 123: 369-90.
Whiston, W.
  1995   *The Works of Flavius Josephus.* 10th printing. Peabody: Hendrickson.
Widengren, G.
  1951   *The King and the Tree of Life in Ancient Near Eastern Religion, King and Saviour IV.* Uppsala: Lundequistska Bokhandeln.
Wildberger, H.
  1997   *Isaiah 13-27: A Continental Commentary.* Trans. T. H. Trapp. Minneapolis: Fortress.
Williams, A. J.
  1976   "The Mythological Background of Ezekiel 28:12 –19." *BTB* 6: 49-61.
Winter, I.
  1968   *The Carmona Ivories and the Phoenicians in Spain.* AM dissertation, University of Chicago, unpublished.
  1973   *North Syria in the Early First Millennium B.C. with Special Reference to Ivory Carving.* Ph.D. dissertation, Columbia University, unpublished.
  1976   "Phoenician and North Syrian Ivory Carving in Historical Context: Questions of Style and Distribution." *Iraq* 38: 1-22.
  1981   "Is There a South Syrian Style of Ivory Carving in the Early First Millennium B.C.?" *Iraq* 43: 101-30.
Wiseman, D. J.
  1958   *The Vassal-Treaties of Esarhaddon* (= *Iraq* 20). London: British School of Archaeology in Iraq.
  1974   *Chronicles of the Chaldean Kings (626-556 B.C.) at the British Museum,* 3rd ed. London: British Museum.
  1984   "Palace and Temple Gardens in the Ancient Near East." *Bulletin of the Middle Eastern Culture Center in Japan* 1: 37-43.

1985   *Nebuchadnezzar and Babylon.* The Schweich Lectures, 1983. Oxford: Oxford University Press.

1989   "The Assyrians." In *Warfare in the Ancient World*, ed. J. Hackett, 36-53. New York: Sidgwick and Jackson.

1991   "Babylonia 605-539 B.C." In *CAH*, 2nd ed. Vol. 3, part 2, *The Assyrian and Babylonian Empires and Other States of the Near East, from the Eighth to the Sixth Centuries B.C.*, eds. J. A. Boardman et al., 229-51. Cambridge: Cambridge University Press.

Wolf, W.
1930   "Papyrus Bologna 1086. Ein Beitrag zur Kulturgeschichte des Neuen Reiches." *ZÄS* 65: 89-97.

Wolff, H. W.
1977   *Joel and Amos.* Trans. W. Janzen, S. D. McBride, and C. A Muenchow. Philadelphia: Fortress.

Wong, K. L.
2001   *The Idea of Retribution in the Book of Ezekiel.* Leiden: Brill.

Wunsch, C.
1999   "Land Use in the Sippar Region During the Neo-Babylonian and Achaemenid Periods." In *Urbanization and Land Ownership in the Ancient Near East*, eds. M. Hudson and B. A. Levine, 2.391-413. Cambridge: Harvard University Press.

Xella, P.
1992   "Eshmunazor." In *DCPP*, ed. E. Lipiński, 160. Paris: Brepols.

1995   "Les sources cunéiformes." In *CPP*, ed. V. Krings, 39-56. Leiden: Brill.

Yadin, Y.
1963   *The Art of Warfare in Biblical Lands.* 2 vols. New York: McGraw-Hill.

1976   "The Historical Significance of Inscription 88 from Arad: A Suggestion." *IEJ* 26: 9-14.

Yalichev, S.
1997   *Mercenaries of the Ancient World.* London: Constable.

Yamauchi, F.
 1982   *Foes from the Northern Frontier. Invading Hordes from the Russian Steppes.* Grand Rapids: Baker.
Yaron, R.
 1960   "A Document of Redemption from Ugarit." *VT* 10: 83-90.
Yon, M.
 1992   "Kition." In *DCPP*, ed. E. Lipiński, 248-49. Paris: Brepols.
 1995a "Les prospections et "surveys" *partim* Orient." In *CPP*, ed. V. Krings, 85-105. Leiden: Brill.
 1995b "L'archéologie monumentale *partim* Orient." In *CPP*, ed. V. Krings, 119-31. Leiden: Brill.
Yoyotte, J.
 1951   "Sur le voyage asiatique de Psammetique II." *VT* 1: 140-44.
 1958   "Nechao ou Neko." In *Dictionnaire de la Bible* (Suppl. 6, fasc. 31) 363-93. Paris: Letouzey et Ane.
Zaccagnini, C.
 1996   "Tyre and the Cedars of Lebanon." In *Alle soglie della classicità il Mediterraneo tra tradizione e innovazione,* ed. E. Acquaro, 1.451-66. Pisa – Rome: Istituti editoriali e poligrafici internazionali.
Zaccagnini, C., ed.
 1989   *Production and Consumption in the Ancient Near East.* Budapest: Chaire d'Égyptologie de l'Université Eötovös Loránd de Budapest.
Zadok, R.
 1978a "Phoenicians, Philistines and Moabites in Mesopotamia in the First Millennium B.C.E. Chiefly according to Akkadian Sources." *BASOR* 230: 57-65.
 1978b *Geographical Names According to New- and Late-Babylonian Texts.* Répertoire géographique des textes cunéiforms 8. Beihefte zum Tübinger Atlas des vorderen Orients B7. Wiesbaden: L. Reichert.
Zimmerli, W.
 1958   "Israel im Buche Ezekiel." *VT* 8: 75-90.

1979   *Ezekiel 1: A Commentary on the Book of the Prophet Ezekiel.* Trans. R. E. of Clements. Hermeneia. Philadelphia: Fortress.

1983   *Ezekiel 2: A Commentary on the Book of the Prophet Ezekiel.* Trans. J. D. Martin. Hermeneia. Philadelphia: Fortress.

Zorn, J. R.

1997   "Mizpah: Newly Discovered Stratum Reveals Judah's Other Capital." *BAR* 23 (1997): 28-38, 66.

Index of Biblical Citations

Index of Authors

Finito di stampare
nel mese di maggio 2002

presso la tipografia
"Giovanni Olivieri" di E. Montefoschi
00187 Roma - Via dell'Archetto, 10,11,12